LOCAL FOCUS

A Japan Guide to Nature, Culture, and Community

鎌倉 江ノ島

Vol.1 Kamakura & Enoshima

2nd Edition 2019

arigatoubooks

INTRODUCTION

Only an hour from Tokyo, the Miura Peninsula is surrounded by sea and mountains and overlooks Mt. Fuji. All of the members of our production team reside on this peninsula, and spend their time at the ocean and on the mountains on a daily basis.

When I travel, I prefer small towns and villages over large cities, and I seek out low-key, small, family-run businesses frequented by local residents as opposed to well-advertised, popular establishments. Instead of searching for photo ops to feed my SNS, I seek out people and places that possess intrinsic charm and experiences that will leave an imprint somewhere deep in the heart. But it can be a challenge to find these places, shops, or people without any local connections or language skills, and I assume that this is the same for non-Japanese who are visiting Japan with interests in local experiences. A surplus of information can be found on the internet, but it's generally time and energy consuming to search endlessly through random sites for information on sightseeing locations, inns, or restaurants. Also, precious time and energy can be wasted while aimlessly searching for WiFi spots on their smart phones.

Our production team is made up of both local Japanese and non-Japanese members. To create this guidebook, our non-Japanese speaking members identified what was necessary to assist foreign travelers who can't speak the language, while our Japanese members compiled their insider information. This was then neatly consolidated into a graphically pleasing and user-friendly, all-in-one practical guidebook that will enable any visitor to efficiently create a travel itinerary to match their interests and schedules and enjoy their travel experience as if they were being guided by a local friend.
We hope this book will serve as a tool for meaningful connections to Japan through the many enterprising and unique individuals who gather here to pursue their visions beyond national or cultural barriers.

Mariko Miki
Founder of arigatoubooks

Standards for Our Selections

The following are the standards for our selections of sightseeing spots or shops for this guidebook.

■ **Sightseeing spots were selected for their richness in nature, culture, and history.**
■ **The interiors of the eateries listed are completely smoke-free.**
■ **The owner/s is/are unique and has/have distinctive appeal.**
■ **For eateries, to the extent possible the establishment uses ingredients that are fresh, local, and organic with authentic flavors, and the dishes are prepared with care.**
■ **The visit to the sight-seeing spot or shop impressed the team enough to want to recommend it to a close friend.**

* There are some selections that do not satisfy all of the above items, but were chosen in consideration of those traveling with small children or in large groups since choices can be limited, and in some circumstances, convenience must take priority; we felt it was better to have some insider information than to have none at all.

The following are reasons why some stores were eliminated from our selection:

■ **The shop is always crowded, and the establishment prefers to maintain a low publicity profile.**
■ **The proprietors or owners could not speak English, and would not grant permission for a write-up.**

For each and every one of these places, there has been no arranged "deal" made between the publishers and the establishment regarding advertisement, selection, or the content of the write-up.

TABLE of CONTENTS

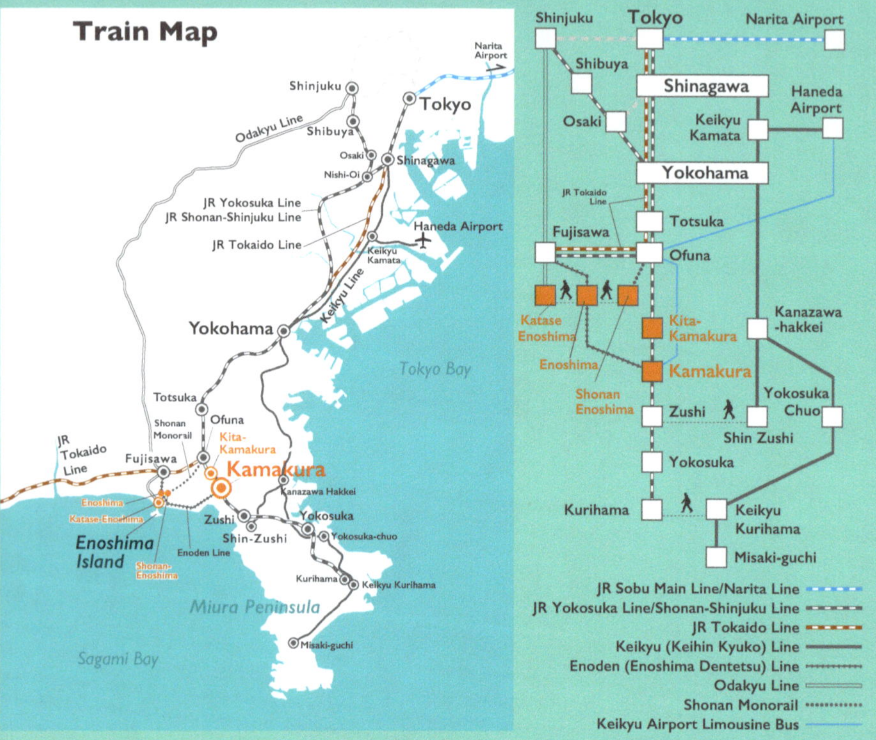

Getting to Kamakura

Kita-Kamakura Station is one station before Kamakura Station.

From Tokyo Station (Two options)

1st Option: JR Yokosuka Line   60 mins. ¥920

The JR Yokosuka Line runs directly to Kamakura Station.

2nd Option: JR Tokaido Line + JR Yokosuka Line   60 mins. ¥920

Take the Tokaido Line to **Totsuka** or **Ofuna** Station and transfer to the JR Yokosuka Line to Kamakura Station.

From Shinjuku or Shibuya Station   60 mins. ¥920

JR Shonan-Shinjuku Line runs directly to Kamakura Station. Make sure to take the train bound for **Zushi** Station.

From Haneda Airport (Two options)

**1st Option: Keikyu Line + JR Shonan Shinjuku Line/
JR Yokosuka Line**   60 mins. ¥820

Take the Keikyu Line to Yokohama Station then transfer to the JR Shonan Shinjuku Line or the JR Yokosuka Line to Kamakura Station.

2nd Option: Airport Limousine Bus   95 mins. ¥1,370

The bus ticket and information counter is located on the **second floor (arrival lobby)** of the **international terminal.** Buses to Kamakura Station depart at 9:15 am and 10:15 am.

Getting to Enoshima

From Tokyo Station (Two options)

1st Option: JR Tokaido Line + Odakyu Line/Enoden
80 mins. ¥1,130/¥1,190

Take the outbound train to **Fujisawa** Station and transfer to either the **Odakyu Line** to **Katase-Enoshima** Station or the **Enoden** to Enoshima Station.

2nd Option: JR Tokaido/Yokosuka Line + Shonan Monorail
80 mins. ¥1,110

Take the outbound train to **Ofuna** Station and transfer to the Shonan Monorail to Shonan Enoshima Station.

From Shinjuku Station (Two options)

1st Option: Odakyu Line   80 mins. ¥630

There are three different lines along the Odakyu Line from Shinjuku Station, so make sure to take the one bound for **Katase-Enoshima** Station via **Fujisawa** Station. The "Romance Car" is the express train that operates a few times a day on weekdays and several times a day on weekends and national holidays. All seats are sold by reservation only and tickets can be purchased at the ticket vending machine at the station. (Shinjuku Sta. to Katase-Enoshima Sta., 70 mins. ¥1,250)

2nd Option: Shonan Shinjuku Line + Enoden   70 mins. ¥1,130/
Shonan Monorail   70 mins. ¥1,230

Take the outbound train for **Fujisawa** Station and transfer to the **Enoden** to **Katase-Enoshima** Station, or transfer at **Ofuna** Station to the **Shonan Monorail** that will take you to **Shonan Enoshima** Station.

Getting Around Kamakura

By Train
Enoshima Dentetsu (Electric) Line ("Enoden" for short)

The Enoden is a charming tram that runs along the coast between **Kamakura** and **Fujisawa** stations via **Enoshima** Station.

By Bus

Many buses for major sightseeing spots depart from the bus terminal at the East Exit of Kamakura Station. Detailed bus information is provided on the maps in the "Places to Visit" section (p. 053~), and a bus terminal map is provided on p. 197.

Here is how to use the local bus:

- Enter the bus either through the front door or rear door (depending on the bus).
- When entering through the front door, tell the driver your destination, and pay the required fare by dropping in the correct change, or get change from a bill (only 1000 yen bills are accepted) by sliding it into the payment box next to the driver, then drop in the exact change); alternatively, place your prepaid Pasmo/Suica card over the IC card reader. When entering through the back door, take a numbered ticket (to determine your fare), or place your Pasmo/Suica card over the reader.
- Pay attention to the screen at the front of the bus that indicates the name of the bus stop in both Japanese and English.
- When your stop is announced, press the button to let the driver know that you want to get off at the next stop.
- When getting off, check the screen for the amount indicated by the number on your ticket (you need this ticket to pay your fare). If you use a Pasmo/Suica card, place it over the card reader.

By Bicycle

Major sightseeing spots are accessible by bicycle in 15-20 minutes. Please see p. 199 for information on rental bicycles.

Weather & When to Go

Japan has four distinct seasons and both Kamakura and Enoshima have plenty to see and do in each season, making them very popular destinations for day trips from Tokyo throughout the year.

The best time to visit Kamakura & Enoshima

In spring to early summer (late March to early June) and fall (late September to November), the weather is mild and stays relatively dry, so it is pleasant to walk around town. Cherry blossoms in late March through the first week of April, and autumn leaves in late November through mid-December enhance the beauty of the old temples and shrines, and are perfect seasons for hiking, too.

Other good times to visit

Mid-June to July is rainy season in Japan, but hydrangea viewing at a temple or shrine, a stroll through a moss garden in the rain, or sipping a bowl of matcha green tea while listening to the rainfall are also memorable experiences.

The new year is also a fun season to visit Kamakura and Enoshima. Japanese natives visit shrines and temples to pray for good fortune, so you can follow alongside them for an authentic experience. Aside from temples and shrines, however, most business are closed from the end of December through around January 3rd, except in the immediate vicinity of Tsurugaoka Hachiman-gu Shrine and on Enoshima.

Summer fun

It gets too hot and humid to walk around town from late July to mid-September, so many go to the beach instead. Temporary beach huts providing food, drink, and shower are open in July and August at the seaside, and give a festive ambiance with many visitors, especially during the week of "Obon" in mid-August, which is a Japanese major holiday (most business in town are closed during the week of "Obon"). (For information on beaches, see p. 193)

Tips to avoid crowds

"Golden Week" (the last weekend of April through around May 5th) is a major holiday in Japan and people go out and travel. Kamakura and Enoshima are popular spots, so you may have to wait for hours to view certain sites or have a meal.

THE HISTORY

INTRODUCTION

With shouldering mountains that embrace the sea and a distant view of Mt. Fuji, this historic town of Kamakura is graced by a gentle climate that enhances the beauty of its distinct seasons throughout the year. Located nearby is the small island of Enoshima, a sacred ground that has been protected since the feudal era.

It was at the end of the 12th century when a major turning point in Japanese history took place here—in Kamakura; at that time, control of the nation's government and authority under the rule of the Imperial Court and aristocrats shifted to a Shogunate system called a *bakufu*, the administration headed by a military dictator, the hereditary leader of the most powerful samurai family. The military nobility, the samurai warriors, who had been despised as savage barbarians and who were exploited by the Imperial Court in Kyoto, gathered in Kamakura from surrounding rural areas to build the new government and culture with their own hands. Inevitably, Kamakura became the site of frequent battles.

The aftermath of endless wars and natural disasters that included earthquakes and tsunamis, and eventual dissolution of the shogunate in Kamakura regrettably left no traces of the sites of administration, samurai residences, or townscapes; however, many of the temples and shrines remain. And fortunately, Zen Buddhism and other religious traditions, along with the culture and arts surrounding the lifestyles of the resident samurai of the past continue to be passed down, not only in Kamakura, but also in Japan on a wider scale.

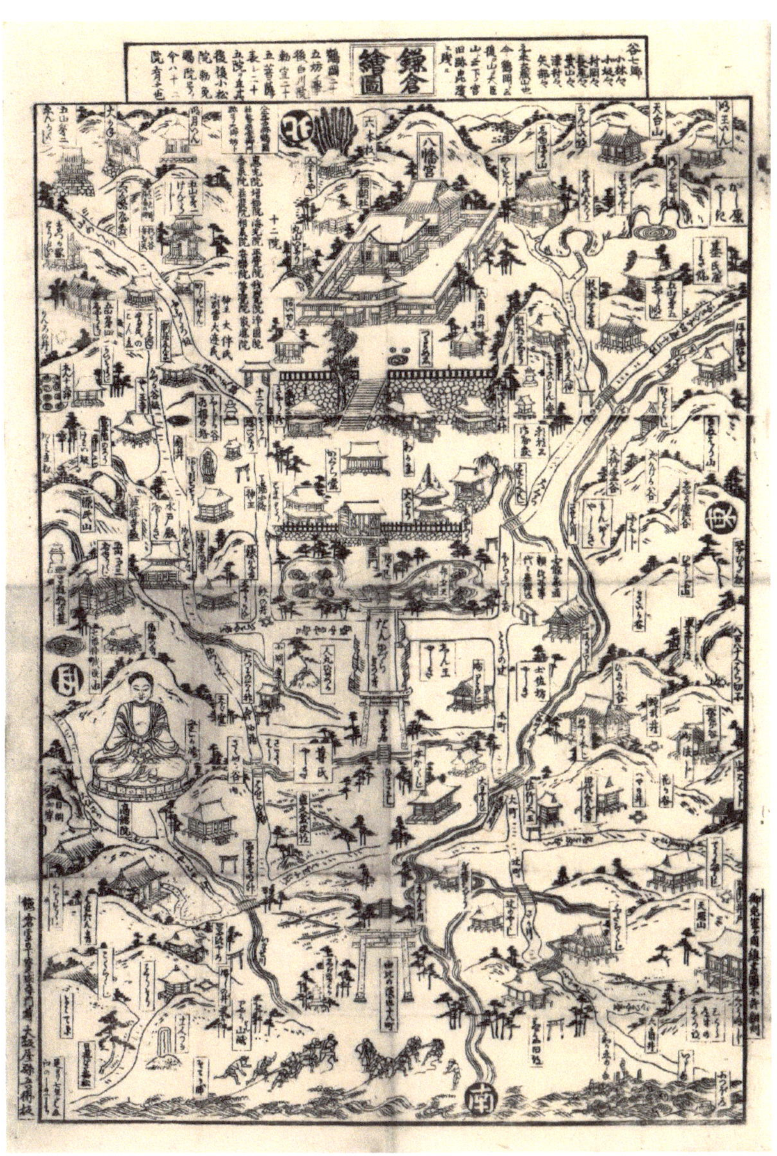

"Kamakura Ezu"
Woodblock print
(Data provided by
Kanagawa Prefectural Library)

This map drawn in the Edo period (1603 to 1868) shows Kamakura surrounded by mountains on three sides, and depicts the Great Buddha, temples, and shrines with Wakamiya-Oji Avenue extending down the center from Tsurugaoka Hachiman-gu Shrine to Yuigahama Beach.

LAUNCHER OF A NEW REGIME

The sequence of events that led to the *bakufu* feudal military dictatorship being established in Kamakura at the end of the 12th century centers on the life and ideals of Minamoto Yoritomo (1147 to 1199), who founded Japan's first real shogunate system.

The third son of the leader of the Minamoto clan, Yoritomo lost his father in a battle with the rival Taira clan when he was only 13, but his life was spared and he was exiled to Izu Peninsula, the land visible from Kamakura across Sagami Bay. Eventually, Yoritomo married Hojo Masako, the daughter of the leader of the Hojo clan, and lived in Izu for some 20 years. In 1180, however, he was commanded to overthrow the Taira clan, so with Kamakura as a base, he assembled samurai warriors throughout the Kanto district and assumed control of the region.

"Yoritomo Ichidai-ki Emaki"
<detail>
Edo period
Picture scroll
(Owned by Tsurugaoka Hachiman-gu Shrine, Data provided by Kamakura Kokuhokan Museum)

It was during this time that Yoritomo unified samurai who had gained power as a new political force and established a capital in Kamakura far from Kyoto, where the Imperial Court's power had been gradually declining. In 1199, only seven years after becoming an influential shogun, Yoritomo died at the young age of 53. There is a small grave near Okura Shirahata Shrine (p. 107), next to the site of Yoritomo's residence.

BUILDING THE CITY

Minamoto Yoritomo was strategic in establishing Kamakura as the headquarters for his new Shogunate government; it was an important location along the old Tokaido road that connected Kyoto to Tokyo Bay since ancient times, and faced a harbor, where timber was brought to build the town. Enveloped by hills to the north, east, and west with a gently sloping beach, its topography is a natural fortress. Yorimoto first established his residence in the Okura area, then transferred the Tsurugaoka-Wakamiya Shrine where his ancestors were worshipped, to the current location of Tsurugaoka Hachiman-gu Shrine, to the west of and adjacent to Okura. Finally, he built Wakamiya-Oji Avenue as a 1.8 km approach road that led from Hachiman-gu to the seashore.

The Hojo clan of regents, who ruled the Kamakura shogunate long after the Minamoto clan had lost power, forged ahead with a development plan for the government, creating *kiridoshi*—excavated valley passes for traffic and defense—other transportation routes, and a port. They also leveled the hills near the entrance to the *kiridoshi* passes and erected large temples there; these temples played a defensive role in preventing invasion by enemies via the *kiridoshi*. Trade ports and commercial areas were also established, and the samurai-backed government strategically created religious, defense, and commercial facilities along with a new political system. Many of the roads, temples, and shrines created in this period still exist in Kamakura and play an active role in the daily life of its residents.

THE DAWNING OF A MODERN ERA

End of the Kamakura Shogunate

After more than a century of rule under the Hojo clan, the shogunate was weakened by two Mongol invasions and extended autocratic rule; taking advantage of that situation, in 1333, under the order of Emperor Godaigo (1288 to 1339), who restored the Imperial House back into power, warlord Nitta Yoshisada (1301 to 1338) led a large army to besiege and capture Kamakura. Without being able to break through the *kidiroshi* roads, the weakened Nitta forces came ashore from the Cape of Inamuragasaki, approached from Wakamiya-Oji Avenue, and cornered the Hojo leaders and the rest of the clan at their family temple of Tosho-ji where over 870 committed suicide. After nearly 150 years of rule, the Kamakura Shogunate came to a close.

And Then....

Although the stage of the government returned to Kyoto, the rule of Emperor Godaigo did not last much longer, and a ruling body called the "Kamakura kubo" shogunate was established in Kamakura. The Minamoto-decended Ashikaga family governed the "Kanto kubo" and ruled the Kanto region. Later, the Kamakura kubo was moved and its function and Kamakura's position as the seat of administration was lost, but the city itself was restored by the succeeding Tokugawa shogunate.

Kamakura and Enoshima Gain Tourist Appeal

At the start of the Edo era in 1603, the capital of the nation moved from Kyoto to Edo (now Tokyo). Because of his reverence for Minamoto Yoritomo as the ideal warrior, the first shogun of the Edo period, Tokugawa Ieyasu, rebuilt many Buddhist temples and Shinto shrines in Kamakura. Over time, visits to temples became popular among commoners as well, and Kamakura and Enoshima gradually became lively sightseeing spots.

Separation of Shinto and Buddhism

The beginning of the Meiji Restoration in 1868 marked the end of the 650-year-long shogunate, causing great change. The Meiji government made Shintoism the official national religion and commanded the removal of Buddhist elements from Shinto shrines; as a result, many temples, Buddhist statues and images were destroyed and lost.

Western Culture and Establishment as a Resort Area

After the establishment of the Meiji restoration, many Westerners came to live in Tokyo and Yokohama, however, had some had fallen victim to tuberculosis. Japan's first sanatorium, Kaihin-In, was built on the shores of Yuigahama in 1887, and a year after its opening, Kaihin-In reopened as a resort hotel. Once the railway was in operation, nobles and members of the wealthy class constructed villas turning Kamakura into a high-end villa resort.

—The Kamakura Kaihin Hotel

Originally built as a sanitorium, Kaihin Hotel was a long-standing landmark in Kamakura, but it eventually was burned down by a fire in 1946. At present, all that exists on this site is Keihin Park and a modest commemorative monument.

The Great Kanto Earthquake of 1923

In 1923, the Great Kanto Earthquake shook the entire Kanto Plain region of Japan, destroying most of the homes, shrines, and temples of Kamakura. Thanks to the power of the financiers with their villas, recovery was speedy.

Post-Quake Kamakura to the Present Day

Primarily because Kamakura evaded air raids during WWII, the prewar architecture and charm that no longer remained in Tokyo or Yokohama was kept well preserved there. The period of rapid economic-growth around the 1960s, however, impacted the appearance of Kamakura since the new architecture lacked character or uniformity. For better or worse, the economic boom came to a halt, and the stagnant business scene produced a populace who came to favor the pastoral lifestyle over one of affluence. Kamakuraites share a common love of the city, and people have been forming connections irrespective of age, race, or social background, sparking the current distinctive trends of the area.

CULTURE

Deepening the Experience

While visiting Japan, it's likely that you'll come across customs and manners completely different from your own or those which you're familiar. In this section of our guidebook, we provide tips and information on appropriate conduct and actions in different situations during your stay.

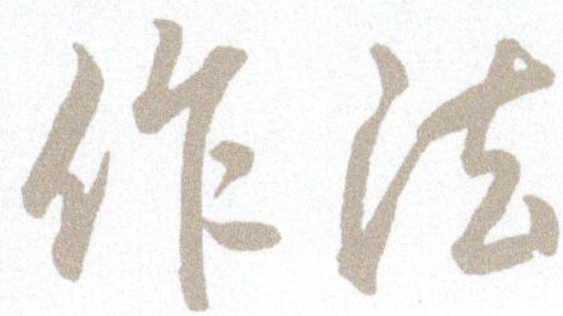

MANNERS & CUSTOMS

As the saying goes, "When in Rome…," traveling in a foreign land is a great chance to immerse yourself in new cultural experiences. While you may not get everything down pat the first time, it's better to have a bit of knowledge up your sleeve than to be stuck not knowing what to do.

I. Greetings

A light nod with a smile is the most basic way to greet someone in Japan. Once you become close to a person, a handshake is acceptable, but for the most part, hugs or kisses are not yet the norm in this country.

2. Removing shoes indoors

Shoes are not worn inside the home in Japan. Once you step inside, you are expected to remove your shoes and put on slippers, if provided. If you enter a room with tatami mats, however, you will need to remove the slippers. If you plan on visiting a Japanese home, we advise you come prepared with hole-free socks.

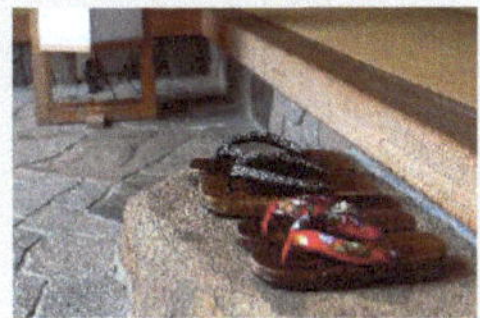

3.Taboos of using chopsticks

Sticking chopsticks into a bowl of rice or passing the food from one's chopsticks to another person's pair are both taboo as they are part of the ritual of Japanese Buddhist funerals for the dead.

4. Eating and walking

When eating outside, it is impolite to eat while walking. We suggest you either stand in one place to eat, or find a park bench to sit down to eat.

5. Restaurant Service and Payment

In Japan, tipping is not practiced in restaurants and therefore you can call on any employee for such services as extra orders or if you need more water. Generally payments are made by bringing your check to the cashier and paying at the front.

6. Hot springs and public bathhouse

Before entering the bathtub, you are expected to thoroughly clean your body. Do not put your washcloth in the bath water. Tattoos are not accepted in many public bathing areas, so be sure to check the rules beforehand.

FOOD

In Japan, it is customary to say 'Itadaki-masu' (literally, "I gratefully partake") before a meal. There are few even among the Japanese who consider the true meaning of this word, the origins of which can be traced back to the existence of the ancient polytheistic religious Shinto faith of Yaoyorozu no Kami (literally meaning "Eight Million Gods"). Condensed into this single word is a vague, but overall gratitude for the ingredients, the person who prepared the food, those who grew and harvested the product, and an appreciation for the ancestors who brought the receiver of the food into this world.

Japanese ingredients are full of the rich blessings of nature due to the variety of food available throughout the four seasons.

In Kamakura, a place blessed with fertile agricultural land and sea, one can also look forward to enjoying the taste of local seasonal produce. Most Japanese cuisine places great emphasis on seasonality, being careful to make the best of the flavors of the raw ingredients. Characteristic to Japanese cuisine is the staple rice, the use of miso (fermented soybeans), and the use of soy sauce. *Dashi* (soup stock), traditionally used as cooking stock, and is commonly made with dried bonito shavings, dried kombu seaweed, small dried sardines and/or dried shiitake mushrooms.

The ingredients, cooking methods, number of items, taste, and aesthetics of the food, and the sense of hospitality and gratitude are all perfectly balanced with *washoku*, the traditional cuisine of Japan ("wa" refers to things Japanese), and in 2013, washoku was added to the UNESCO Intangible Cultural Heritage list. In addition to a traditional menu that focuses on simple food and is basically comprised of a bowl of rice, miso soup, and one main dish, in recent times there is a richer variety of choices because of the introduction of cuisine from other countries such as China, Italy, France, and more exotic countries.

In Kamakura, one can enjoy various types of traditional Japanese style fare such as the vegan *shojin-ryori* cuisine which was adopted by the temple monks during training; traditional dishes that optimize the use of fresh, local ingredients; popular Japanese food such as sushi and eel loved by world famous Kamakura culture mavens; Italian cuisine prepared by young, creative chefs; and casual, but high-quality ramen or curry.

CHA-NO-YU
Japanese Tea Ceremony

Cha-no-yu, the Japanese tea ceremony, (or literally, "the Way of Tea") is essentially about the enjoyment of drinking tea, and it eventually developed into a traditional cultural art form called *sado*.

At a tea ceremony, tea is made by pouring hot water into a bowl of matcha green tea powder made from tea leaves ground in a stone mortar; this is then whipped with a bamboo whisk into a frothy beverage. Matcha is more concentrated than regular green tea, and there are two types of tea depending on the thickness: *usu-cha* and *koi-cha*. Usucha is a weak tea presented in individual tea bowls and is received by a single guest. The thick and concentrated *koi-cha* is prepared for more than one guest, and is passed around for others to drink from.

The standard actions of the tea ceremony are to eat a tea cake or other confection before imbibing the tea. To drink the tea, lift the tea bowl that has been served in front of you with your right hand and place it in palm of   your left hand, turn the bowl around twice with your right hand in a clockwise direction and then lift the tea to your lips, take a sip, then lower the bowl to admire its beauty, then repeat until the tea is completely consumed. After you are done, place the bowl directly in front of you and once again admire its form, illustration or pattern, and the color and texture of the glaze.

The *wabi-cha* style of the Japanese tea ceremony that continues today was perfected in the 16th Century by Sen no Rikyu (1522 to 1591), the tea master who had the most profound influence on the tea ceremony. Prior to its development as an art, samurai warriors of the Sengoku (Warring States period) period frequently performed the tea ceremony believing it held special significance. Because they faced mortal danger on a daily basis, it was the one time that they could feel at ease and enjoy the simple pleasure of the tea ritual. Without exception, it was forbidden to bring swords and other weaponry into the small tea room; it was the one ritual where both rivals and allies could gather in peace. In that space bound by a gentleman's agreement, the ultimate beauty of simplicity existed, and those once-in-a-lifetime encounters were valued as precious experiences.

Recommended book: "The Book of Tea"(1906) by Kakuzo (Tenshin) Okakura

神社 SHRINES

Shrines are places of worship and the dwellings of *kami* (Japanese Shinto deities). Long before Buddhism had been introduced to Japan, the native people had faith in a polytheistic religion called "Shinto," where almost any natural object is worshipped as a "kami," or a divine spirit. Shintoism has no doctrine, founder, or idolized figure. Even today, shrines venerate natural objects including ancient trees, boulders, and natural springs.

Although it is anomalous to the religious practices of most other nations, for over 1,000 years, the Japanese in parallel worshipped both Buddhism and Shinto in a system called *Shinbutsu-shugou*, or the syncretism of Shinto and Buddhism, and many still visit shrines and temples depending on the occasion. Typically, visits to shrines are made for New Year's celebration, weddings, and rituals to celebrate the birth of a child and pray for good health, to ward off evil spirits, and to pray for good fortune, family safety, wellness, or prosperity. Shrines are most easily distinguished from temples by their *torii*, or gate structures that symbolize the entrance to a sacred place.

A visit to any shrine calls for proper etiquette. It begins by bowing once to show respect to gods before passing underneath the *torii*. Near the entrance, there is a stone basin filled with water (called "Chozu-ya" or "Temizu-ya"), where you are expected to perform the following purification ritual:

1. Hold the *hishaku* wooden dipper with your right hand.
2. Scoop enough water to wash your left hand.
3. Switch hands and repeat the same for your right hand.
4. Switch again and pour water into the cupped palm of your left hand and rinse out your mouth, then spit the water out outside of the basin.
5. Once you reach the front hall of worship, bow once and shake the end of the rope with a bell attached where available. Show gratitude to the deities by tossing a coin or two into the offertory box.
6. If you feel comfortable imitating the Japanese ritual, bow twice, press your palms together together as if in prayer, clap twice, and give gratitude with one last bow. Shrines sell what is known as *omikuji* as a way of fortune telling.

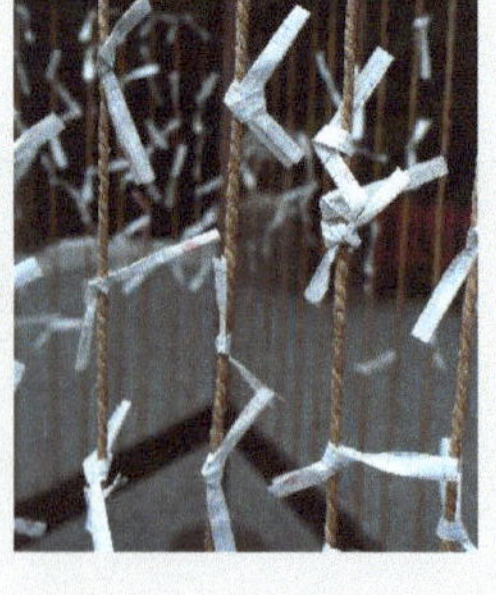

We hope you'll have the chance to get your own *omikuji* since some shrines have English versions (p. 076). If you happen to receive an undesirable fortune, it is customary to tie the *omikuji* onto a tree branch or frame for such purpose provided at the shrine to rid yourself of it.

TEMPLES

Instead of *torii*, entrances to temples have a main gate, and towards the back of the temple complex is the main hall (Buddha hall) where the principal image (Buddha statue) is displayed. Toss a coin or two into the offertory box in front of the main hall as a symbol of detachment from money, then, again, if you feel comfortable imitating the Japanese tradition, bow and bring your hands together to display gratitude. If there is an incense burner, light a joss stick and let it burn for a few seconds before fanning it out with your hands.

When removing your shoes upon entering the main hall, place your shoes in the shoe rack, if available. Otherwise, if plastic bags are provided, put your shoes in a bag and enter the temple hall. It is considered good manners if you wear socks.

There are about 110 temples of various sects located in Kamakura, from the grand temples built by shoguns and other powerful figures, to the smaller back alley temples that have been dear to the local residents for ages. One large difference from shrines is that temples have graveyards, and so many renowned historical figures rest at the temples of Kamakura.

Regardless of one's own religious beliefs, temples generally allow anyone to experience Buddhist practices for themselves, such as *zazen* (Zen sitting meditation), where practitioners will sit and meditate, or *sha-kyo* (sutra copying), in which practitioners will copy the Buddhist scriptures once preached by the Buddha himself. Many temples require the presence of a Japanese-speaking person, but for those who are able, your *zazen* or sutra copying experience at a peaceful temple deep in the hills or overlooking a rock garden will be a special time of calm introspection. Many temples have well-maintained gardens, and some have *karesansui* rock gardens. If you don't have a chance to try *zazen* or *shakyo*, just gazing at a *karesansui* garden at a temple should be peaceful enough.

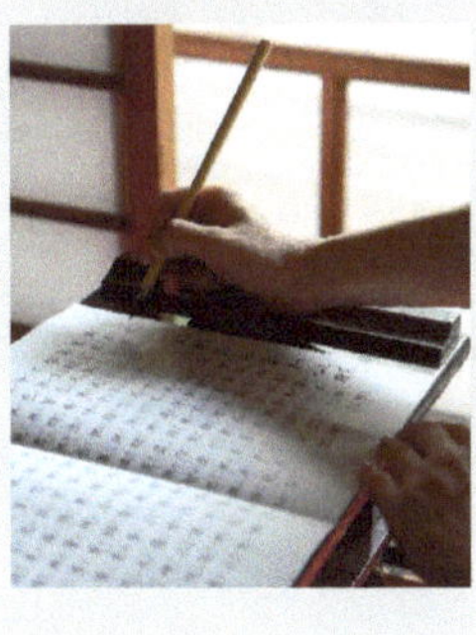

(Information on temples where *zazen* or *sha-kyo* can be practiced are on p. 205.)

ZEN

Zen was introduced to Japan in the 8th century. Buddhist monks in Japan traveled to China in pursuit of authentic knowledge that was available only close to the source of the religion; as a result, Buddhism was brought back to Japan in various forms depending on where the monks trained. Eventually, Japanese monks Myoan Eisai (1141 to 1289) and Eihei Dogen (1200 to 1253) spread teachings from the Rinzai and Soto schools, respectively, the latter of which was based on the principles of Zen philosophy. These teachings were dispersed on a wide scale throughout the country during the Kamakura era (1185 to 1333). In the 11th century, due to feudal wars and famine throughout the nation, people were led to various sects of Buddhism including Zen, Jodo (Pure Land), and Jodo-Shin (True Pure Land), and Nichiren by their earnest desire to be saved from extreme poverty. For the samurai class in Kamakura, Zen was the flavor of choice.

In Zen Buddhism, the aim is for one to awaken to the dignity and pure human nature that is inherent within themselves (or "Buddha nature," referring to one's Buddha-like qualities) through practices that may involve *zazen* sitting meditation or koan meditations, sutra-chanting, or *sha-kyo* work. Every aspect of daily life is considered to be practice, and even the perception of something in terms of morals, or as good or evil, is considered an earthly desire, and is what keeps one from attaining enlightenment; it is easy to understand why Zen came to be fully embraced by samurai warriors who lived in the ephemeral interval between life and death in the Kamakura era.

In basic ascetic practice, *zazen* is performed by sitting in a prescribed posture and concentrating on the breath. Depending on which denomination of Zen, the meaning and purpose of the practice of *zazen* varies, but the type that general temple visitors can experience is a type of discipline or mental training. The aim is to eliminate self to the extent possible, passively experiencing the existence of all that is "other" than self, and spirituality returning to the recognition of a self that emerges from the existence of that which is other than self.

Zazen meditation is often translated as "meditation," but in fact its principles are spiritually based and are fundamentally different from the style of meditation typically done with the eyes closed. In *zazen* meditation, one can experience relaxation, and achieve better concentration, and relief from stress. According to scientific studies, the proper breathing, posture, and concentration that occurs during *zazen* meditation activates the neurotransmitter serotonin and stabilizes the mind. With a spotlight on this effect, the practice of "mindfulness" is nowadays incorporated as a form of mental and physical therapy, but this also is not the same as *zazen*. Information on temples that offer *zazen* meditation for beginners is available on p. 205.

D. T. Suzuki
Daisetz Teitaro Suzuki

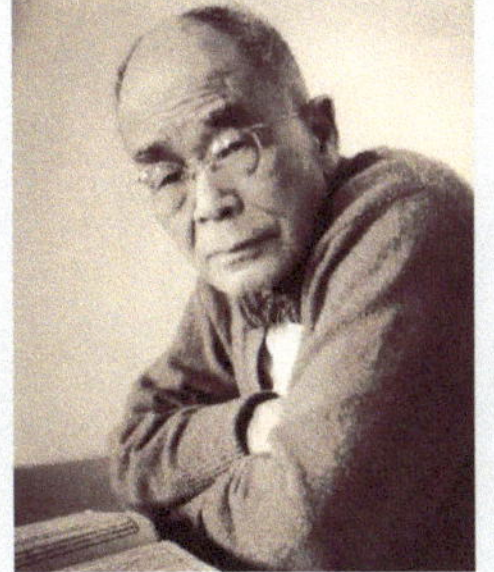

Reputed as the foremost important figure in spreading Japanese Zen Buddhism and culture in the West through his English publications, eminent Buddhist scholar D. T. Suzuki (Daisetz Teitaro Suzuki) (1870 to 1966) first sat *zazen* (Zen-style sitting meditation) here in Kamakura in 1891, and it is also where he lived out his later years. In 1946, based on the vision stipulated in the will of his master, Soen Shaku, Suzuki founded a library in Kita-Kamakura that he began focusing on Zen and devoted himself to studies on the spirituality of the Japanese and Eastern philosophy.

In addition to teaching at Columbia University in NY as a visiting professor from 1952 to 1957, Suzuki lectured at many other prestigious colleges throughout the US including Yale, Harvard, and Princeton. As a result, he left a large imprint on culture even outside the religious sphere, as seen in the works of composer John Cage in music, as well as in dance, literature, and other forms of art.

(Photo data provided by
The Matsugaoka Bunko Foundation)

KAMAKURA GOODIES

When visiting the town of Kamakura, what should you eat? And what sort of souvenirs can you bring home to immortalize the memories of your trip?

In this chapter, we introduce a variety of goods that are distinctively Kamakura. While there are antiques and various crafts common to many parts of Japan made using traditional techniques, there are also those that are unique to Kamakura alone, made by local craftspeople.

To satisfy the tummy, on top of Japanese cuisine and confections, there are also a variety dishes of non-Japanese origin that have been given a local twist though the creativity and skill of Kamakura food experts.

Access to fresh and delicious vegetables and seafood from family-run or independent local farmers or fishers is also one of the charms of this town. Kamakuraites take great pride in the superior quality of these crafts and foods that are part of their daily lives. We encourage you to experience the essence of the daily lives of the locals by sampling these Kamakura goods.

Fresh Produce

Kamakura Yasai (Vegetables)

This has become a famous brand name in the market to indicate vegetables grown in Kamakura. Kamakura is known for having small quantities of a large variety of vegetables. The vegetables grow in the warm local climate and are raised in a soil rich of minerals from the nearby ocean. Most of these vegetables are raised with reduced amounts of agricultural chemicals or none at all, so many restaurants in town use Kamakura Yasai that are freshly harvested in the morning .

Kama-age Shirasu

Kama-age shirasu means "young sardines boiled in salt water." People eat the young sardines in this way or even raw when they are in season. (Fishing is closed January through mid-March.)

Unagi no Kabayaki

Unagi no kabayaki is filleted and deboned eel that are glaze-grilled after steaming by skilled chefs. The basting sauce is made with soy sauce, sugar, and savory seasonings (p. 130).

Jizakana

Jizakana means "locally caught fish." It's very easy to enjoy freshly caught fish procured directly from the local fishing harbor. Try their in-season selections.

Wakame

Kamakura is famous for a kind of seaweed called *wakame*. As a tradition of the early spring, you'll see *wakame* hung to dry on the beaches of Kamakura, and the taste of freshly harvested *wakame* can only be enjoyed at its place of production.

Sweets

Mame-kan

A Japanese traditional confection, *mame-kan* consists of cube-shaped *kanten* (agar gelatin) that are made from a type of boiled seaweed (*tengusa*). It's enjoyed with chilled red beans and is served with sugar cane syrup (p. 161).

Warabi-mochi

This is a confection made from bracken starch, and has a chewy yet soft, jelly-like texture sprinkled with *kinako* (roasted soybean flour) topped with sugar cane syrup (p. 059).

Kaki-gori

Kaki-gori is the name for shaved ice and is a typical treat in the summertime. The smooth and fluffy flakes of ice have the consistency of freshly fallen snow (p. 166).

Hato-Sabre

This pigeon-shaped sable cookie is sold by the long-established Japanese confectioner in Kamakura, "Toshimaya" (p. 060). The cookies are baked using fresh eggs and butter.

An-pan

This bread with sweet red bean paste inside combines the cultures of both East and West. Most bread shops sell *an-pan*, but Paradise Alley bakery (p. 065) takes it to a whole other level with its unique twist of adding dried fruit.

Drinks

Hand-Drip Coffee

There are many people in Kamakura who are very particular about the quality of everyday food and objects. Considering this, you may imagine the quality to which coffee shops strive, from the selection of coffee beans to the roasting process (p. 084).

Kamakura Beer

The wonderful taste of locally crafted beer comes from its freshness. The brewery of this Kamakura Beer is located just a 10-minute drive from the center of Kamakura.

Matcha/Ryoku-cha/Hoji-cha (Tea)

Steamed and dried young tea leaves are used to make *ryoku-cha*, or green tea. *Hoji-cha* leaves are made using same method as green tea but the leaves are then roasted. Green tea leaves that are ground into powder are called "matcha." *Matcha* is not only for drinking, but is also used in cooking and baking.

Shopping

Kamakura-Bori (lacquerware)

This sculptured lacquerware is a traditional art that originated in the Kamakura era. Objects of art in themselves, the functional artworks possess a rich beauty acquired from a long process that starts from carving the designs into a wood base, which is then lacquered in several layers, and polished up to a shiny finish.

Kotto sara (antique dishes)

These antique (*kotto*) blue-on-white chinaware platters (*sara*) "dyed" with a special glazing technique called "sometsuke" were in wide use a half century to a century ago, but can still be found today at reasonable prices. Set out to find one with Mt. Fuji to bring home as a memory of Kamakura.

Furudougu (secondhand goods)

Furudougu are *mingei* folk art handicrafts created as tools for living. No matter where you may come from, if you are a tool lover, these time-tested simple utensils seasoned from long use will hold unlimited charm. Shops specializing in *furudogu* carefully restore the tools and display them for sale in a gallery-like setting.

Tenugui (hand towels)

Tenugui are traditional versatile cloth towels that are used for drying the hands, face, and body. They can also be fashioned in various ways as a head scarf, "hachimaki" headband for festival participants, quick-to-dry washcloths, and as a *furoshiki* wrapping cloth. Dyed using a distinctively traditional Japanese method, they come in various prints and colors and make suitable gifts.

PEOPLE

One of Kamakura's main features is the personality of the people that live there. Individuals who are responsive to the times and who uphold the value of authenticity are what give the town of Kamakura character and allure.

People create history .... Joji Fujikawa

Ensconced within the deep greenery and quietness of Kita-Kamakura there is a Japanese restaurant called "Hachinoki". This ideal environment is not accidental—along with the town administrators, Joji and other residents organized a preservation committee and established the area as a "scenic zone" with building ordinances under which newly built structures must go through a preliminary assessment of their design and usage to determine whether they can be built. In this way, staunch town preservation activity is supported by a clear vision and civil pride. With a gentle smile, Joji explains, "Even still, we're not bound by tradition and formality, and residents are involved in their own activities—but we collaborate when necessary. Kamakura became desolate after the period of provincial wars, but since the Meiji era (1868 to 1912) many have taken up residence here. Kamakuraites maintain that everyone is an outsider, and thus everyone is welcome...its many residents work together toward what's good for our community." Just as Joji himself asserts that "people create history," through his daily efforts in transmitting Japanese culture globally through Hachinoki's dishes, he is playing his part in creating a piece of Kamakura's history.

Sea and culture are what make Kamakura
.... Taisuke Yokoyama

"Although there are better waves elsewhere and Tokyo is the best place to be for work, I never considered leaving Kamakura—because we have both sea and culture here," Taisuke explains. Through the blessings of his father's Leica as well as his father's favorite phrase "Seek true value," Taisuke's photographs of the ocean nearby garnered him with recognition, and from then onward, the fusion of surfing and photography became his lifework and career, grounding him to this area.
Issuing sighs of regret, however, Taisuke laments the changes to the Kamakura townscape over the years—a hodge-podge of nondescript

buildings and electrical wires obstruct scenic views. Fortunately, Taisuke says, "Now there is an exciting return of the younger generation who, after getting their fill of urban or overseas life, have awakened to the value of living in peaceful coexistence with nature, and are now acting on their visions that herald the creation of a new Kamakura. Taisuke has taken on the role of his community's "big brother," passing down the regional beach and land culture to younger generations.

Where one senses the unseen .... Junsho Nakada

In an age overflowing with technology and never enough time, Junsho considers that one of the roles of the temples is to "be a place where one can discover a sense of the unseen." As an alternative to pushing religion through words, preserving the sanctity of the temple grounds by keeping it neat and tidy is an effective way to "purify the hearts of the visitors, and allow them to experience something that is different from the outside world" and guide worshippers with care.

As it is clear in Junsho's commitment to regularly meeting with his Shinto, Buddhist, and Christian counterparts on the Kamakura Worshippers Committee, he is dedicated to establishing Kamakura as a firm base of peace. Since prayer is the universal stance of holding value in sensing what is unseen, on this committee, they maintain that people should not clash over their differences, but should surpass them and connect through prayer.

Conveying the beauty of old Japan with younger-generation sensibility .... Megumi & Sayuri Ikeda

Megumi tells their story: "A housing development that was being planned on forested land behind Tsurugaoka Hachiman-gu Shrine in the 1960s was protected by an opposition movement of Kamakura residents, and brought about the Japanese National Trust movement. Since we were born and raised in this place where our ancestors had thus maintained the beauty of Kamakura's nature and scenery, we couldn't just stand back and watch it deteriorate before our eyes."

They settled on the idea to make use of traditional Japanese folk houses and hold workshops such as brush calligraphy and how to properly wear kimono. The sisters manage a similar space in Kyoto, but say they feel more at ease and relaxed in Kamakura. In their spare time, when the waves are good, Megumi and Sayuri go out surfing; otherwise, they head to the hills for trail running.
The Ikeda sisters sum up in saying, "The delight of travel and the transfer of cultural value—each of these happens on a personal level. We want to help transmit the value of Japan from person-to-person."

Joji Fujikawa

President of Hachinoki (Limited Private Company)

Born and raised in Kita-Kamakura, after university graduation and training at a well-established Japanese restaurant in Kyoto, Joji Fujikawa succeeded the small Japanese restaurant his mother had opened in his hometown, and brought it to its current thriving status, regularly hosting VIPs from overseas. Despite his restaurant's time-honored traditional food offerings, Joji (a Mac devotee since the first generation iBook) is known for flexibly keeping up with the times, as demonstrated in his website's pioneering launch in English ahead of other local establishments.

www.hachinoki.co.jp/english/

Taisuke Yokoyama

Photographer

Raised in Kamakura, Taisuke Yokoyama has been a wave rider since the dawn of the surfing era in Japan.
Taisuke was brought up in a rich cultural milieu centered on his famed cartoonist father (Taizo Yokoyama) and uncle (Ryuichi Yokoyama), who would meet up with Kamakura's most celebrated cultural figures including film director Yasujiro Ozu and author Yasunari Kawabata. Known for his iconic photograph collection, *surfers*, Taisuke launched *Surf Magazine* in 2017.

taiseye.com

Junsho Nakada

Chief abbot of Kakuon-ji Temple,
Shingon sect

Born in Kamakura, Junsho Nakada
was brought up at Kakuon-ji
Temple, a Shingon Buddhist
temple established in Kamakura
in 1218, where his father served
as the chief abbot.
After graduating from university
and a year of Buddhist training at
Mt. Koya in Wakayama Prefecture,
Junsho returned to Kakuon-ji
Temple to become its vice abbot
and follow his father's footsteps in
protecting its sacred value and
became its chief abbot in 2018.
Triggered by the Great East Japan
Earthquake and Tsunami, he was
involved in establishing the
Kamakura Worshipper's
Committee, whose members are
connected through prayer regardless of religion or denomination.

kamakura894do.com

Megumi & Sayuri Ikeda

President and Vice President of
Viages Inc.

Twin sisters born and bred in
Kamakura, after both working for
large corporations, Megumi and
Sayuri Ikeda founded their own
business with some friends
renovating old folk houses in
Kamakura and Kyoto and planning
and organizing events and exchange
programs. Through the fresh lenses
of a younger generation, they are
transmitting the values of old Japan
both inside and outside the
country.
The Ikeda sisters opened a
Japanese style breakfast restaurant
in Kamakura in the spring of 2018.

www.corporate.viajes-jp.com

COMMUNITY

Although Kamakura is an area blessed by sea, mountains, and culture, those merits alone don't keep it from having its share of problems. Thankfully, this town is also endowed with many residents who readily move towards action, and Kamakura is known to have high number of NPO and NGO organizations among its local government. Among those organizations are those started by communities comprised of Kamakuraites who were born and raised in this town who promote the culture of the area through their unique approaches, overlapping one another within this small town. Here, we introduce three communities that have love and pride for their local town, and that were established through valued connections among one another.

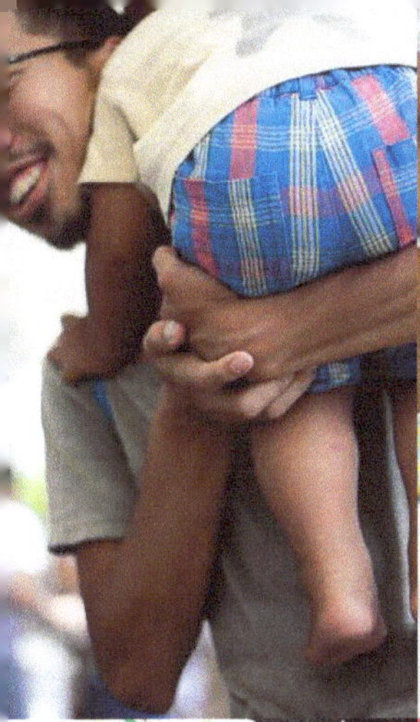

GREEN MORNING KAMAKURA

Like an extension of one's home, this community strives toward serving as a town gathering space where all residents, from children to adults, can drop in and have social exchange with others. Live music events called "Green Morning Kamakura" are held in three different shops including Cobakaba (p. 058) on the third Sunday of each month; and an event called "Green Morning Market" is held in town irregularly.

Event runs from 9:00 am to 1:00 pm
www.facebook.com/GreenMorningKamakura/

Photos by Yuko Okoso

ROOT CULTURE

Root Culture is a group of resident artists and creators from Kamakura that gather to hold events such as symposiums or workshops that cross the genres of music, art, and literature. This organization also actively participates in inter-local activities, establishing exchange with cultural organizations both domestic and abroad, such as with groups in the US and in Palestine. Root Culture also holds events at Tsurugaoka Hachimangu Shrine and temples around Kamakura in order to build a foundation for local cultural exchange. It is truly a unique academic community, the likes that could only be found in Kamakura.

rootculture.jp/

Photos: courtesy of ROOT CULTURE
Takamitsu Sakamoto

TRANSITION TOWN KAMAKURA

The "Transition Town" movement is a global grassroots movement that practices cooperation among the people of a local region to create a shift to a sustainable society. In Kamakura, the owner of Sông bé Cafe (p. 083), Kaoru Uji, plays a key role in the local Transition Town activities through such events as holding DIY solar panel workshops or hiking tours to search for local potential.

www.facebook.com/TransitionTownKamakura/

Although these organizations are limited in the amount of information they share in English, events such as the Green Morning gatherings are open to the public and anyone is welcome, and the owners and employees of the shops that serve as the hubs for these communities invite non-Japanese participants to share in the experience. Members of these warm communities of Kamakura would certainly be thrilled to make new connections, so don't be afraid to join in!

THE HAPPY VISITOR
Recommended Routes

First-time visitors

History lovers

Zen seekers

Overnight stayers

"Happy Visitor" Day Tours

Kamakura has a surplus of wonderful sites and bites. For those unfamiliar with the area and who want to make effective use of their visit, we came up with three day plans and an overnight plan. Select whichever plan suits your needs depending on your interests and the amount of time you have available. We hope they serve as a guide to give you a little taste of Kamakura.

First-time visitors

For those visiting Kamakura for the first time, we came up with a fail-safe plan that covers the must-sees of the area.

① 10:00 am   JR Kamakura Station

It's best to start out early while the air is clear —if you get to the famous temples and shrines before the sightseeing tour buses arrive, you'll be able to enjoy their serene atmosphere at leisure.
First, set off in the direction of the popular Hase-dera Temple on the small and charming Enoshima Electric Railway, more affectionately known as the "Enoden."

② Enoden: 5 mins.

10:10 am   Arrive at Hase Station

🚶 5 mins.

③ 10:15 am   Hase-dera Temple (p. 151)

As one of the oldest temples in Kamakura, Hase-dera is also referred to as "the Temple of Flowers," with gardens filled with flora that blossom all year round. Follow along the path until you reach the Kannon-do ("Hall of the Goddess of Mercy"), in which is enshrined a statue of the eleven-faced goddess. In the many faces of the Kannon goddess who brings prosperity to humankind, you may discover a calm worldview that surpasses the boundaries of religion. Follow the path that leads to an overlook, and you will find a spectacular view of Kamakura and the sea, with a bird's-eye view ofthe Miura Peninsula.

Let's go visit the Kamakura Daibutsu (Great Buddha), the must-see of the area.

5 mins.

④ 11:00 am Kamakura Daibutsu (Great Buddha) (p. 149)

Despite the floods of tourists at this spot, the enormity of the Daibutsu will not disappoint. Stand before this Great Buddha statue, and take in its calm yet awesome presence.

It's time to grab lunch!

5 mins.

⑤ 11:30 am Yuigahama-Dori Street

A stroll down Yuigahama-Dori Street would be an ideal way to search for the perfect bite as you take in the charm of the intermingling of old buildings and cafes and restaurants run by young proprietors. Once your tummy is satisfied, head off to the shrine in the mountain.

25 mins.

⑥ 1:00 pm Sasuke Inari Shrine (p. 101)

Entering this tunnel-like arrangement of "torii" gates is like a passage to a different dimension. Minamoto Yoritomo, founder and first shogun of the Kamakura Shogunate, established this shrine in gratitude to the gods for his successful defeat of the Taira Clan. Note the number of "inari" foxes, who are considered messengers to the gods. Next stop is another Yoritomo-affiliated shrine.

(7) 1:30 pm   Zeni-arai Benzaiten Ugafuku Shrine (p. 100)

This shrine built by Yoritomo to bring peace to the people is situated upon Kamakura's valuable water source. According to ancient legend, if you wash your coins in the spring water, your wealth will multiply. Why not give it a try?

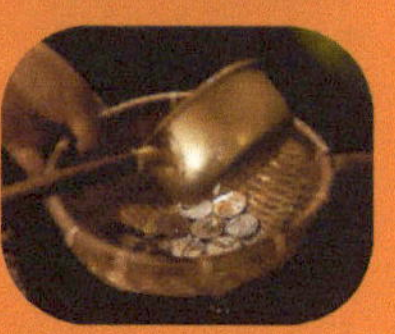

(8) 2:00 pm   Genji-yama Park (p. 102)

There is a lot to see along the pleasant trails within lush Genji-yama Park. Take your time to enjoy the view of Mt. Fuji, see the statue of Yoritomo, or just stretch your legs and relax at the picnic area.

> **Ready to move onto the final destination?**
>
> We recommend a walk along the historic Kewai-zaka *kiridoshi* mountain pass, however, the dirt path is rough and steep with exposed tree roots in certain areas, and tends to become slippery. If you don't feel comfortable with taking this path, then walk to the end of the park and take the paved road following the sign to Jufuku-ji Temple. Walk across the train track in front of Jufuku-ji Temple and follow the sign to Tsurugaoka Hachiman-gu Shrine.

(9) 2:30 pm   Tsurugaoka Hachimangu Shrine (p. 075)

Since the days of the samurai until present times, the Tsurugaoka Hachimangu Shrine has been considered the center of Kamakura. After climbing the steep steps and putting your hands together to show respect to the shrine deity, turn around and take in the panoramic view of the town of Kamakura that extends from the shrine approach to the sea.

After checking your fortune by purchasing an *omikuji* or boosting your luck with an *omamori* amulet, stroll down Wakamiya-Oji Avenue or Komachi-dori Street to enjoy some souvenir shopping and Japanese treats before heading for home from Kamakura Station.

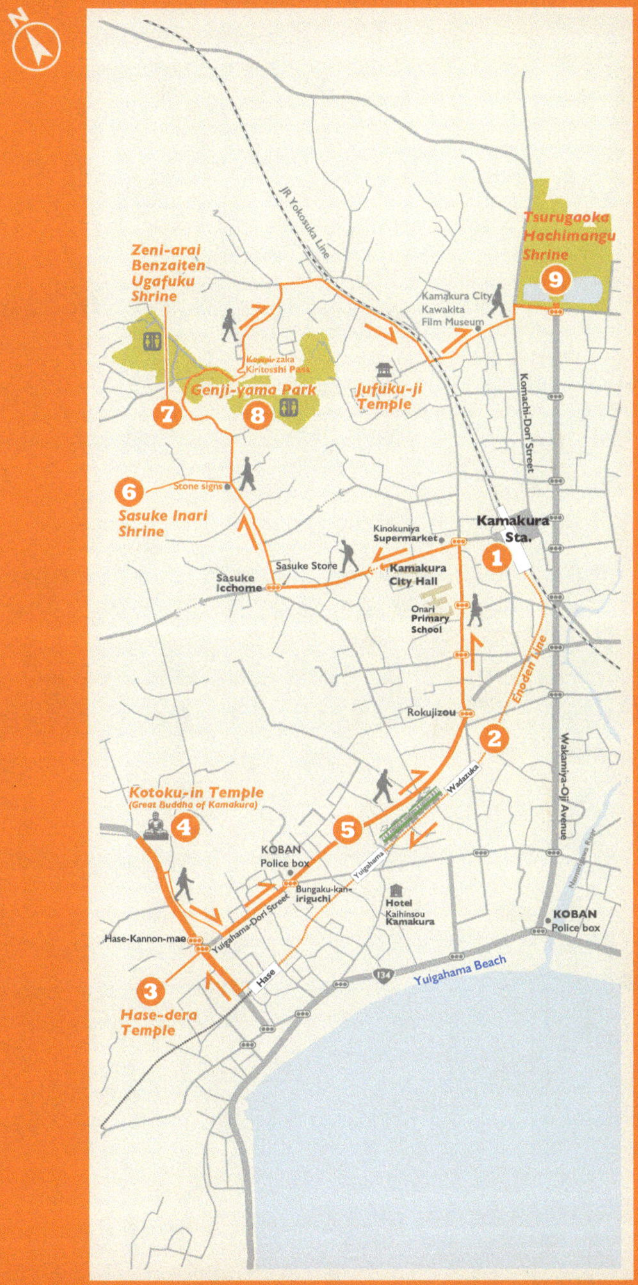

N
JR Yokosuka Line
Zeni-arai Benzaiten Ugafuku Shrine
Tsurugaoka Hachimangu Shrine
9
Kamakura City Kawakita Film Museum
Kenpi-zaka Kiritoshi Pass
Genji-yama Park
8
7
Jufuku-ji Temple
Komachi-Dori Street
Stone signs
6
Sasuke Inari Shrine
Kinokuniya Supermarket
Kamakura Sta.
1
Sasuke Store
Sasuke Icchome
Kamakura City Hall
Onari Primary School
Enoden Line
Rokujizou
2
Wakamiya-Oji Avenue
Kotoku-in Temple
(Great Buddha of Kamakura)
4
Wadazuka
5
KOBAN
Police box
Bungaku-kan-iriguchi
Yuigahama
Hotel Kaihinsou Kamakura
KOBAN
Police box
Hase-Kannon-mae
Yuigahama-Dori Street
Hase
134
Yuigahama Beach
3
Hase-dera Temple

History lovers

Traces of the lives of the samurai who once lived in this town are faint, but still visible. The deeper you delve into the history of Kamakura, the more you will know about the circumstances of the samurai who resided here and what makes this town unique.

(1) 10:00 am   Kamakura West Exit   → 🚶 7 mins.

(2) 10:07 am   Kamakura Museum of History and Culture (p. 099)
Let's start here, where you can scan the history of Kamakura in just half an hour.
After that prelude, pass through the tunnel from the West Exit side of the station to the East, make a left onto Wakamiya-Oji Avenue, then cross to the median to stroll the Dankazura pedestrian path (p. 043).   → 🚶 15 mins.

(3) 11:00 am   Tsurugaoka Hachimangu Shrine (p. 075)
Make sure to visit "Houmotsu-den," the small museum located next to the Main Hall, where swords, arrows, and other relics from the Kamakura era are on display. They offer various *omamori* amulets—even one shaped like a sword (¥1,000).

(4) 11:30 am
To avoid a long wait, it's best to find a place for lunch before noon. Try the soba at Kosuzu (p. 059) or a light lunch at the Kamakurabori Museum cafe (p. 078).

(5) 12:30 am   Stone monument of Okura Bakufu
The "Okura Bakufu" was the first government of the shogun Minamoto Yoritomo. A private school now occupies the site of the government offices and Yoritomo's residence.   → 🚶 I min.

(6) 12:35 am   Yoritomo's tomb (p. 107)
Above the steep flight of stairs by the Okura Shirahata Shrine, you will find Yoritomo's tomb surrounded by those of his retainers.

(7) 12:45 pm
Make a left onto the narrow road in front of the shrine onto Kanazawa-Kaido Road that has connected Kamakura to Tokyo Bay since ancient times.   → 🚶 10 mins.

(8) 12:55 pm Sugimoto-dera Temple (p. 107)
A castle once occupied the site behind this temple to control the area between Kamakura and Mutsuura Port. About 300 samurai committed suicide here during a battle over the Ashikaga clan.

(9) 1:05 pm Jomyo-ji Temple (p. 110) → 5 mins.
This temple was the family temple for the Ashikaga clan who had their residence next door. Kisen-an tea house, where monks from Kamakura Gozan (Five Zen Temples) gathered to have tea in the 1500s, is open to the public and serves green tea.

(10) 1:30 pm Hokoku-ji Temple (p. 111) → 3 mins.
The last stand of the Ashikaga clan in the Kanto region. *Yagura* cave tombs were created for the Ashikaga clan who ended their lives here in battle, but now it is a place to enjoy peaceful moments with a bowl of matcha green tea while gazing out at the bamboo forest.

(11) 2:00 pm Tosho-ji Temple Ruins → 15 mins.
Turn left to walk along the narrow road for 10 minutes before you hit Kanazawa-Kaido Road, cross the O-mido Bridge, then make a left onto Kanazawa-Kaido Road. Go straight, passing Hokai-ji Temple, then follow the sign to the Tosho-ji Temple Ruins. The *yagura* cave tombs and flat area beyond the fence is the site where 870 samurai from the Hojo clan took their own lives when they learned their enemies had reached Wakamiya-Oji Avenue, and lit fire to Tosho-ji Temple, the family temple of the Hojo clan. It was the last stand of the Kamakura shogunate that had lasted for 150 years. The sign by the *yagura* says "Only worshippers allowed beyond this point," so please be respectful of that instruction.

On the way back to Kamakura Station, window shop or stop in to see the artisans of samurai-history related craftware such as **Kamakura-bori lacquerware** (p. 073) **and swords** (p. 094).

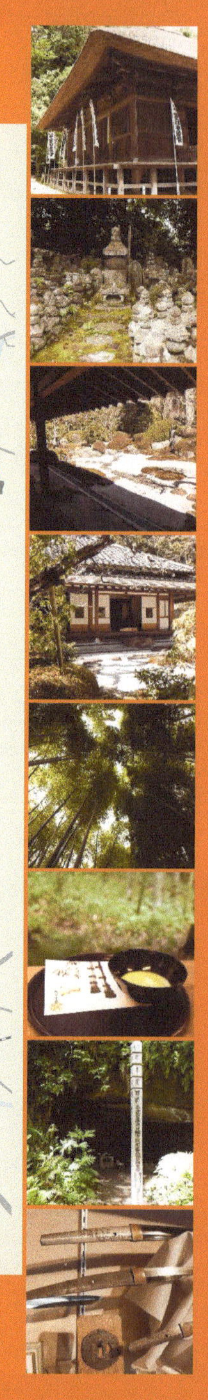

N
Zuisen-ji Temple
Jomyo-ji Temple
9
Jomyo-ji
Hokoku-ji Iriguchi
Kakuon-ji Temple
Kamakura-gu Shrine
Sugimoto-dera Temple
8
10
Daito-no-miya
Sugimoto Kannon
Hokoku-ji Temple
KOBAN Police box
Stone monument of Okura Bakufu
5
Tenjin-mae
7
Yoritomo's tomb
6
O-naito Bridge
Wakare-michi
Kanazawa-Kaido Rd. Prefectural Rd. 204
Daigaku-mae
Tosho-ji Temple Ruins
11
Tsurugaoka Hachimangu Shrine
3
Hokai-ji Temple
Hakkodo
Kamakura City Kawakita Film Museum
Kosuzu
4
Myohon-ji Temple
Kamakurabori Museum, cafe and store
Komachi-Dori Street
Jufuku-ji Temple
Masamune Sword and Blade Workshop
Kamakura Sta.
1
Hotel New Kamakura
2
JR Yokosuka Line
Kamakura Museum of History and Culture
Kinokuniya Supermarket
Kamakura City Hall
Onari Primary School
Wakamiya-Oji Avenue

Trivia to Boost Your Appreciation of Kamakura

The Three Great Clans that Ruled Kamakura

Family crest   Name of the clan   (The years that each clan ruled the Kamakura shogunate)

Minamoto (Genji) clan (1180-1219)

A noble family with Imperial blood. The Minamoto lineage is full of famous generals and distinguished people, and Minamoto Yoritomo established Japan's first full-scale samurai caste in Kamakura.

Hojo clan (1219-1333)

A samurai family based in Izu. Hojo Masako came to prominence as the wife of Yoritomo and subsequently assumed power for a long time over the Minamoto clan government. The Hojo clan became devout believers in Zen Buddhism and built large Zen temples along with building ports and carving out *kiridoshi* passages through the hills of Kamakura.

Ashikaga clan (1338-1455)

After the end of the Kamakura shogunate, the Ashikaga clan (descended from a branch of the Minamoto clan) became the reigning family and moved the shogunate to Kyoto. Kamakura became the jurisdiction that governed the Kanto district and the Ashikaga clan served as rulers by succession.

Kamakura History Map   (Road map is made based on the map made in late 1800s)

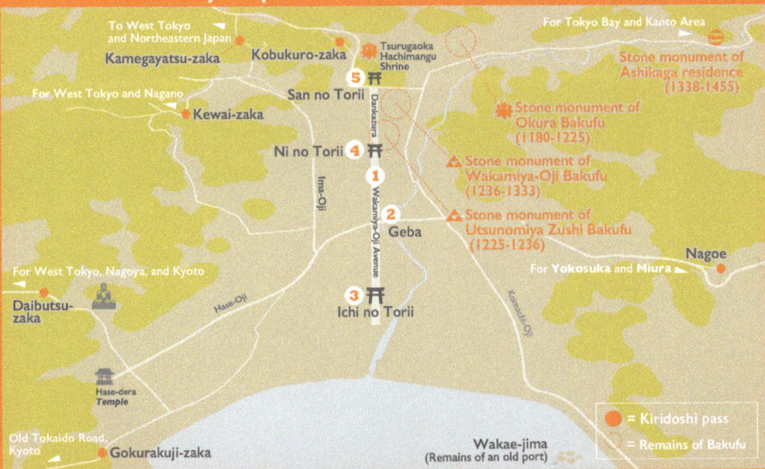

1 **Wakamiya-Oji Avenue**   The shrine approach built by Minamoto Yoritomo. By clever use of perspective, the avenue appears longer than it actually is due to the width of the road being narrower towards the end as seen from the beach.

2 **Geba**   This name means "to dismount a horse" and it is here that horsemen had to dismount to show their respect toward the sacred grounds.

3 **Ichi no Torii**   The coastline allegedly used to be located here, at the First Gate.

4 **Ni no Torii / Dankazura**   From here, the Second Gate, to San no Torii, Yoritomo built a raised path called "Dankazura" that leads to the shrine.

5 **San no Torii**   The Third Shrine Gate to Tsurugaoka Hachimangu Shrine.

Zen seekers

Kita-Kamakura is where monks from the Song Dynasty were invited by the Hojo clan creating a home base of Zen Buddhism in Japan. Take time to relax at each Zen temple and absorb yourself in the ancient atmosphere. Information on Zen is available on p. 021. Icons indicate where matcha green tea is served, or where "shakyo" (sutra copying) is available. See details on p. 205.

① **10:00 am   Kita-Kamakura Station, West Exit** ➡ 🚶 1 min.

② **10:01 am   Engaku-ji Temple** (p. 171)
Engaku-ji introduced Zen to the common people. Soyen Shaku, a priest who introduced Zen overseas, and his pupil Daisetz Suzuki, a renowned scholar of Buddhism lived and practiced here.

➡ 🚶 5 mins.

③ **11:20 am   Tokei-ji Temple** (p. 173)
This is where Soyen Shaku and Daisetz Suzuki established a library specializing in Buddhism. They both rest in peace at this temple ground.

➡ 🚶 5 mins.

④ **11:40 am   Hachinoki Kita-Kamakura-ten** (p. 167)
Enjoy *shojin-ryori*, a vegan cuisine that originates in the food served for Buddhist monks during their training.

➡ 🚶 10 mins.

⑤ **12:50 pm-1:20 pm   Meigetsu-in Temple** (p. 175)
The round window at the Hojo building is said to symbolically express enlightenment, truth, and the universe in its circular shape.

➡ 🚶 5 mins.

⑥ **1:30 pm   Jochi-ji Temple** (p. 174)
This quiet temple surrounded by deep greenery has a small bamboo forest and a dynamic rocky backdrop created through an excavation.

➡ 🚶 10 mins.

⑦ **2:15 pm   Kencho-ji Temple** (p. 177)
Kencho-ji Temple is the oldest Zen training monastery in Japan. Many training dojo are not open to the public and the strict Zen training continues since the samurai days.

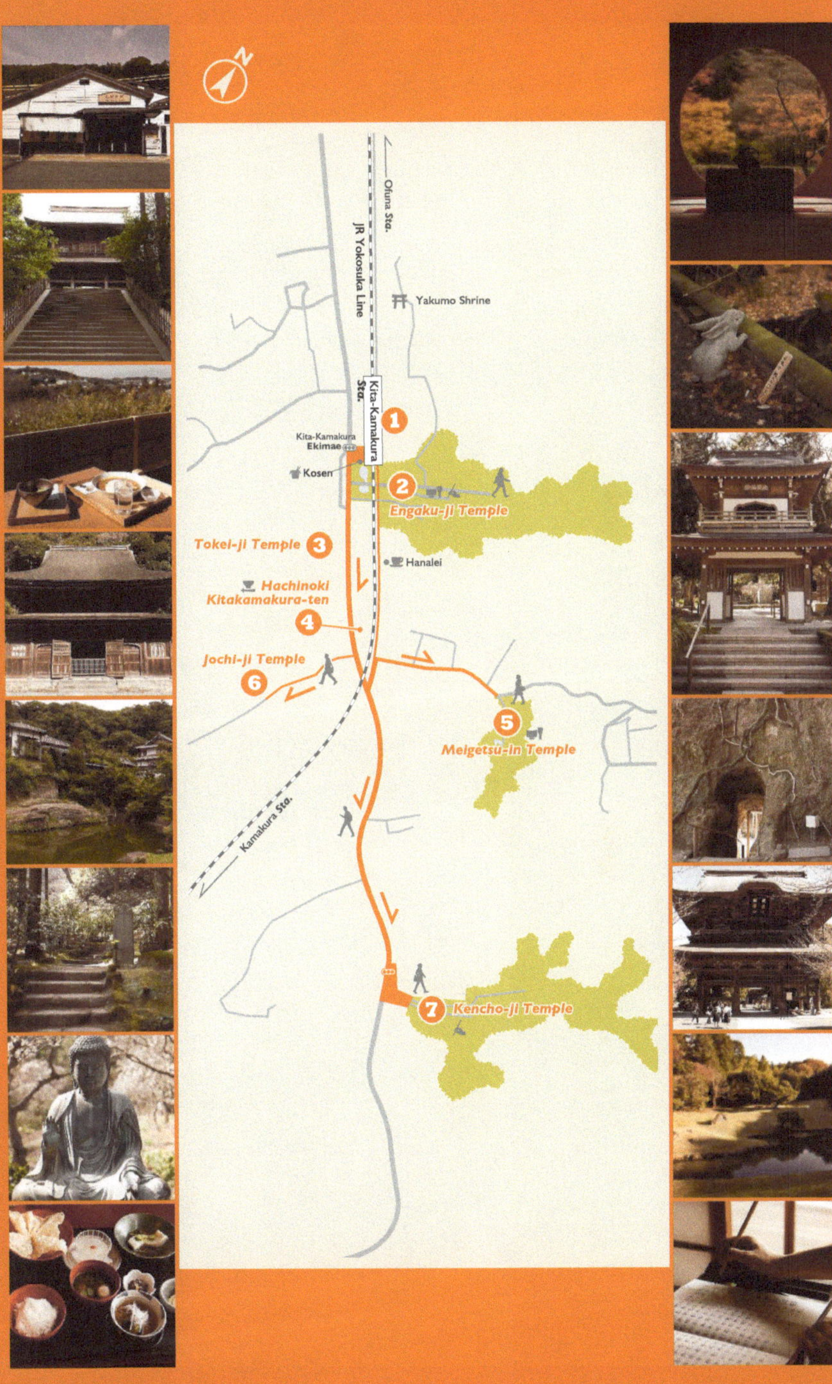

Ofuna Sta.
JR Yokosuka Line
Yakumo Shrine
Kita-Kamakura Sta.
1
Kita-Kamakura Ekimae
Kosen
2
Engaku-ji Temple
Tokei-ji Temple 3
Hanalei
Hachinoki Kitakamakura-ten
4
Jochi-ji Temple
6
5
Meigetsu-in Temple
Kamakura Sta.
7 Kencho-ji Temple

Overnight stayers

If staying overnight, you can enjoy the luxury of witnessing the ordinary lives of local people in addition to sightseeing.

Day 1

Morning to evening: select one sightseeing plan from the routes on the previous pages and enjoy your day. Watch the sunset at the beach in the evening, then pick a restaurant for a dinner. After dinner, join the locals at the public bath, Shimizu-yu (p. 116), Hideyoshi yakitori bar (p. 064), or at the Yorozuya Shoten general store (p.116).

Day 2

(1) 8:30 am **COBAKABA** (p. 058) Enjoy a Japanese-style breakfast, then stop by Renbai, the local vegetable market next door.

(2) 9:30 am Take the Enoden (Enoshima Dentetsu Railroad) to Hase Station from Enoden Kamakura Station located next to the West Exit of JR Kamakura Station.

(3) 9:40 am Walk from the Hase area to the Gokuraku-ji area through Hoshinoi Street. Visit the Daibutsu (Great Buddha), if you have not visited him yet.

(4) 9:45 am **Jojuin-in Temple** (p. 158) Walk up the steep stairs and enjoy the view of the bay. Walk along the Enoden train tracks to Kaihin Park Inamuragasaki.

(5) 10:10 am **Kaihin Park Inamuragasaki** Take a break on the grassy park or on the beach. Walk a few minutes to Inamuragasaki Station to catch the Enoden to Enoshima Station.

(6) 10:45 am Walk for 10 minutes to Enoshima Island over the long bridge.

(7) 11:30 am **Enoshima Island** (p. 179) Enjoy strolling around the island, and try lunch at Eno-maru (p. 185) or iL Chianti Cafe (p. 184).

(8) 1:30 pm **The Market SEI** (p. 183) Be sure not to miss their homemade gelato.

(9) 2:00 pm **Enoshima Station** Head back to Kamakura. Check R Old Furnitures (p. 156) on the way, or else take the Odakyu Line from Katase Enoshima Station that heads back into Tokyo.

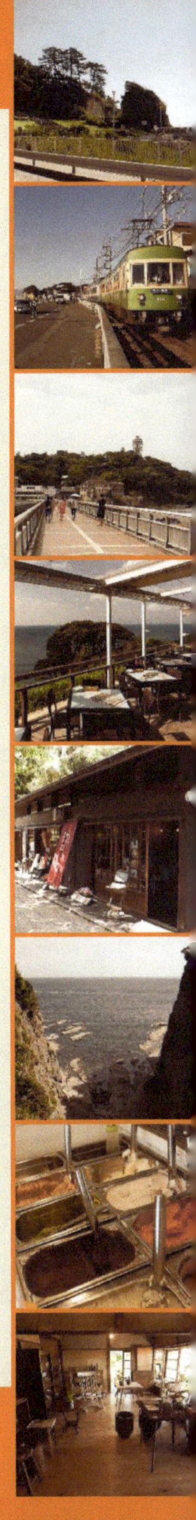

Tsurugaoka Hachimangu Shrine
COBAKABA
1
Renbai
Hideyoshi
JR kamakura
Shimizuyu
Yorozuya Shoten
Enoden Kamakura
2
Yuigahama Beach
134
Hase Sta.
Hoshinoi St.
3
Jojuin-in Temple
4
Gokurakuji Sta.
Kaihin Park Inamuragasaki
5
Inamuragasaki
R Old Furnitures
9
Shichirigahama Beach
Shichirigahama Sta.
Enoden Line
Shonan Monorail Line
Kamakura Kokomae Sta.
Koshigoe Sta.
Koyurugi Cape
Shonan Enoshima Sta.
The Market SE1
8
Enoden Enoshima Sta.
6
Enoshima Island
Odakyu Line
Katase Enoshima Sta.
iL Chianti
7
Eno-maru
134

WHERE TO GO?

Here, we present nine sightseeing areas—the settings for our production team's hand-picked recommendations. The selections include shops we frequent or spots we bring friends visiting from abroad.

To plan effectively for a meaningful experience, refer to the icon list (pp. 051-052) and detailed charts provided on (p. 201).

Map of Kamakura and Enoshima

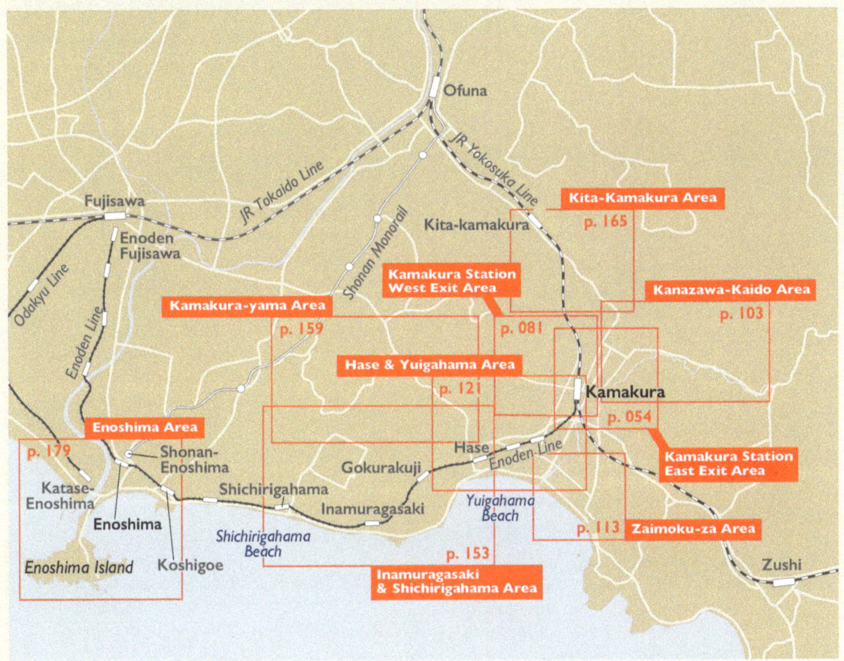

Walking is the best way to explore Central Kamakura, which is located near Kamakura Station.
To travel west to Enoshima, we recommend taking the charming train known affectionately as "Enoden." Bus service from Kamakura Station provides convenient access to other areas, and rental cycles are available for fair-weather travel. Information on transportation and sightseeing is available at the information center located directly to the left of the station's East Exit.

All of the content for sites and shops listed in this section have been checked and confirmed for accuracy by the owners, temple/shrine priests, or public relation representatives of each establishment.

Icons & Symbols

 **Cafe** Drinks, snacks and sweets are served. Some cafes also serve light meals

 **Japanese food** Eateries serving Japanese meals of refined traditional cuisine; Japanese soul food, such as *okonomiyaki* savory pancakes or *yakitori*; or more standard home-style cooking, such a rice, miso soup, and grilled fish

 **Other food** Italian, French, American, Chinese, Southeast Asian, and fusion cuisine

 **Take-out food** Take-out food sold at delis, food stands, or shops

 **Shopping** Retail shops selling confectionaries, processed food, fresh food, crafts, home accessories, gift items, etc.

 **Hotel** Lodgings such as hotels, hostels, B & Bs, or guest houses

 **Shrine** Shinto places where *kami* (Shinto deities) are housed and Shinto rituals are performed

 **Temple** Buddhist places of worship, where funerals and other Buddhist services are performed

 **Museum** Museums that hold collections of art or other historic, natural, archaeological, or scientific artifacts

 **Park and other facilities** Public parks and business complexes

 **Activities** Facilities for learning traditional Japanese cultural arts and crafts or for various sports

 **Spa** Traditional Japanese bathhouses with communal bathing areas

 **English Menu** English menus are available

 **English Speaker** English-speaking staff are always available
(Reduced size icon): Minimal amount of English spoken

 **Flexitarian** Eateries where the menu has at least one option for which seasoning, broth, or soup stock may be meat- or seafood-based, but morsels of meat or seafood are not served in the dish itself. Eggs and dairy might be used

 **Vegan** Eateries with at least one menu item completely free of animal or seafood, including eggs or dairy products. The dishes may not be "Buddhist vegan," which excludes onions, garlic, chives, green onions, and leeks (In small cafes, there may be options with flexitarian or vegan snacks or sweets but the icon might be not indicated since menus frequently change)

 **Wi-Fi** Free Wi-Fi is available
(Reduced size icon): Indicates that free Wi-Fi is available in limited areas

 **Credit Card** Credit cards accepted (primarily Visa and MasterCard)
(Reduced size icon): Indicates that credit cards are accepted with a minimum purchase amount. Check before ordering

 **Parking** Parking lot with more than 4 free parking spaces
(Reduced size icon): Indicates one of the following: 3 free parking spaces or less available; compact cars only; or paid parking available

 **Group** Seating capacity or take-out is available for a party of 10 or more people
(Reduced size icon): Indicates seating capacity for group of 10 or more people only with reservations or during non-peak hours

 **Barrier-Free** Facilities, including restrooms, are barrier-free
(Reduced size icon): Barrier-free accommodations are possible if accompanied by a helper, but toilets do not meet barrier-free standards

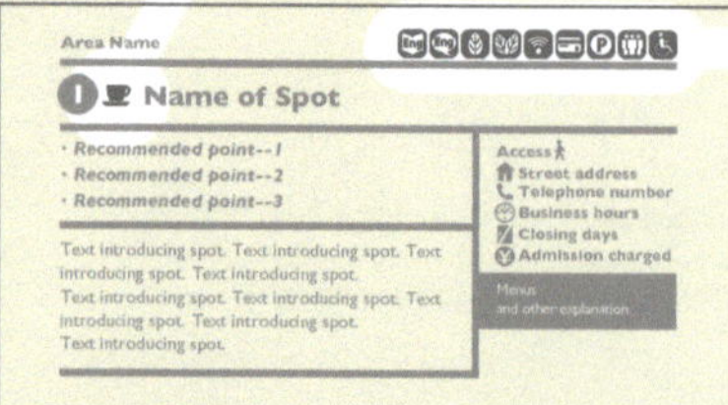

Icons & Symbols

 **Walking figure icon** Time required on foot from nearest train station or bus stop

 **House icon** Street address ("Kamakura City, Kanagawa Prefecture" is omitted)

Telephone icon Telephone number (for domestic calls) (If calling from abroad, precede the number with 81-467) Caveat: Most businesses do not have English-speaking staff

Clock icon Business hours
L.O. =Last order
C/I =Check-in
C/O =Check-out
D/C =Closing time (Most museums, temples, and shrines close 30 minutes prior to closing time)

 **Door icon** Closing days
(*) When regular closing days fall on a national holiday, the following day will be closed. (Check Japanese calendar in advance to confirm national holidays)
IR =Closing days are irregular (Many independent business operations have irregular schedules, thus there is always a risk of an unannounced holiday or closure. We recommend visiting a tourist information center where they can confirm operation in advance.)
wk =Week
~ Used to indicate prices that are not fixed, but have a base rate (eg. "¥500~" means "¥500 or more")

Res. only Advanced reservations are necessary

 **Yen Icon** Admission charged (Some temples, shrines, and museums offer discounted rates for students and children)
Ele =Elementary schoolers
Mid =Middle schoolers
HS =High schoolers

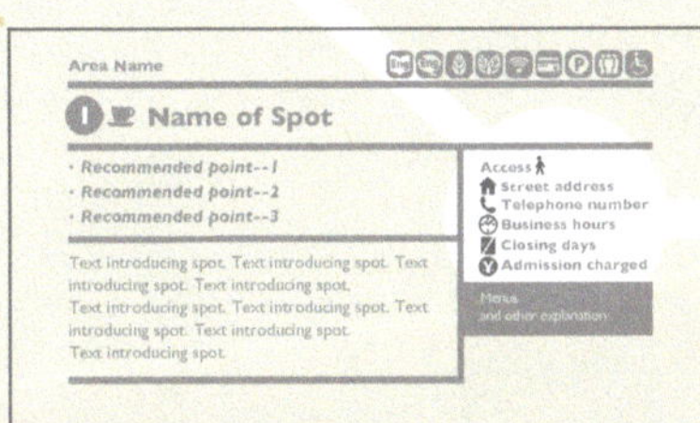

All prices listed include 8% tax.
Tax rates are subject to change.

Icons on Area Maps

 **Bus stop**

 **Rental bicycles**

 **Antique fair, Flea market**

 **Public toilet**

Wise must-know tips from the Great Buddha

1 Travel in small numbers.

2 Driving is not recommended especially since streets are narrow and parking is limited.

3 Few shops or sightseeing spots are baby-stroller or wheelchair accessible. (Refer to Barrier-Free icon)

4 Credit cards are not always accepted.

5 Public trash bins are not provided on the streets, so on principle your waste should be taken home for disposal.

6 When eating at the beach or outdoors, kites (hawk-like birds) will grab food from your hands or bag, so eat under a roof.

Kamakura Station East Exit Area

Since the Kamakura Era, the East Exit Area of Kamakura has been the city center; now, the bus terminal at JR Kamakura Station serves as the gateway.
A visit to Kamakura is never complete without a walk along Wakamiya-Oji Avenue or the souvenir-shop-packed Komachi Street.

Naruto-ya＋Tenzo

Tempura Hiromi

RENDEZ-VOUS DES AMIS

COBAKABA

Kosuzu

Toshimaya Honten

floresta

Kamakura Ham Tomioka Shoukai Komachi Honten

Renbai (Kamakura Farmer's Market)

Hideyoshi

PARADISE ALLEY BREAD & CO

DAILY by LONG TRACK FOODS

Kamakura Chiffon

IKUSTAM

FUNIKURA

Patagonia Kamakura

nugoo kamakura Ninotorii Store

Kimono Kuroudo Miyamoto

Hakko-do

Hachiman-do

Myohon-ji Temple

Tsurugaoka Hachimangu Shrine

Tsurugaoka Museum, Kamakura

Kamakura Kokuhoukan (National Treasure) Museum

Kamakurabori Museum, Cafe, and Shop

M's Ark Kamakura (Pay toilet)

Kaburaki Kiyokata Memorial Art Museum

Kamakura City Kawakita Film Museum

Kamakura Station East Exit Area

 Naruto-ya+Tenzo なるとや ＋ 典座

- *Japanese restaurant with a simple menu*
- *Featuring fresh, local vegetables*
- *Carefully selected miso, salt, and soy sauce*

Kamakura Sta. East Exit, 2 mins. 🚶
🏠 **2F 1-6-12 Komachi**
📞 **0467-23-7666**
🕐 **11:30am-3:00pm**
   (L.O. 2:30)
   6:00pm-9:00pm
   (L.O. 8:30pm)
▨ **Tue, 2nd & 4th Wed**

Monthy special set ¥1,728
Kudzu udon ¥864
Udon set: Udon noodles with three deli dishes ¥1,728

Tenzo is the title given to a chef at a Zen Buddhist temple; their role is to oversee all matters concerning food preparation. This restaurant, which takes the word *tenzo* as part of its name, serves dishes that completely bring out the delicious flavors and freshness of local, seasonal vegetables. Proprietor Yosuke Ichikawa's motto is: "You are what you eat." Using skills he developed at a Kyoto restaurant that serves *kaiseki ryori* (traditional Japanese course meals) and ideas borrowed from *shojin ryori* (Buddhist vegan cuisine), he serves dishes that are simple yet have refined flavors not commonly found in home-style cooking, and food that is nourishing for both the body and the mind.

Naruto-ya+Tenzo offers a list of items that balance flavor, color, and cooking technique in keeping with a fundamental concept of Japanese cooking called *gomi-goshiki-goho* ("five flavors, five colors and five cooking methods"). In the spring, Naruto-ya+Tenzo's popular set menu may include such items as *goma doufu* (puréed sesame seeds chilled in tofu-like cakes), rice steamed with bamboo shoots, spring cabbage soup, young wakame seaweed with new potatoes, or baby carrots with tomatoes. The menu changes depending on the ingredients in season, and many customers travel long distances to find out what is being served. The tableware is crafted by artisans and gives character to the experience. Visit Naruto-ya+Tenzo to experience scrupulously prepared Japanese cuisine.

2 Tempura Hiromi 天ぷら ひろみ

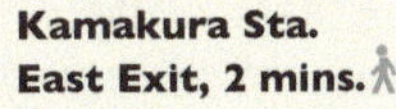

- *Tempura loved by legendary Kamakuraites*
- *Top-grade ingredients and frying oil*
- *A 3-minute walk from the station*

**Kamakura Sta.
East Exit, 2 mins.**
🏠 2F 1-6-13 Komachi
📞 0467-22-2696
🕐 11:30am-2:00pm,
   5:00pm-7:30pm
▨ Wed(*)

Ozu-don (Bowl) ¥3,800
Lunch set ¥1,950~¥2,800
Dinner set ¥2,500~¥3,780
"Kaede" (early bird special)
¥6,480
"Omakase" course ¥10,800
*Reservations required for
"Kaede" and "Omakase"

Over 60 years old, this tempura restaurant loved by Kamakura's famous cultural figures was relocated from its nearby location by the current owner, Masao Sato, who is the second generation to continue this family-owned operation, with his wife and son.

Sato hand-selects seafood and vegetables fresh from the market, and uses oil from unroasted golden sesame seeds that has been "pressed" by a traditional method, resulting in a crisp and aromatic finish. The rice is cooked in an iron kettle, and the miso is a special *akadashi* red miso, which has a dark color and tastes stronger than typical miso soup.

For lunch, the three choices of tempura set meals offer a selection from a variety of fish, shrimp, and vegetables with miso soup and pickles. For dinner, there is a choice of three set meals, and they also serve five different course meals for which advanced reservations are recommended. Bowl menus are available at both lunch and dinner.

If you prefer counter seating to witness the tempura master's culinary skills, we recommend reserving the "Kaede" early bird special course for which reservations are between 5:00-6:00pm. Another option is the "Omakase course" with 13 tempura items from among the owner's pick of the day. Enjoy the added luxury of a counter seat where you can feast your eyes and chat with the chef.

3 🍴 RENDEZ-VOUS DES AMIS

- *Stand-up bistro near the East Exit*
- *Comfortable eatery for solo diners*
- *Perfect wine accompaniments*

**Kamakura Sta.
East Exit, 1 min.** 🚶
🏠 2F 1-4-24 Komachi
📞 0467-24-2214
🕐 6:00pm–12:00am
(L.O. 11:30pm)
Thu

Porchetta ¥800
Wine by the glass ¥500~
(Wine by the bottle also available). No table or chair seating, only standing at the counter.

As you emerge through the East Exit of Kamakura Station, take an immediate right down a narrow alley, and on the second block to your right, you will find the bistro's small square sign for this bistro next to the stairs of an old multi-use building. Climb up the stairs to reach this quaint wine-and-dine bar on the second floor.

At first glance, Ren-Vous des Amis may seem like a local hideaway-type joint, but customers are made to feel comfortable even when visiting solo and/or for the first time.

Owner-chef Mou Soejima is a rising star in the food biz, and is the subject of interest particularly for his catering supervision for a Hollywood film crew. With the concept of making dishes that go well with wine, Soejima, whose experience ranges from serving as chef at a leading French restaurant to assisting with research on French cuisine, opened this restaurant in Kamakura because of it's cultured community.

With its inviting and casual appearance that lures people inside, its fine selection of wine and reputation for laboriously prepared dishes with authentic flavors, Rendez-Vous des Amis is always thriving.

Casual snack-like items are ¥300 to ¥1,800, while more substantial ones such as porchetta (a kind of pork roast) are from ¥800 and up. A glass of wine ranges from ¥500 to ¥1,000. Items are clearly listed by price on the user-friendly menu.

4 COBAKABA

- *Japanese home-style breakfasts*
- *Operates from 7:00am*
- *Choice of rice or bread*

Kamakura Sta. East Exit, 4 mins.
🏠 1-13-15 Komachi
📞 0467-22-6131
🕐 7:00am-2:00pm
Wed

Rice set (Choice of raw egg, "natto," tofu, smoked bacon & fried egg, and grilled fish, served with five-grain rice, miso soup, pickles, a vegetable side dish and organic herb tea) ¥820~

Bread set (Choice of fried egg, smoked bacon, seasonal jam, served with homemade pain de champagne, salad, and a drink) ¥720~

A Kamakuraite from birth, Keisuke Uchibori opened this home-style eatery 10 years ago with the idea to create a hub-like spot for locals. After renewing his shop in 2017, he focused on developing his operation as a breakfast joint. He serves straight-up and simple breakfasts prepared with tender care, like those traditionally served in the average Japanese home. Each (except for the "Bread set") serving is rounded out with the basic set of rice, a bowl of miso soup, and *otsukemono* (rice bran fermented) pickles. Uchibori pays particular attention to creating dishes that reflect the qualities of traditional home cooking, or in other words, dishes that harness the gifts of nature and the seasons. He relies on a hand-picked network of vendors from various parts of Japan to procure basic ingredients such as organic rice and homemade miso and soy sauce. He also uses fresh seasonal vegetables from the Kamakura Renbai market next door.

The breakfast menu is simple: a choice between a traditional meal with rice or a Western meal with bread. If you're adventurous and want to try the "real deal," you can ask for your rice to be topped with a fresh raw egg, a long-standing Japanese staple breakfast item. In support of Kamakura culture, the restaurant also serves as a performance space and gallery for local artists.

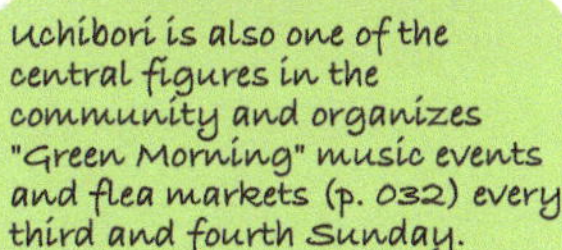

Photos by Yuko Okoso

5 Kosuzu こ寿々

- *Homemade soba noodle restaurant*
- *Japanese dessert "warabi-mochi" to go*
- *Local cafe and shop franchise*

Opened in 1996, this noodle shop operates out of what used to be a specialty store for tea ceremony goods. With charm apropos to Kamakura, it maintains the appearance of a traditional tea house. To enjoy the taste of freshly milled, handmade soba, we recommend you try a cold soba item. The most popular one is their specialty, Kosuzu Soba, a cold noodle dish with a variety of toppings including grated Japanese radish, fried batter, *mitsuba* (Japanese wild parsley) and *nori* seaweed. Instead of dipping the soba in sauce, pour the sauce over the toppings and enjoy. One of their dessert items is *warabi-mochi,* made of bracken and has a mildly sweet jello-like texture. Also be sure to sample their healthy vegan take-out sweets at the counter.

<Sister Shops>

Kosuzu has two other sister shops.

Yuigahama (Japanese sweets cafe) (p. 122)
This modern interior cafe does not serve soba, but you can enjoy *warabi-mochi* and other Japanese sweets along with hot and cold matcha green tea drinks.
Try the "Azuki Warabi-mochi" in a sweet adzuki bean paste and matcha green tea sauce.
**(3-3-25 Yuigahama, Open: 10:30am~5:30pm
Closed on Mondays)**

CIAL Kamakura (p. 054)
(Warabi-mochi take-out shop)
This shop in the mall next to Kamakura Station East Exit sells take-out *warabi-mochi.*
**(1-1-1 Komachi, Open: 9:00am~8:00pm
Open 7 days/wk)**

**Kamakura Sta.
East Exit, 6 mins.**
2-13-4 Komachi
0467-25-6210
11:30am-6:30pm
Mon(*)

"Warabi-mochi" to go
(9 pieces) ¥756
Kosuzu-soba ¥1,080
Zaru soba ¥864
Sake ¥540

6  Toshima-ya Honten 豊島屋

- *An old and famous sweets store*
- *Popular dove shaped cookies*
- *Made using high-grade ingredients*

Kamakura Sta. East Exit, 5 mins. 🚶
🏠 2-11-19 Komachi
📞 0467-25-0810
🕐 9:00am-7:00pm
▧ Wed(*), IR

Hato Sable (bag of 5 cookies) ¥648
Kamakura no Irodori (Colors of Kamakura) ¥972
"Kobato Mameraku" (Dove-shaped powdered sweet beans) ¥432

Established in 1894, Toshima-ya is a confectionery that creates Japanese sweets with scrupulous care using top-grade ingredients. Its trademark product is a cookie called "Hato Sablé" that is shaped like a dove ("hato" means "dove"), the symbol of Tsurugaoka Hachiman-gu Shrine. Hato Sablé has been the most iconic and popular sweet of Kamakura for over 100 years. The background story is that the founder had learned the recipe for shortbread cookies after his delightful discovery of the taste from a non-native acquaintance.

One bite of these cute, crunchy textured, and sweet Hato Sablé will make you an immediate fan. Sold individually wrapped, the cookies also make great souvenirs along with the fun dove-shaped stationery (sold at the main store), sure to put a smile on the face of their recipient.

Toshima-ya also specializes in traditional Japanese confections, such as *nama-gashi* (soft and moist cakes made with sweetened bean paste) and *hi-gashi* (dried cakes made with sugar, beans, and nut flour) that elegantly reflect the seasons. In addition to the main shop that faces Wakamiya-Oji Avenue, there are other locations in Kita-Kamakura—one near the Great Buddha in Hase and the other near the bus rotary at the east exit of Kamakura Station.

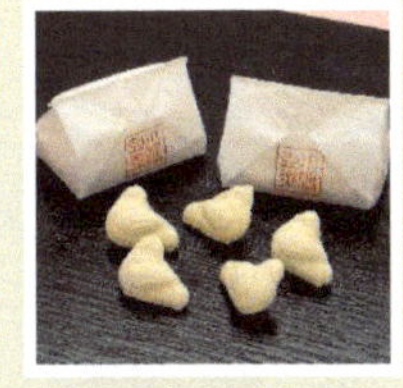

7 floresta

- *All-natural homemade donuts*
- *Adorable animal-shaped donuts*
- *3 minutes from the station*

**Kamakura Sta.
East Exit, 3 mins.**
1-3-4 Komachi
0467-73-7371
11:00am-6:00pm
IR

Sugar donut ¥130
Earl Gray donut ¥160
Daibutsu donut ¥190
Animal-shaped donut ¥210

Floresta is a take-out donut shop along Wakamiya-Oji Avenue, a short walk from Kamakura Station in the direction of the coast.

Shelves are lined with donuts of fun shapes and colors, all made using vegetables such as *kabocha* pumpkin and fruit such as strawberries, without the use of any additives, preservatives, or artificial coloring. Every ingredient is carefully selected—in addition to using soymilk, sea salt, and aluminum-free baking powder. The owner rises early each day to make the donuts by hand. The fluffy and delicate taste will fill your mouth with flavors that never fail to put a smile on faces of adults and children alike.

Despite their high quality, the donuts are kept at reasonable prices since the owner believes that children should be able to enjoy them as a daily snack. It's a shop loved by everyone. Why not mingle with the locals to get your fill of these delightful donuts?

8  Kamakura Ham Tomioka Shoukai Komachi-honten

鎌倉ハム富岡商会

- *Long-established ham manufacturer*
- *Traditional flavors*
- *Top sanitary quality*

Kamakura Ham's secret recipe was brought to Kamakura by an Englishman named William Curtis, who landed in Yokohama Port soon after it opened in 1863. After its flavor and quality became popular, "Kamakura Ham" was named after its place of origin, then took root throughout the region.

Shuzo Tomioka, a manufacturer and engineer brought up in the ham industry, eventually established "Kamakura Ham Tomioka Co., Ltd." This brand inherits the tradition of producing flavors that can only be created by hand, for which craftsman at the production plant carefully manufacture daily to protect the time-honored taste. Leading in sanitary quality management, their innovative packaging methods seal in the delicious ham essence. Each product goes through a scrupulous manufacturing process and strict sanitation checks before they are labeled and shipped. Retort pouch products are available in addition to ham, bacon, sausage, and hamburger patties. Keep an eye out for their goods sold widely at supermarkets and other specialty stores.

Kamakura Sta.
East Exit, 4 mins.
🏠 1F 2-2-19 Komachi
📞 0467-25-1864
🕐 10:00am-6:00pm
(Jun-Jul:10am-7pm)
Jun-July, Nov-Dec
Open 7 days/wk
Jan-May, Aug-Oct
Wed

kamakura-ni (Stewed pork) ¥594
Sausage ¥648~
Ham ¥432~
Traditional roasted ham wrapped in cloth ¥5,400

9 Renbai (Kamakura Farmer's Market)　鎌倉農協連売所

- *Market of freshly harvested local vegetables*
- *Sold directly from farmers*
- *A 4-minute walk from Kamakura station*

Kamakura Sta. East Exit, 4 mins.
🏠 1-13-10 Komachi
📞 N/A
🕐 8:00am-til products are sold out
Open 7 days/wk
Jan.1-Jan.4

If there is a particular farmer you prefer to buy from, then check the calendar on the wall that indicates which group they are in and which days they are scheduled to sell.

This farmer's market known to the locals as "Renbai" started out in 1928. At a time when local Japanese farmers were struggling with sales, a pastor from overseas taught them about the European market system in which farmers sell directly to customers at a set place and time. This inspired the local farmers to organize their own direct-sales system, resulting in Renbai—Japan's first farmer's market. Farmers are organized in groups of 4 and take turns in shifts (every 4 days) to proudly display and sell their produce.

The daily use produce sold here are known as "Kamakura vegetables" since they are grown locally and according to the season. Other than those used for daily meals, they also sell hard-to-find veggies, such as those used in European cuisine, which are produced upon request by the chefs of restaurants near and far, who arrive in the early morning to make their purchase.

There are no labels or signage to distinguish organic produce from the conventionally grown produce, but most of the veggies found here are grown without pesticides or with a reduced amount of pesticides in comparison to those in supermarkets. For the widest selection, it's best to arrive at the market before noon—the vendors close up their stands as soon as their items are all sold out.

10 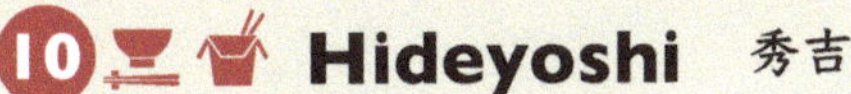 Hideyoshi 秀吉

- *Take-out char-grilled "yakitori"*
- *Eat-in counter for nighttime dining*
- *Guaranteed use of fresh chicken daily*

This small *yakitori* shop has been in operation nearly 20 years and is run by a couple who were raised in Kamakura. Always packed with local customers who come for the popular charcoal-grilled *yakitori* ("yaki" means "grilled" and "tori" means "chicken") and other skewered items, the grill's master insists on using only fresh chicken, never frozen, and carefully rotates the skewers until they are done grilling. During the day, *yakitori* is sold only for take-out, but after 5:00pm (4:00pm on weekends) several counter seats are made available as a traditional style Japanese bar inside their store.

The main menu consists of "kushi-yaki" ("kushi" means "skewer"), with ingredients such as vegetables, pork back ribs, or unique foie gras. For a la carte items, there is number of dishes including cabbage with miso paste, onion salad, or giblet stew. Enjoy sampling these while you wait for your *yakitori* items to arrive.

Lined up along the counter are a variety of bottles of "shochu" (distilled spirits made from grains and vegetables) such as the house original or one made with chili peppers, both of which go well diluted with hot water. In the evening, the proprietors set up tables and chairs outside the store for additional seating. Why not join in for a *yakitori* happy hour experience at this compact, but tasteful and lively traditional Japanese bar environment, while dining on *yakitori*.

Kamakura Sta. East Exit, 4 mins. 🚶

🏠 1-13-10 Komachi

📞 0467-24-1616

🕐 <Take-out>
11:00am-9:00pm
<Eaat-in>
Weekdays:
5:00pm-9:00pm,
Sat, Sun, Holidays:
4:00pm-9:00pm

▨ Tue, IR

Average price for "yakitori": ¥120~¥150, with some gourmet items over ¥600.

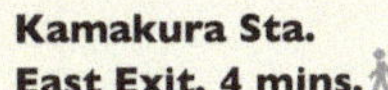

PARADISE ALLEY BREAD & CO

- *Bread served with philosophy*
- *Perfect marriage of wheat flour and yeast*
- *The hub of contemporary Kamakura culture*

Kamakura Sta. East Exit, 4 mins.
🏠 1-13-10 Komachi
📞 0467-84-7203
🕐 **As soon as the first batch of bread is ready-6:00pm (closing time)**
▨ IR

Anpan ("an" means "sweet bean paste"), Bread stuffed with raisins (plain/bamboo charcoal powder): ¥216, Bagels: ¥324, Pain de Campagne: ¥205/100g

This bakery is owned by Junpei Katsumi, one of the leading figures of contemporary Kamakura culture who was born and raised locally.

While the bread is delicious on its own merit, it has been baked with a pinch of philosophy to give it extra flavor. The yeast is thriving with live cultures, the wheat is the highest quality available, and the most important ingredient—love—is kneaded into the bread before it is baked. Through their bread products, Paradise Alley strives to communicate a message for everyone to live peacefully as humans should—a message from Kamakura to rest of the world.

Everyone should visit this bakery and taste the bread that is guaranteed to satisfy both taste buds and hearts.

Bread items are delivered to the shelves fresh out of the oven. Supplies are limited, so it's best to get there as early as possible.

From the sheer amount of event announcements and stacks of flyers on the counter and walls, you can tell this is a hubs for many Kamakuraites. (There is an adjoining cafe but it is not non-smoking)

12 DAILY by LONG TRACK FOODS

· *Tasty, stylish delicatessen with handmade*

This deli serves all natural, non-processed items that are guaranteed to garner a following since they only use carefully picked ingredients and are very particular about serving home-made goods. Product highlights include pickles made with locally harvested vegetables, vegetable dips and dressings that taste best with fresh vegetables sold at the nearby local market, and healthy and tasty baked goods. There is also a variety of hand-made items that are perfect for souvenirs or gifts.

To those in the know, the Daily is where you will always find quality, as indicated by the dedicated customers who come from near and far.

Kamakura Sta.
East Exit, 4 mins.
🏠 1-13-10 Komachi
📞 N/A
🕐 10:00am–5:00pm
Mon

13  Kamakura Chiffon

· *All-natural chiffon patisserie*

The chiffon cake on the menu of Satoko Aoki's coffee shop became so popular among customers that she decided to open a take-out shop. The soothing taste of this melt-in-your-mouth chiffon is made with domestic wheat and high-quality eggs, eliminating the need for baking powder or other leavening agents. The wide variety of flavors includes plain, matcha green tea, banana, earl grey tea, chocolate, and seasonal offerings such as cherry blossom and *yomogi* (Japanese mugwort). Each cake is made one by one with meticulous care, and flavors are all additive- and preservative-free so that the natural and delicate tastes can be fully enjoyed.

Kamakura Sta.
East Exit, 4 mins.
🏠 1-13-10 Komachi
📞 0467-23-1833
🕐 10:00am–5:30pm
Mon

Slice of cake ¥280
Whole cake ¥1,680
Standard flavors: Plain and tea (other flavors available by ordering in advance)
Cakes will last up to two weeks if kept frozen.

Marushichi Shopping Alley 丸七商店街

· *Shopping alley like the time has stopped*

Walk the opposite direction of Komachi street through the rotary in front of Kamakura station, a large white signboard will be visible. Past there will start a narrow alley with approximately 10 stores, with a Japanese street corner atmosphere that feels like time has stopped in the 1940s to 1950s.

The locals who are in their 60s and 70s speak of nostalgic times when they were kids after World War II, when the shopping alley was "Crowded with fish store, vegetable store, bars, milk store, flower shops, imported cosmetics store, and snacks store."

With the trace of those times left, each owner is committed to their own small space even after shops change over time. Cake shops, knick-nap shops,

restaurants are open during the day, and when the night gets closer, standing bars open up and turn this place into a "Drunkers' alley," a place where cigarette smoke drifts.

The big white signboard is easy to find just a door away from Tokyu Store supermarket.

14 🛍 IKUSTAM

· *Miniature specialty shop*

In the depths of the retro back alley of Marushichi, you will discover this fantasy world overflowing with thousands of teeny tiny fruit, vegetables, flowers, cake, snacks, bottles, cooking ware, books, furniture, and many, many other items all looking like shrunken replicas of the real thing. Since the owner was a child she built up a wide collection of miniatures, and after it became substantial enough, she opened up this shop. She and her staff travel around the world looking for more miniature items to add. Some of the kitchen items are unique in that they can actually be used for cooking a mini meal. Take home one of their vintage items—at least you won't have trouble finding space for it!

**Kamakura Sta.
East Exit, 3 mins.** 🚶
🏠 1-3-4 Komachi
📞 050-1453-2739
🕐 12:00pm-6:00pm
Open 7 days/wk

Fruit ¥300
Flowers ¥20~¥50

15 🛍 Funikura

· *A vintage variety shop*

With a shop-front display of nostalgic kitchenware serving as its signage, this variety vintage shop possesses important iconic value in maintaining the retro atmosphere of the Marushichi Shopping Street. Finding delight in the extra special appeal of everyday items of yesteryear, the shop owner has dedicated her life to sharing her selection of charming kitsch items from Japan and other parts of the world. Here you will find a variety of Mid-century modern thermos bottles, anodized aluminium "Alumite" lunch boxes, hot pots, and baskets. Your inner child is sure to be tickled by the charm of the early modern wares and various hand-made accessories.

**Kamakura Sta.
East Exit, 3 mins.** 🚶
🏠 1-3-4 Komachi
📞 N/A
🕐 11:00am-6:00pm
Mon-Thu, IR

16 Patagonia Kamakura

- *Outdoor apparel and gear store*
- *Supports local grassroots activities*
- *Kamakura Store original T-shirts*

**Kamakura Sta.
East Exit, 4 mins.**
🏠 1-13-12 Komachi
📞 0467-23-8970
🕙 10:00am-6:00pm
Open 7 days/wk

Kamakura Store original
"tenugui" washcloth ¥1,998

Patagonia is an international outdoor apparel company founded by legendary climber and environmentalist Yvon Chouinard who defines his effective management style in his memoir "Let My People Go Surfing." Products sold are based on encouraging a sense of social and environmental responsibility, efficiency, flexibility, and cooperation. The company's first Japanese headquarters founded in the 1990s was based at this location for about 20 years, but have since moved elsewhere.

What remains in its place is their signature retail shop with the relaxed atmosphere of their flagship store in Ventura, CA. The "communication space" on the second floor has sofas for leisurely shopping with the family. In keeping with its agenda to support grassroots organizations, the shop has ties to the local community and plays an active role in preserving Kamakura's environment.

This shop's selection includes sportswear for trail running, yoga, and surfing, and also ecologically designed outerwear and other comfortable items.

17 nugoo kamakura Ninotorii Store 拭う

www.grap.co.jp/nugoo/home.html

- *Traditional "tenugui" hand towel store*
- *2 shops along Wakamiya-Oji Avenue*
- *Adjoining cafe*

The name of the store "nugoo" is based on the Japanese word meaning "to wipe." Here, you can find traditional Japanese *tenugui* hand towels that are very versatile in use; for example, they can be used as tea towels, scarves, decorative wall hangings, or gift wrapping.

nugoo's original *tenugui* are unique in that they are dyed using a special traditional technique called "chuu-sen" ("chuu" means "pour" and "sen" means "dye") in which both sides are dyed, vividly revealing the colored patterns.

The first store along Wakamiya-Oji Avenue carries more than 300 patterns including original designs. With varying combinations of colors, materials, and sizes, there are all together more than 700 items on sale.

Aside from *tenugui*, they also sell items made using the *tenugui* cloth, such as small cloth pouches, fans, and other stylish accessories. Be sure to ask for their handy English pamphlet on the many ways to use *tenugui*, an explanation of the *chuu-sen* technique, and other dyeing processes.

Their Ni-no-torii shop is closer to the Kamakura train station and carries food-themed items such as bento boxes and bento wrappers made with *tenugui*. These *tenugui* products are not only beautiful and practical, but are also compact, making them perfect souvenirs or gifts from Japan. On the second floor of this shop is a Japanese tea cafe serving tea and seasonal sweets, so you can shop and rest in one visit. (Credit cards not accepted at the cafe.)

<Ni-no-torii Store>
Kamakura Sta.
East Exit, 5 mins.
🏠 2-10-12 Komachi
📞 0467-22-4448
🕐 <Store>
Weekdays:
10:30am-7:00pm,
Sat, Sun, Holidays:
10:00am-7:00pm
<Cafe>
11:00am-6:30pm
(L.O.6:00pm)
Open 7 days/wk

<Wakamiya-Oji Store>
🏠 Kamakura Sta.
📞 East Exit, 6 mins.
🕐 2-12-32 Komachi
0467-22-5551
Weekdays:
10:30am-7:00pm,
Sat, Sun, Holidays:
10:00am-7:00pm
Open 7 days/wk

Hand towels ¥972~
Pouches ¥1,296~
Bento wrappers ¥1,944~

Tenugui are used not only for drying your hands or sweat, but are also used to wrap around the head as "hachimaki" sweatbands during festivals as a symbol of focus or collective spirit. Be sure to check out their stoles made with tenugui cloth, too.

18  Kimono Kuroudo Miyamoto 着物 蔵人宮本

http://www.kuroudo.co.jp/en/

- *A long-standing luxury kimono shop*
- *Authentic one-of-a kind kimono*
- *Kimono rental and photo studio services*

Kamakura Sta. East Exit, 8 mins.
🏠 1-8-20 Omachi
📞 0467-22-0602
🕐 10:00am-6:00pm
Open 7 days/wk

Kuroudo was established in 1877 as a producer of dyed cloth for temple flags and banners, as well as for providing a kimono service known as "arai-hari" (the washing and stretching of kimonos). Currently operating under its fourth generation since they began selling high quality kimono made using traditional techniques, their business covers a wide range of services related to the art of kimono wearing.

For those interested in trying on kimono without the fuss, they provide kimono rental and fittings, and even arrange for hair styling and make-up to go with the look. You can choose from among their wide selection of pure silk kimono displayed inside the store, get fitted, and have your photograph taken by their professional photographers at the photo studio in the back or in the garden. They also offer outing tours for a more authentic kimono experience, such as visits to iconic Kamakura sights, participation in a tea ceremony, or rickshaw rides. The most popular request from their kimono renters is to be photographed posing among the historic scenery of Kamakura.

Kimono rental & fitting service ¥10,800~ (Price includes accessory rental, but you are requested to purchase your own pair of "tabi" split toe socks for ¥1,080~)

In the summertime (July and August) "yukata" cotton kimono are available. Rental and fitting service ¥5,400~ (Price includes accessory rental)

English website available. Reservations and inquiries in Engish accepted by email. kimono@kuroudo.co.jp

19 Hakko-do 博古堂

http://www.kamakurabori.org/english.html

- *Kamakura-bori lacquerware shop*
- *Modern Japanese interior design*
- *Directly in front of Hachiman-gu Shrine*

**Kamakura Sta.
East Exit, 10 mins.**
🏠 **2-1-28 Yukinoshita**
📞 **0467-22-2429**
🕐 **Mar-Oct:
9:30am-6:00pm
Nov-Feb:
9:30am-5:30pm**
Open 7 days/wk

Hand mirror ¥14,500
Rectangular tray ¥39,000
Round black tray ¥54,000
Other items include cups,
plates and tea caddies.

During the Kamakura era, sculptors of Buddhist images of Zen temples were very active artisans. The founders of this Kamakura-bori lacquerware shop, the Goto family, have been passing on the heritage of one of the most notable sculptors of that period, Unkei, through 29 generations to the present day owner.

The present owner is the first female heir. She carefully maintains her family tradition while introducing touches of modern design. Her vision for the craft is not to produce traditional lacquerware for display, but to create functional items that can be appreciated even by younger people for daily use. Hand mirrors and small platters are examples of the useful, but beautiful items you can find here among the breathtakingly elaborate work that is tastefully displayed in this shop here in front of the large torii gate of Tsurugaoka Hachiman-gu Shrine.

Created through a lengthy and time-consuming process, Kamakura-bori lacquerware has a beauty that is best enjoyed through years of usage, as it takes on richer shades and textures. If you find an item that suits your taste, it is sure to be a lifelong treasure to remind you of Kamakura with each use.

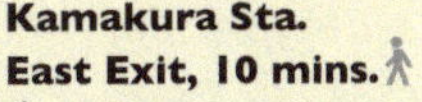

20 Hachiman-do 八万堂

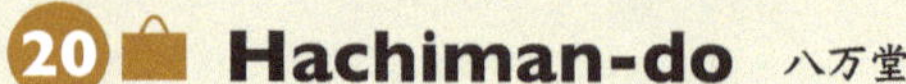

- *Antique shop established in 1925*
- *Authentic and refined items*
- *Close to Tsurugaoka Hachiman-gu Shrine*

Kamakura Sta. East Exit, 8 mins.
🏠 1-8-33 Yukinoshita
📞 0467-55-5594
🕙 11:00am-7:00pm
Wed

Small plates ¥900~
Small sword (without blade) ¥280,000

Occupying its prominent location in front of the main torii gate of Tsurugaoka Hachiman-gu Shrine for over 90 years, this antique shop has steadily maintained a refined selection of wares in line with its reputation.

Although situated along the city's bustling thoroughfare, the entrance and show windows of this charming shop emanates the quiet and refined ambiance of a small tea room.

Once inside, you are greeted by a 600-year-old statue of Benzaiten (the goddess of music) seated in the middle of the small shop; on the surrounding shelves are stacks of small chinaware platters more than 100 years old at reasonable prices from ¥900 since their decorations were not painted by hand, but from copperplate printing. With each illustration unique from the next, tableware and various decorative containers have endless possibilities for use.

Other offerings of modest beauty and refined quality lining the shelves are authentic tea ceremony articles, decorative swords for display, and other small items selected with a keen aesthetic sensibility. For those who are interested in acquiring genuine Japanese antiques, this is the place for you.

22 **Myohon-ji Temple** 妙本寺

http://www.myohonji.or.jp/english/

- *A temple surrounded by a thick grove*
- *Quiet temple with few tourists*
- *10 minutes from Kamakura Station*

**Kamakura Sta.
East Exit, 10 mins.**
🏠 1-15-1 Omachi
📞 0467-22-0777
🕘 9:00am-4:00pm
¥ Free

Established in 1260 by Nichiren Shonin, a Buddhist priest and founder of the Nichiren sect, Myohon-ji Temple is one of the oldest Nichiren temples. The temple was built by Hiki Daigaku Saburo Yoshimoto in

this valley where fellow Hiki clan member, Hiki no Ama, Minamoto Yoritomo's wet nurse had lived. Eventually, it became the site of the Hiki Rebellion, where the Hiki were destroyed by the Hojo clan who were scheming to retain power of the Kamakura Shogunate. Yoshimoto's life was spared since he was taken to Kyoto for safety; after his return to Kamakura as an adult, he encountered Nichiren, and believed that only he could pray for the repose of souls of his clan. He donated his property to Nichiren to build this temple. Despite the tragic history of the location, visitors will find nothing but peace at this temple next to a dense forest. The trees are modestly pruned as a show of respect to nature and produce a tranquil environment.

Hiki Yoshikazu was adopted by Hiki no Ama, Minamoto Yoritomo's wet nurse, and served as Yoritomo's right-hand man. Yoshikazu and his wife served Yoritomo's son, Yoriie, as a wet-nurse and their daughter Wakasa became Yoriie's mistress and gave birth to Yoriie's first son. After Yoritomo's death, Yoshikazu gained power as relative of Yoriie, which posed a threat to the Hojo clan, so Yoriie, his infant son, and the Hiki clan were all assasinated by the Hojo clan.

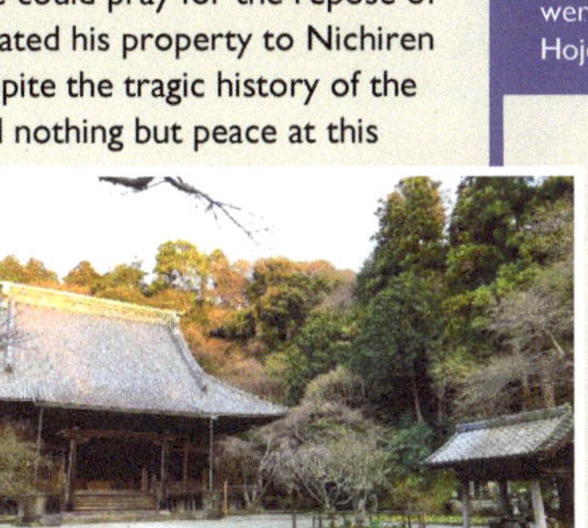

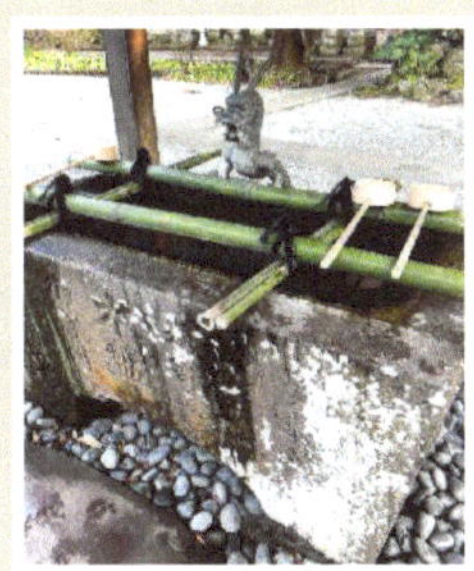

Nichiren Shonin
(1222-1282):
A Japanese Buddhist priest who lived during the Kamakura period when the city was suffering from natural disasters and famine. He is known for preaching to commoners on the street and also for his predictions of Genko (the Mongol invasion of Japan), which occurred twice.

21 ⛩ Tsurugaoka Hachimangu Shrine 鶴岡八幡宮

http://www.tsurugaoka-hachimangu.jp

- *Founded by Minamoto Yoritomo*
- *Spiritual base of Kamakura warriors*
- *800-year old symbol of Kamakura*

**Kamakura Sta.
East Exit, 10 mins.** 🚶
🏠 **2-1-31 Yukinoshita**
📞 **0467-22-0315**
🕐 **Apr-Sep:
5:00am-9:00pm
(D/C: 8:30pm)
Oct-Mar:
6:00am-9:00pm
(D/C: 8:30pm)**
**Open 7 days/wk
*Jan 1st-3rd:
Open 24 hours**
💴 **Free**

To maintain the power of the Minamoto clan, Minamoto Yoritomo, the founder of the first feudal government (shogunate) in Japan, built this magnificent shrine in 1180 for Hachiman, the tutelary god of warriors, who was worshiped by his ancestors. Initially it was known as Tsurugaoka Wakamiya Shrine, thus, the main avenue of Kamakura City that stretches from the shrine's main torii gate (The third torii) to the beach was named Wakamiya-Oji.

The symbolism of particular elements of the shrine shows us how serious the Minamoto clan was about retaining glory. For example, the ponds collectively known as the Genpei-ike pond just inside the main torii gate—the Genji pond to the east and the Heike pond to the west. Possessing three islands, Genji pond represents the Minamoto clan, while Heike pond has four islands symbolizing the Taira clan, the rivals of the Minamoto clan. The east is symbolic of the direction of ascension (sunrise), and the west is the direction of descent (sunset). There is hidden meaning in the number of the islands: three, or *san* in Japanese, means birth and success, and four, or *shi*, means death. Before the Meiji period, Shintoism and Buddhism were worshiped together, since Buddhism was incorporated seamlessly into Shintoism, thus Buddhist temples were built around the Genpei pond. None of those structures remain, however, the pictorial map exhibited in the shrine museum reveals the happy coexistence of both religions during that period.

Tsurugaoka Hachimangu served as the political center as well as the spiritual hub for Kamakura warriors; and today it is still regarded as a sanctuary retaining the spirit of Bushido, or the "Way of the Warrior." With over 800 years of history, the shrine continues the rituals and festivals that were held in the days of Yoritomo, and attracts many visitors throughout the year.

The text on Tsurugaoka Hachimangu Shrine was edited at the request of their publicity representative, thus we are not responsible for any grammatical inconsistencies. Thank you for your understanding.

A **Main Shrine**
The main shrine enshrines Emperor Ojin, Hime-gami, and Empress Jingu; these three are enshrined together as the Hachiman *kami*, or deities. After a fire in 1191 that destroyed the entire precinct, the main shrine was rebuilt the same year. Yet again, it was attacked in 1821, and so the present structure dates from an 1828 restoration ordered by the eleventh Tokugawa shogun, Ienari.

B **Wakamiya Shrine**
The relatives of Emperor Ojin are enshrined here—his wife (Nakano-hime), son (Emperor Nintoku) and daughter-in-law (Nintoku's wife), and grandson. The old juniper tree planted next to is said to have been imported from China by Minamoto Sanetomo, the son of Yoritomo about 800 years ago.

C **Museum of Shrine Treasures**
Located to the left side of the main shrine. Displays shrine treasures such as portable shrines (*mikoshi*), arrows and bows, and Japanese armory. Ticket vending machines are located just outside the main shrine (Adult ¥200, Child ¥100).

D **Maruyama-Inarisha Shrine**
Maruyama-Inari had been worshiped by the local people prior to the founding of Tsurugaoka Hachimangu.

E **Amulet Office**
A variety of amulets and *ema* (votive tablets) are provided here. At the far end of the amulet office, you can draw paper fortunes (English version available), and you will find pamphlets in English.

F **The Great Ginkgo Tree**
A giant 1000-year-old ginkgo tree that existed on this spot was toppled in a strong wind on 10th March, 2010. Young saplings have emerged from its roots.

G **Lower Worship Hall / Maiden**
Rituals and other events are held here throughout the year.

H **Shirahata-Jinja Shrine**
Minamoto Yoritomo and his son Sanetomo, the third shogun (and also a talented poet), are enshrined here.

J **Guest House / Saikan**
Shrine priests stay here before important rituals in order to purify their bodies and spirits. This building is also used to welcome emissaries and special guests. Unless ceremonies are being conducted, it generally operates as a tea house serving matcha green tea (¥1,000). To preserve the stillness and peace, young children or large groups are discouraged from entry.

K **L** **M** **Rest House**
Snacks and small meals are available here. Food and beverages from off-site are not permitted.

N **Genpei pond**
Excellent for viewing cherry blossoms in spring, lotus flowers in summer, and autumn leaves in the fall.

O **Hata-age Benzaitensha Shrine**
Hata-age means "to raise an army." This shrine was built to pray for Yoritomo's victory.

P Tea Salon "KAZENOMORI" 茶寮 風の杜

This glass-walled cafe looking across Heike Pond toward the Tsuru-gaoka museum is a tranquil space with a simple modern Japanese design. Managed by a time-honored traditional Japanese restaurant, it serves refined, high-quality modern dishes and Japanese-style sweets, along with green tea and other beverages. The menu features "ochazuke," a long-time favorite dish at traditional Japanese restaurants. Ochazuke is made from various toppings on rice with hot tea poured on top. Topping choices at "KAZENOMORI" include sea bream flavored with a homemade sauce and seasonal sashimi. The beautiful table presentation includes rice served in wooden containers called "ohitsu" and dainty teapots. Tea is made with water boiled in a large tea ceremony style iron pot in the center of the café giving extra cultural flair. The delicious flavor of the extra high-grade green teas and the peaceful ambiance are sure to soothe anyone after a long tour around town.

📞 **0467-61-3106**
🕙 **10:30am-5:00pm**
Open 7 days/wk

"Tai Chazuke Zen" set ¥2,000
"Zenzai" (sweet adzuki red bean soup with "mochi") ¥850
Matcha green tea ¥700

Q  Tsurugaoka Museum, Kamakura

鎌倉文華館
鶴岡ミュージアム

• *History of the shrine, samurai, and more*

This modern building facing Heike Pond on the precincts of Tsurugaoka Hachimangu Shrine was designed by Japanese architect Junzo Sakakura, who apprenticed under the pioneering Modernist Le Corbusier in Paris. In its former use as a modern art museum it was long cherished, but has now been renovated and has reopened as a facility introducing the history of the shrine, its seasonal rites, the events leading up to the establishment of a military government in Kamakura, the culture and religion left behind by the warriors and the transition to modern Kamakura, centered on artifacts from the shrine's collection. Most of the displays, including exhibited items, panels, and videos, have English explanations, and change on a seasonal basis. A museum café is slated to open August 2019. We recommend a visit to those who want to learn more about Kamakura as well as to those who prefer to be indoors when the weather is not so pleasant for walking around.

🏠 **2-1-53 Yukinoshita**
📞 **0467-55-9030**
🕐 **10:00am-4:30pm (D/C 4:00pm)**
Mon, IR
Open 7 days/wk
¥ **¥300, Ele/Mid ¥100 (Varies depends on the exhibition)**

1  Kamakura Kokuhoukan (National Treasure) Museum 鎌倉国宝館

• *Museum of Buddha statues and more*

When valuable statues and art stored at temples and shrines were destroyed in the 1923 Great Kanto Earthquake, wealthy businessmen with villas in Kamakura donated money to the city to establish this museum in 1928. Regular exhibitions of Buddha statues from the Kamakura era are not encased in glass, but are placed freestanding so that visitors can observe them from all angles to appreciate the powerful energy of their creators who lived 700 years earlier. Every few months, special theme-based exhibitions are held, such as Ukiyoe paintings or Zen art. English information is scant, but if you are a fan of Buddhist art, it is well worth a visit.

🏠 **2-1-1 Yukinoshita**
📞 **0467-22-0753**
🕐 **9:00am-4:30pm (D/C 4:00pm)**
Mon(*), IR
Varies depends on the exhibition
¥ **¥200~, Ele/Mid ¥100~**

23  Kamakurabori Museum, Cafe, and Shop 鎌倉彫資料館

http://kamakuraborikaikan.jp/museum/information

- *Kamakura-bori style lacquerware museum*
- *Vegan lunch served in Kamakura-bori ware*
- *Shop selling Kamakura-bori items*

Kamakura Sta.
East Exit, 5 mins. 🚶
🏠 2-15-13 Komachi
📞 0467-25-1502
🕘 9:30am-5:00pm
(D/C 4:30pm)
Mon(*), IR

Regular exhibition
¥300
Ele/Mid ¥150

<Cafe Menu>
"Shojin" (vegan) lunch set ¥1,620
Hamburger lunch set ¥1,296
Honey pound cake ¥626
Credit cards are accepted both at the cafe and shop.

This museum located on the third floor of the Kamakurabori Assembly Hall provides information on Kamakura-bori lacquerware, an art that has been passed down locally through the generations, spanning approximately 800 years since the beginning of the Kamakura period in parallel with Zen Buddhism. For greater appreciation of the art, we recommend viewing the exhibit after learning about the painstaking production process of Kamakura-bori. Videos explain all you need to know about the elaborate wood carving techniques and the time and effort involved in the lacquering process.
Their permanent exhibition showcases approximately 50 fine works, including Buddhist statues, tea utensils, trays, and bowls from the Muromachi period (1336-1573) through to the present day.

On the first floor facing Wakamiya-Oji Avenue is a glassfront cafe that serves various lunch items including vegan dishes, coffee, and cakes. The food is served in Kamakura-bori ware, enabling customers to experience firsthand their warmth and beauty. In the museum shop located next to the cafe, there are items for sale including tableware and stationary based on patterns used in the lacquerware. This is a great place for those interested in fine quality art and design.

24   M's Ark Kamakura

· *Information spot with a clean pay toilet*

A long-established local restaurant business, Minemoto established this unique complex in 2016 for tourist to enjoy a comfortable break between sight-seeing spots.

On the first floor, there is an exhibit of ruins from the home of the Hojo clan, panel displays introducing the history of Kamakura, as well as videos in English. On the second floor, comfortable barrier-free toilets can be used for a fee of ¥100, and the information counter has computer tablets with sightseeing information in six languages. A perfect oasis for the tired traveler!

Kamakura Sta. East Exit, 9 mins.
🏠 1-12-5 Yukinoshita
📞 0467-81-4410
🕙 10:00am-5:00pm
Open 7 days/wk
¥ Toilet: ¥100

25  Kaburaki Kiyokata Memorial Art Museum 鏑木清方記念美術館
www.kamakura-arts.or.jp/kaburaki/english/

· *Museum of traditional Japanese paintings*

This museum was built on the site of the former residence of Kiyokata Kaburaki (1878-1972), who is famous for his Ukiyoe art, traditional Japanese paintings, and literary writing. Born in Tokyo, Kiyokata had a passion for the stylish air of Edo period (1603-1686) and downtown brothels. Pained by the steady loss of that character of Edo, he began expressing them in his paintings. He moved to Kama-kura after his home in Tokyo was burned down in an air raid during WWII, and spent close to 20 years of his last years there. Through the works and environ ment of the artist that reflect the rich flavors of Edo, one can capture a sense of "the essence and beauty of everyday life" from an era left behind.

Kamakura Sta. East Exit, 7 mins.
🏠 1-5-25 Yukinoshita
📞 0467-23-6405
9:00am-5:00pm
(D/C 4:30pm)
Mon(*), IR
¥ ¥200~,
Ele/Mid ¥100~

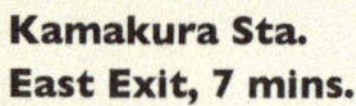
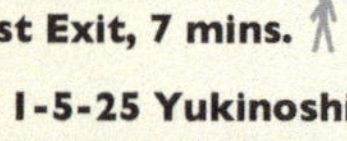

26 Kamakura City Kawakita Film Museum 川喜多映画記念館

http://www.kamakura-kawakita.org/en

- *Museum serving the art and film community*
- *Exhibitions related to the movies*
- *Location of "Tokyo-Ga" movie*

Kamakura Sta.
East Exit, 8 mins.
🏠 2-2-12 Yukinoshita
📞 0467-23-2500
🕘 9:00am-5:00pm
  (D/C 4:30pm)
Mon(*)
¥200~,
  Ele/Mid ¥100~

This museum was built on the site of the former residence of the couple, Nagamasa and Kashiko Kawakita who from 1928 imported and distributed many foreign movies into Japan, and also introduced Japanese movies overseas starting with the works of Kenji Mizoguchi, Yasujiro Ozu, and Akira Kurosawa. In addition to exhibiting materials such as photographs and letters that document their exchanges with movie stars and directors both in Japan and abroad, such as Charlie Chaplin, Alain Delon, Jean Cocteau, and Kurosawa, there are also special exhibitions held throughout the year and movies related to these special exhibitions are shown in the museum's theater.

The interview with Japanese actor Ryu Chishu in the film "Tokyo-Ga" by director Wim Wenders, a fan of Ozu was filmed at a detached building located on the grounds. Although this is a small facility, film fanatics will be sure to enjoy it.
Unfortunately, there is little English information available in the museum, so we advise visiting with a friend or tour guide who can speak Japanese.

Kamakura Station West Exit Area

Since days of old, the quietness of this area with its large residences and public institutions has been maintained. Along the Genji-yama Hiking Trail that runs between Sasuke (immediately beyond the city hall) and Kita-Kamakura, you can still find ancient shrines and "kiridoshi" (excavated roads) from samurai battles.

SÔNG BÉ CAFE

THE GOOD GOODIES

Kokuriko Onari-dori Store

Bun Bun Kochaten

Tsukui

Latteria BeBé Kamakura

Bistrot Orange

Katsuretsu-an

Garden House

HAPPY DELI Kamakura

Sasuke Store

Masamune Sword and Blade Workshop

Yuko-do

Moyai Kogei

Hotel New KAMAKURA

Kamakura Museum of History and Culture

Jufuku-ji Temple

Zeni-arai Benzaiten Ugafuku Shrine

Sasuke Inari Shrine

Genji-yama Park

Samurai are the children of the central aristocracy who arrived in the provinces and those who organized themselves into a self-styled national defense force (similar to knights in the Western world) amidst the abolition of the old military regime. It was Genji (Minamoto clan) and their rivals, the Taira clan, who assumed power over the samurai class.

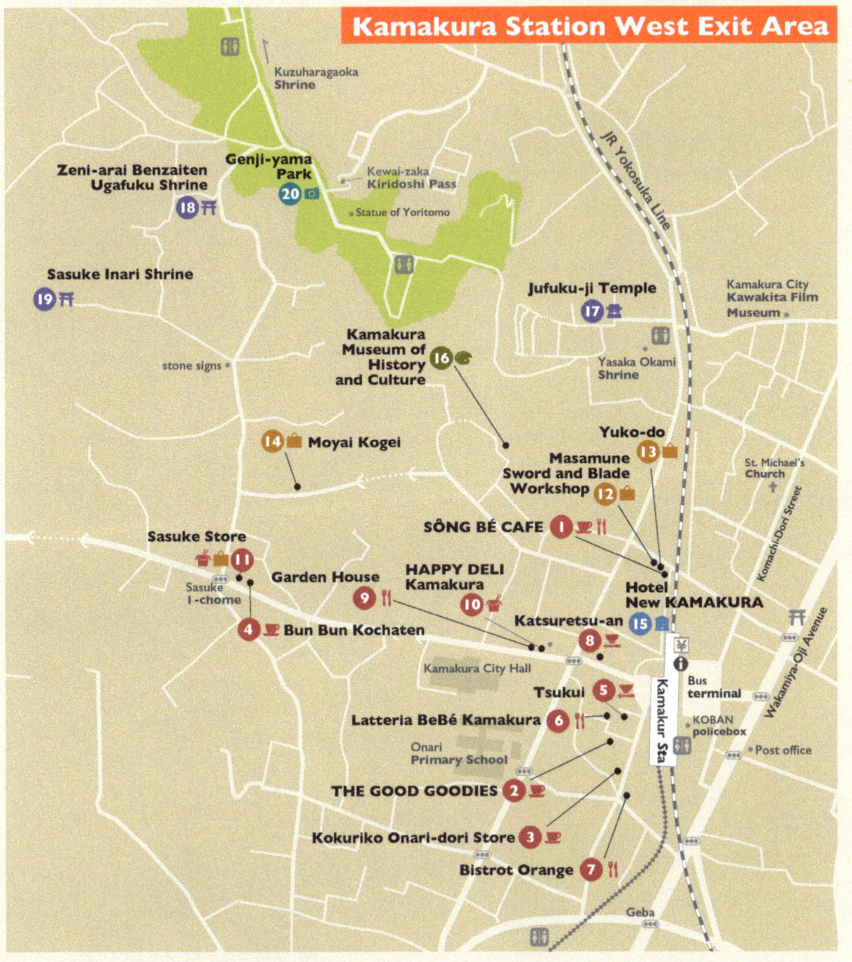

Kamakura Station West Exit Area
Kuzuharagaoka Shrine
Kewai-zaka Kiridoshi Pass
Statue of Yoritomo
JR Yokosuka Line
Zeni-arai Benzaiten Ugafuku Shrine
Genji-yama Park
18
20
Sasuke Inari Shrine
19
Jufuku-ji Temple
17
Kamakura City Kawakita Film Museum
Yasaka Okami Shrine
stone signs
Kamakura Museum of History and Culture
16
14 Moyai Kogei
Yuko-do
Masamune Sword and Blade Workshop
13
12
St. Michael's Church
SÔNG BÉ CAFE 1
Sasuke Store
11
Sasuke I-chome
Garden House
HAPPY DELI Kamakura
Hotel New KAMAKURA
9
10
Komachi-Dori Street
4 Bun Bun Kochaten
Katsuretsu-an
8
15
Kamakura City Hall
Tsukui 5
Bus terminal
Latteria BeBé Kamakura 6
KOBAN policebox
Onari Primary School
Kamakur Sta
Wakamiya-Oji Avenue
Post office
THE GOOD GOODIES 2
Kokuriko Onari-dori Store 3
Bistrot Orange 7
Geba

Ⅰ 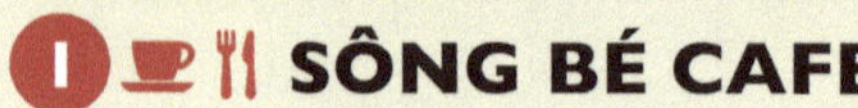 SÔNG BÉ CAFE

- *Health- and eco-conscious Asian cuisine*
- *A hub of local community activists*
- *A 3-minute walk from the station*

Kaoru Uji, owner of this quaint cafe serving Asian treats, is a strong promoter of Kamakura's natural and cultural environment. As one of the key persons of Kamakura's local community (p. 034), he uses local organic produce to the extent possible.
Pad thai and green curry are the owner's signature dishes, learned while traveling around Asia. We also recommend the tasty and authentic homemade desserts, chai, and Vietnamese coffee.

Just a few minutes' walk from the station, this cafe has a warm interior of natural finishes with an ad-hoc blend of second-hand furnishings from Japan and Southeast Asia create a nostalgic and relaxed ambiance. An assortment of handmade fair-trade crafts and goods are also for sale at the entrance, where you can also peruse flyers and announcements of local events on ecology conscious activities in the area. A natural gathering place for like-minded locals. Enjoy a chat with the owner while resting your feet!

**Kamakura Sta.
West Exit, 3 mins.**
13-32 Onarimachi
0467-61-2055
Sun, Mon, Thu, Fri:
11:30am-8:00pm
(L.O 7:00pm)
Sat:
11:30am-9:00pm
(L.O.8:00pm)
Tue, Wed

Pad Thai ¥850
Chicken pho ¥800
Coconuts Ice Cream ¥450

Behind the curtain, there is a cozy lounge where you can take your shoes off and sit on the floor.

2  THE GOOD GOODIES

- *Hand drip-brewed coffee and desserts*
- *Opens at 7:00am on weekdays*
- *Located a 2-minute walk from the station*

Kamakura Sta. West Exit, 2 mins.
🏠 10-1 Onarimachi
📞 0467-33-5685
🕐 **Weekdays: 7:00am-6:00pm**
Sat, Sun, Holidays: 9:00am-6:00pm
Wed, last Tue of the month

Since there are very few stores that open early in Kamakura, this coffee shop is a true rarity.
The owner established the early opening hour to add a certain value to Kamakura mornings. The self-service "Good Morning Coffee" selections available from 7:00am to 9:00am on weekdays are very reasonably priced, from ¥100 and up.
For those who have time to relax, we recommend a cup of hand drip-brewed coffee. Homemade American-style organic desserts produced by the owner's friend make a perfect coffee accompaniment. Sit at the bar to enjoy a chat with the owner or sit outside on the bench to soak up the sun.
This small coffee shop also serves as a comfortable community space where locals hang out to catch up on the latest news and peruse an information board overflowing with flyers for local events. Add a touch of color to your day with a bouquet of fresh flowers, which are sold at the storefront a few days a week.

Original blend coffee ¥421
Masara chai ¥540
Cookies ¥140~, Scones ¥375
Cake ¥388~

Check out the variety of stylish and practical iron fixtures made by the owner, who happens to also be an artist in metalwork.

3  Kokuriko Onari-dori Store

- *Freshly prepared crêpes*
- *Both take-out & eat-in available*
- *Time-honored local crêperie*

In the late 1970s, before crêpes were well-known in Japan, the founder of this crêperie became enamored with this French snack that he tasted on a street corner in Paris—so much so that he imported some grills and decided to introduce them to Japan.
His first shop along Kamakura's Komachi Street brought surprise and delight to the Japanese, and in no time, its long lines exposed revealed its popularity. From there onward, Kokuriko became Kamakura's go-to place for crêpes, and locals have grown up on them as a soul food treat of sorts.

Since their original shop on Komachi Street became very popular among tourists, this shop on Onari Street was established 7 years ago so that the locals could enjoy crêpes while having tea. Just like their flagship location built close to 40 years ago, they maintain the value of home-cooked flavors and each crêpe grilled immediately upon ordering—not prepared in advance—using fresh ingredients of flour, eggs, and milk. Grilled to a heavenly crispiness, they also somehow maintain a rich fluffiness.

The most popular item is their "lemon sugar filled crêpe", which uses freshly squeezed lemons.
In addition to crêpes filled with chocolate, fruit jam, fresh whipped cream, or ice cream, there are also savory crêpes served with vegetables and ham.

<Onari-dori Store>
Kamakura Sta.
West Exit, 2 mins.
🏠 **10-6 Onarimachi**
📞 **0467-23-8551**
🕐 **10:30am-6:00pm**
Mon

<Komachi Store>
(p. 054)
Kamakura Sta.
East Exit, 6 mins.
🏠 **1-6-4 Yukinoshita**
📞 **0467-22-7286**
🕐 **10:30am-6:00pm**
Open 7 days/wk

Crêpes ¥350~¥600
<photo> Raspberry cream cheese crêpe ¥450
Coffee ¥300

4  **Bun Bun Kochaten**　ぶんぶん紅茶店

- *Cozy British-style tea house*
- *Finest quality selection of black tea*
- *Delicious homemade sweets*

One step inside makes you feel you have wandered into a teahouse somewhere along the British countryside. Possessing a fondness for black tea and British cars, owner Sakae Ogiso's teahouse is casually adorned with antiques picked up from his travels, with a full lineup of fine quality tea leaves from selective tea plantations.

A regular spot for residents of the area as well as a perfect rest stop for sightseeing travelers, this tea house has a relaxing ambience. Nearly 15 different varieties of teas are selected from India, Africa, Sri Lanka, and China, and the menu lists 40 different types of teas and tea concoctions. Sure enough, their careful brews are a taste of bliss.

You'll also find a piece of heaven in a bite of their signature snowflake cake, the owner's enhanced version of a British recipe from a dessert prepared at Eton College. Be sure and try it!

Kamakura Sta. West Exit, 8 mins. 🚶

🏠 1-13-4 Sasuke

📞 0467-25-2866

🕙 10:00am -7:00pm (L.O.)

Tue

<Photo> Snowflake cake

<Menu>

Tea & cake set ¥900~
Pot of tea ¥540~ Lunch set: (Choice of Sandwich, Curry or Pasta with a small salad and tea) ¥900~¥1,400

5 Tsukui 津久井

http://www.291.co.jp/eng_index.html

- *Japanese savory pancake restaurant*
- *Self-service table-top cooking*
- *A 1-minute walk from Kamakura Station*

**Kamakura Sta.
West Exit, 1 min.**
🏠 11-7 Onarimachi
📞 0467-22-1883
🕐 **Weekdays:**
   10:30am-2:30pm (L.O.)
   5:00pm-9:00pm (L.O.)
   Sat, Sun, Holidays:
   11:30am-9:00pm (L.O.)

IR

Tsukui-ten "okonomi-yaki" with seafood and vegetables ¥1,026
Tofu-yaki (Fried tofu with eggs and vegetables) ¥756

Established in 1968, Tsukui is a restaurant specializing in Japanese-style savory *okonomi-yaki* pancakes. Duck under the cloth *noren* hanging at the entrance and remove your shoes to experience the traditional ritual of an old Japanese wooden home. The black luster of the ceiling and columns from years of ambient grilling oil shine like a badge of time-honored prosperity, and the greenery of the garden beyond the rows of low-seated individual tables provides a pleasant backdrop.

Okonomi-yaki are savory pancakes made with a batter of flour, eggs, and cabbage, and your choice among various seafood or meat items. This is a "make-it-yourself" style eatery with cooking oil, a selection of sauces, dried bonito flakes, and powdered *ao-nori* seaweed provided at the side of the griddle. To prepare *okonomi-yaki*, mix up the ingredients in the bowl delivered to your table, pour batter onto the griddle like a large pancake, and when it's cooked on one side, flip it over. If you need any assistance, the servers are happy to lend you a hand, or cook it up for you, if necessary.

Once it's cooked, top it with your choice of condiments including *okonomi-yaki* sauce, soy sauce, or mayonnaise, and eat up! Time-honored flavors and filling dishes make this establishment popular among locals and tourists alike. In addition to other classic items like *yaki-soba* fried noodles, *teppan* grilled beef and fish, the owner-chef's original and tasty dishes, such as chicken wing Chinese dumplings are also divine.

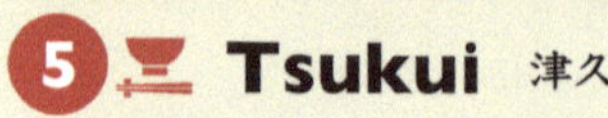

6 🍴 Latteria BeBé Kamakura

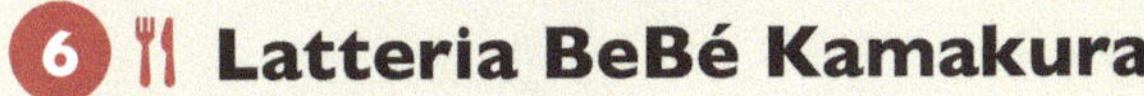

- *Italian restaurant & cheese factory*
- *Owned by a pair of surf-riding brothers*
- *A 3-minute walk from the station*

**Kamakura Sta.
West Exit, 3 mins.** 🚶
🏠 11-17 Onarimachi
📞 0467-81-3440
🕐 11:00am-10:00pm
  (L.O. 9:00pm)
▨ Mon

Only a few minutes from the station's west exit, this Italian restaurant is located inside a tastefully renovated traditional Japanese house that sits amidst a quiet residential area.
The owners, a pair of surfer brothers who share a love for the coastal waters of Kamakura, established this store with an adjacent cheese factory where fresh cheese is made without additives or preservatives.

In addition to over 10 different pizza varieties each of bianca and rossa baked in an oven they tiled by hand, the Italy-trained brothers also serve rare homemade cheese treats such as burrata and stracciatella that are not easily found in Japan.
The antipasto and pasta dishes are made with locally produced vegetables and seafood.
The popular lunch set with salad, pizza or pasta, dessert and a drink is such a bargain that it may be hard to be seated without a reservation, so you may want to aim for a late weekday lunch to avoid waiting in line.
Take-outs are also available as a high-end alternative to your typical pizza-chain fare.

Lunch set ¥1,512~
Salad with burrata cheese, cherry tomatoes, proscutto parma ¥1,944
Pizza margherita ¥1,274
Wine by the glass ¥648~
Mozzarella (100g) ¥529
Burrata (150g) ¥1,058

Don't miss their fresh cheese deli.
A 10% discount is offered
if you bring your own container!

7 🍴 Bistrot Orange

- *Casual French bistro and wine bar*
- *Solo diners are welcome for wine or a meal*
- *A 2-minute walk from the station*

Kamakura Sta. West Exit, 2 mins. 🚶
🏠 2-13 Onarimachi
📞 0467-23-9337
🕐 11:00am-3:30pm
(L.O. 2:30)
5:00pm-11:00pm
(L.O. 10:00pm)
▨ Open 7 days/wk

The bistro is named after a town in Northern Provence, and the eponymous color is used as their trademark, catching the attention of passersby. The allure of this eatery is not only its casual yet authentic French bistro style food and wine list but also its convenient operating hours; light meals and wine are served at any time of the day, accommodating flexible itineraries with late lunches or early or late dinners.

Their reasonable lunch set is always enjoyable, and the wine list features French wines to enjoy with patés, slow-cooked cuisine, and traditional bistro dishes. Also notable is the proximity to the station, and their late-night hours until 11 pm are a plus for Kamakura, where most establishments close early.

Roasted vegetables ¥1,274
Assorted meat hors d'oeuvre ¥1,814
Wine by the glass ¥518~
Lunch set: (Choice of Today's meat, fish, pate with bread and soup) ¥1,296~

8  Katsuretsu-an 勝烈庵

- *Delicious cutlet with secret recipe*
- *Woodblock artist Shiko Munakata's artworks*
- *Convenient for late lunch*

Kamakura Sta. West Exit, 1 min.
🏠 12-10 Onarimachi
📞 0467-23-2772
🕐 11:00am-8:30pm
  (L.O. 8:00pm)
Open 7 days/wk

Pork fillet cutlet set ¥1,728
Pork lion cutlet set ¥1,728
Okonomi set (deep fried shrimp, bite size pork cutlet) ¥2,376
Kamakura Gozan set ¥1,998
Pork cutlet bento to go ¥1,728, Sake ¥432~

The name "Katsuretsu-an" comes from the word "katsuretsu" meaning "cutlet." As a branch of a restaurant that was established in Yokohama in 1927, they continue to use the traditional secret recipe created by its founder. They prepare the skewers with rectangular pieces of meat, use homemade bread crumbs, and create their sauce with a stew of fresh vegetables and fruit.

For a hearty serving, we recommend the "Katsuretsu set meal" with pork fillet cutlet, or the set with pork loin cutlet. If you wish to enjoy a variety, try the "Okonomi set meal." For more local fare, try the Kamakura original "Kamakura Gozan set meal" that uses seasonal ingredients.

The savory sauce that clings to the crunchy coating and tender meat gives an extra zest. If you like, ask for an extra helping of rice and cabbage. The chopsticks are made from timber from forest thinning along the Kumano Kodo trail and are free if you'dlike to take them home.

The signage printed on the restaurant's *chochin* paper lantern and *noren* entrance curtains are created by the famous woodblock printmaker, Shikou Munakata, and a number of his original prints also decorate the restaurant interior.

The second generation of owners knew Shikou Munakata personally, since he had a studio in Kamakura-yama area and often stopped by the main Yokohama restaurant. It's a true treat to enjoy a tasty meal while enjoying these fine art works.

9 🍴 Garden House

www.ghghgh.jp/gardenhouse/kamakura

- *Northern California style restaurant*
- *Suitable for couples or groups alike*
- *A 5-minute walk from the station*

Kamakura Sta. West Exit, 5 mins. 🚶
🏠 15-46 Onarimachi
📞 0467-81-5200
🕐 9:00am-10:00pm
(L.O. 9:00pm)
📶 IR

Morning toast set ¥950～
Morning buttermilk pancake set w/ bacon & eggs ¥1,500
Weekday lunch set ¥1,600～
Roasted "Satsuma" chicken w/ home made harissa ¥2,800
Gardener's green salad ¥1,400

Since early days, Kamakura has served as a hub for scholars and people of culture with refined sensibilities. Carrying on this trademark, this restaurant/event space connects the local community and provides a venue for establishing a new culture through gastronomic experiences. With a spacious interior that opens out into the garden, this eatery bustles with both locals and tourists from breakfast to dinner time.

Without sticking to any particular type of cuisine, the seasonally appropriate dishes have a Northern California flair. Popular menu items are pizza, pancakes, veggies, and ice cream.

Operating under the concept of using local ingredients to the extent possible, the Garden House menu features plentiful amounts of produce from nearby areas. Likewise, the restaurant's originally flavored ham was created together with local ham manufacturer, Kamakura Ham Tomioka Shoukai (p, 062). Wash down these delights with locally crafted Kamakura beer to fully enjoy the local sensibility and quality.

Stop at their gardening shop on the way out to find a gift or souvenir from a selection of items.

The restaurant is a renovation of a well-known Japanese cartoonist, Ryuichi Yokoyama, where Kamakura's cultural figures used to gather.

 10 HAPPY DELI Kamakura

- *Reasonably priced all-natural delicatessen*
- *Take-out and eat-in menu items available*
- *A 3-minute walk from the station*

Kamakura Sta.
West Exit, 3 mins.
2F 15-7 Onarimachi
080-5591-0135
10:00am-6:30pm
Sun

A practiced chef of French cuisine, the owner of this establishment became familiar with the delicatessen style experience from travels in the US and created this casual dining spot.
Salads made with fresh ingredients are available as cold deli dishes, while curries and tacos are among the hot deli items. Although the menu is casual, the offerings have a refined taste, made free of artificial additives or preservatives.

Take-out meals are also sold in three sizes of bento boxes in addition to single deli items sold by weight. For eating in, there is a choice between two lunch plates—the "2 item plate" or the "3 item plate." This is a perfect stop for a quick lunch, a healthy take-out, or for teatime with sweets.

<Bento boxes to-go>
S (2 deli items) ¥470
M (2 deli items) ¥570
L (3 deli items) ¥670
<Eat-in>
S (2 deli items) ¥470
L (3 deli items) ¥670
*All come with rice.
<Deli>
Thai green curry,
Veggies and chicken,
Grilled veggie salad, etc.
¥250/100g~

upper shelf: Standard menu,
ower shelf : Today's specials

Sasuke Store

- *Local seasonal vegetables and seafood*
- *Delicious homemade deli*
- *Smoothies and healthy drinks to go*

Kamakura Sta.
West Exit, 10 mins.
1-13-7 Sasuke
0467-61-1430
10:00am-7:00pm
Tue, Wed

Skewered tuna tail cutlet
¥190/1 skewer
Fresh local eggs
¥300/half dozen
Smoothie ¥540

Sasuke Store is the place for fresh produce grown in the rich environment of the Miura Peninsula and fresh seafood caught in the Misaki Harbor, the southernmost tip of the peninsula. Vegetables that arrive directly from the farmers are packed into the tiny 15-square-meter shop. Since the vegetable items sold here are exclusively seasonal and only grown outdoors, the selection is different from other grocers in the area. You will find completely new offerings at various times of the year. They also have a take-out counter, where you can order a smoothie made with fresh seasonal fruit or a homemade dish from their deli. If you need a break, sit outside the shop and enjoy a light snack before moving on to your next destination.

Hailing from Tokyo, the owner formerly worked in the retail industry for a high-end Italian fashion brand, an experience of Italian culture that inspired in him the value of transmitting the excellence in the quality of a product. With its easy access to Tokyo, Kamakura was chosen as the perfect spot for sharing the harvests of the vast southern area of the Miura Peninsula. In addition to the locally produced items, a fine selection of other goods, such as Italian food products and wine are also available.

12  **Masamune Sword and Blade Workshop** 正宗工芸

http://www.sword-masamune.com/en/info.html

- *Historic swordsmith workshop*
- *Descendants of a master swordsmith*
- *High quality scissors and other items*

**Kamakura Sta.
West Exit, 3 mins.** 🚶
🏠 **13-29 Onarimachi**
📞 **0467-22-3962**
🕐 **8:30am-5:00pm**
Tue

Kitchen knives ¥2,800~
Small scissors ¥3,100~

In the Kamakura period, the shogunate called competent swordsmiths to assemble in Kamakura, but the most famous among them was Masamune. The current owner, Tsunahiro Yamamura, is the 24th generation to inherit this craft, which extends back roughly 700 years since the workshop was founded by Masamune.

Swords made using Masamune's characteristic technique have a beautiful *hamon* (blade pattern) and are also highly valued as works of art.

Yamamura focuses on leveraging his skills to produce daily necessities such as kitchen knives and scissors using traditional techniques, and he also makes swords at a rate of about two a year.

Japanese cutlery is characterized by the special smelting process called "tatara," using ironsand, as used by Princess Mononoke in the eponymous Studio Ghibli movie.

Given that there are complicated procedures involved in bringing Japanese swords abroad, we recommend that travelers make smaller purchases, such as a pair of scissors that you can easily bring home as a memento of Japan and use for the rest of your life. Since the swordsmith does not speak English, it is requested that you bring along someone who can speak Japanese if you have an interest in visiting or making a purchase.

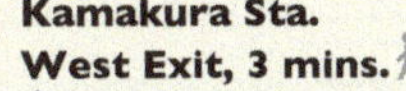

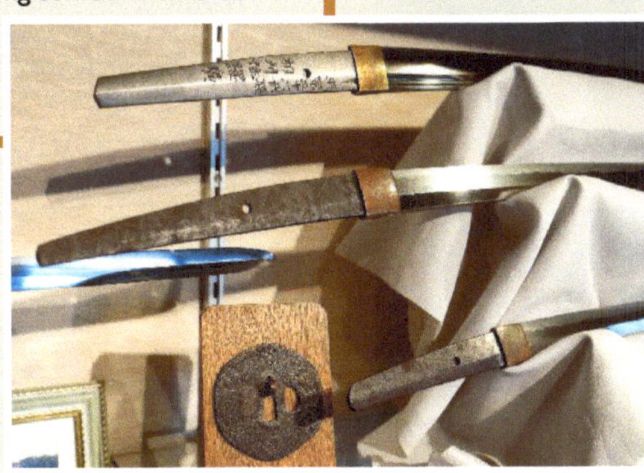

13  Yuko-do 遊古洞

- *Upscale antique and vintage treasures*
- *Affordable bargains guaranteed*
- *Located across the railway crossing*

One step inside this shop, where 2/3rds of the items are used books and the rest are antiques, and you find yourself sniffing out an exciting bargain. Its early morning operation, the piles of antique ceramics, paintings, and other secondhand items outside the storefront are reminiscent of a flea market.

The shop window display brims with an assortment of tableware. In addition to antique Imari ceramic ware, small dishes and pottery from the Edo (1603-1868) and Meiji (1868-1912) eras, you'll also find vintage Noritake ware. They also have *kakejiku* hanging scrolls and prints from the Edo Period, which they are happy to show interested customers. The female proprietor takes pride in her affordable prices, which she claims are more reasonable than others in the area. Starting out over 20 years ago as a secondhand bookshop when the owner's part-time job grew into a full-fledged operation, this shop owes its success to her refined connoisseurship and the support of her friends.

Kamakura Sta. West Exit, 3 mins. 🚶
🏠 13-30 Onarimachi
📞 0467-23-1967
🕙 10:30am-6:00pm
📐 Mon(*), IR

Plates displayed outside
¥300~¥2,000
Higher quality tableware is sold inside.
Woodblock prints ¥1,000~
(Prices vary depending on the age or condition)

14 Moyai Kogei もやい工芸

- *Folk-crafts collected from all around Japan*
- *Large stock of long-cherished wares*
- *Resplendent with the spirit of folk art*

**Kamakura Sta.
West Exit, 10 mins.**
🏠 2-1-10 Sasuke
📞 0467-22-1822
🕙 10:00am-5:00pm
Tue

Japanese-style teacups
¥1,200~
Western-style teacup
and saucer set ¥1,200~
Platters ¥800~
Earthen crock pot ¥5,000~
Large plates or vases
range from ¥50,000
to ¥100,000

Moyai Kogei has graced the Sasuke area with its presence for nearly 50 years.

The founder, Keiichi Kuno, was a strong supporter of the movement to maintain the folk-crafts of Japan. "Mingei," the Japanese word for "folk-crafts" refers to daily wares that are created by nameless artisans intended for everyday use, not to be merely handled as works of art. (The word "mingei" itself is an abbreviation for of "minshu-teki," or "grass roots" and "kogei," or "craftwork".) The Mingei movement is known for its efforts in passing on the value of careful handwork that tends to be forgotten in contemporary society.

The current owner, Tamiju Kuno, the second generation to succeed the cherished pursuits of the founder, ensures a full stock of handmade wares created by craftspeople around the country in the traditions and techniques rooted in the climate of the land. Ceramic, glass ware, baskets, bamboo ware, furniture, and wood work from northern Aomori to southern Okinawa in the south line the shelves of this tasteful Japanese-style interior with deep wooden beams.

Each item on display possesses beauty and refined taste. The universal forms of wares that have been treasured through the ages are timeless and color the everyday lives of their users with a sense of high quality and richness.

HOTEL NEW KAMAKURA
Välkommen

15  Hotel New KAMAKURA

www.newkamakura.com/index_en.asp

- *The oldest Western-style hotel in Kamakura*
- *Family-run operation*
- *A 1-minute walk from the station*

Kamakura Sta. West Exit, 1 min.
🏠 13-2 Onarimachi
📞 0467-22-2230
🕐 C/I 3:00pm
C/O 10:00am

<Original Wing>
14 rooms
<New Wing>
9 rooms
Room rate for one guest
¥5,000~
Room rate for two guests
¥5,000~
*Rate varies depending
on the season.
*Reservations:
Check their English website.
*Parking: ¥1,000/day

This long-time Kamakura landmark is located directly across from the station. At the time of its opening, it was surrounded by villas and mansions of the Imperial family, nobles, and financial elite. Established in 1924 by a cinema actor, it was built as a Western-style hotel to suit its affluent clientele. The present owner's grandfather subsequently bought the business, and while preserving the original design, the family has undertaken restoration of the damaged and outdated sections of the facility by hiring local carpenters and recycling structural members and other materials from local mansions.

The original exterior appearance has been maintained for the most part unchanged, and on the interior, details such as the hung sash windows and the 2nd floor stairwell area preserve the 100-year grandeur of the former era, while also adding tasteful touches of modernity.

In the main building, there are 14 rooms between the 1st and 2nd floors. The guestrooms are given names such as *Sakura* or *Ume-no-ma* ("Plum" Room), which give each room a different theme that is reflected in the interior. Toilet and bathing facilities in the original wing are shared. The staff

kitchen facilities on the 1st floor can be used for heating up a snack or light meal.

The new annex built in 2003 has 10 rooms, 7 of which are equipped with a bath and toilet.

Effuse with family-run hospitality spanning over three generations, the character of the hotel that maintains the flavor of Kamakura culture is felt throughout in the welcoming and warm ambience created by the owners and staff.

16 Kamakura Museum of History and Culture 鎌倉歴史文化交流館

• Display of Kamakura history & culture

Learn the history of Kamakura chronologically through displays, videos, and dioramas. The main building holds a chronological exhibition, and a medieval, modern, and postmodern exhibition, and the annex holds an archeological exhibition. The displayed items of artifacts that were excavated from the ruins give hints of ordinary life such as the local customs surrounding food as well as prayers and spells. Most of the displays have English explanations. The building was designed by the famous British architect Norman Foster, who designed the Apple Headquarters, "Apple Park," in the US. Not only the displays but also the building and spatial designs are unique.

For the architect's design concept of "blending into the historic city of Kamakura," see:
https://www.fosterandpartners.com/projects/kamakura-house/

Kamakura Sta. West Exit, 7 mins.
🏠 1-5-1 Ogigayatsu
📞 0467-73-8501
🕐 10:00am-4:00pm (D/C 3:30pm)
Sun, Holidays, IR

17 Jufuku-ji Temple 寿福寺

• The third rank of Kamakura Gozan Temples

This Zen temple was founded in 1200, the year following Minamoto Yoritomo's death, by his wife, Masako, who selected Buddhist priest Eisai to establish it in commemoration of her husband.
Eisai is known for traveling to China during the Song Dynasty to study Zen and returning to Japan to introduce green tea and spread the Rinzai sect of Zen Buddhism. When Jufuku-ji was established, it was one of the nation's prominent Zen temples with several well-known priests as its followers.
Although the inner grounds beyond the central gate are closed to the public, the distinctive stone paving leading directly from the temple gate to the central gate is exquisite.

Kamakura Sta. West Exit, 8 mins.

🏠 1-17-7 Ougigaya
Not open to Public
(The approach area is open)

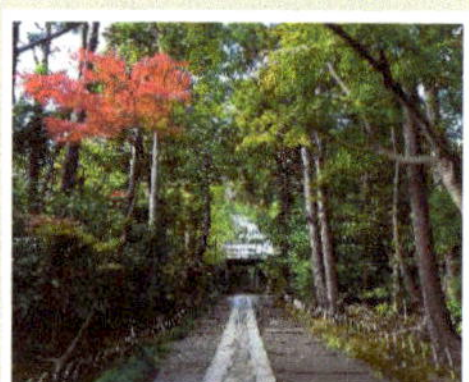

18 ⛩ Zeni-arai Benzaiten Ugafuku Shrine 銭洗弁財天宇賀福神社

- *Shrine associated with Minamoto Yoritomo*
- *Unique money-rinsing ritual*
- *Legend of snakes*

Kamakura Sta. West Exit, 20 mins. 🚶
🏠 2-25-16 Sasuke
📞 0467-25-1081
🕐 8:00am-4:30pm
📅 Open 7 days/wk
¥ Free

Founded by Minamoto Yoritomo in 1185 in efforts to bring peace to the commoners affected by disaster or poverty. The tradition of rinsing money here is said to have been started by Fifth Regent Hojo Tokiyori, when he washed his money in the sacred spring to pray for the prosperity of his family. It is believed that rinsing your money under the spring water here will make it multiply; be sure to familiarize yourself with the meaning of the ritual and respect the shine's instructions.

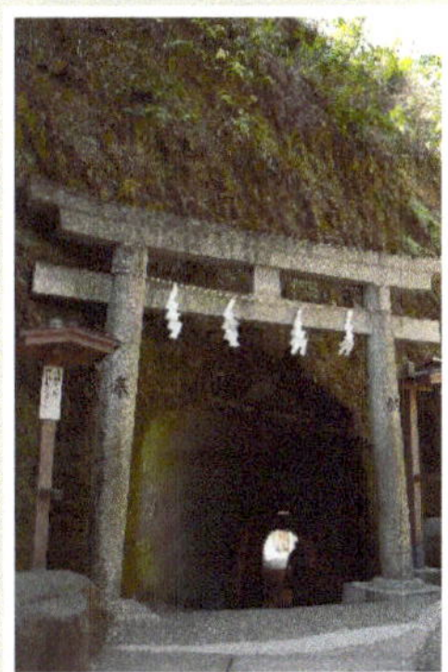

<How to "wash" your money>

1. In exchange for ¥100 at the shrine office, you will be given a set of 3 items: a candle, a bundle of incense sticks, and a basket to borrow.

2. Light your votive candle (symbolizing "the light of wisdom that shines in the darkness") from the large candle in the candle stand, and place it in any of the stands available.

3. Light your incense stick and place it in the incense stand (symbolizing "purification of the body").

4. Go to the main shrine.

5. Inside the cave, where you "wash" your money, place your cash in the basket and pour three ladles full of spring water over it.

Note: You will see raw eggs sold in a set of 5 at the shrine stand; there are two legends behind this: One is that Yoritomo was said to have been led to this shrine in a dream on the hour, day, month and year of the snake, and the other is that snakes are the messengers of the enshrined Benzaiten. No matter the reason, since snakes love eggs, there is a place for offering them in front of each of the five small shrines within the precinct.

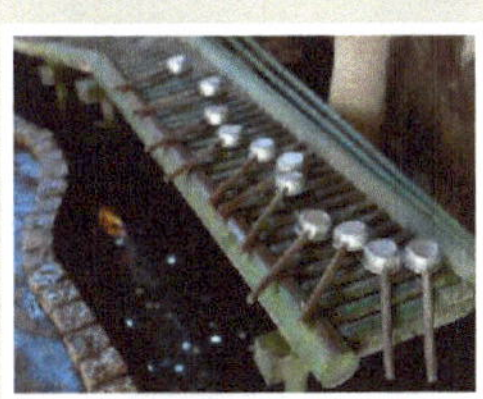

19 ⛩ Sasuke Inari Shrine 佐助稲荷神社

www.sasukeinari.jp

- *Primitive spiritual place*
- *A sacred water source to the area*
- *Founded by Minamoto Yoritomo*

Kamakura Sta. West Exit, 25 mins. 🚶
🏠 2-22-12 Sasuke
📞 0467-22-4711
🕐 Sunrise-Sunset
Open 7 days/wk
¥ Free

This shrine was founded by the young Minamoto Yoritomo. According to legend, while hiding in exile in Izu, a province west of Kamakura, after his father was killed by the rival Heike clan, Yoritomo was visited by an old man in a dream who announced that the time was ripe to avenge his enemies. He had introduced himself as Inari, the god of harvest, residing in Kamakura, and so Yoritomo dedicated this shrine in gratitude after his success of destroying the Heike and establishing the Kamakura Shogunate.

"Inari" means "to bear grain," and since foxes are said to come down to the villages when grain is ready for harvest, foxes are the guardian deities and messengers for Inari shrines. Similar to the head shrine of Inari in Kyoto, Fushimi Inari Shrine, this shrine also has rows of red torii gates and hundreds of white foxes guarding the shrine.

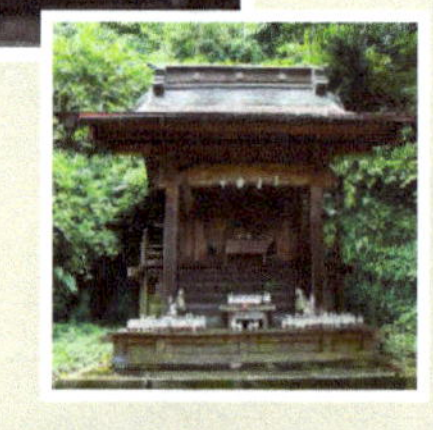

Because this shrine was established due to Yoritomo's historical victory, it is believed that visits here will bring good fortune in career or work, but there are other attractions as well. Since ancient times, Reiko-sen, the natural spring behind the shrine office, had served as the water source for the fields and paddies. You can also find an old ritual ground in a grove up a small path within the shrine precinct, where a sacred rock marks the protection of the water source and was a place to pray for productive harvest.
Unlike many large temples and shrines in the area, this is a primitive spiritual place where the deep roots of animism are preserved.

20 📷 Genji-yama Park 源氏山公園

- *Vast park spreads over Mt. Genji*
- *Hike trails, picnic areas, shrines and more*
- *Seasonal flowers and a view of Mt. Fuji*

Kamakura Sta.
West Exit, 20 mins. 🚶
🏠 4-649-1, Ougigaya
📞 0467-23-3000
🕐 Sunrise-Sunset
📅 Open 7days/wk
¥ Free

A 25- to 30-minute walk from either Kamakura Station's west exit or Kita-Kamakura Station, this park spreads over a hilltop on Mt. Genji (Genji-yama), so named for the land that had been owned by the Genji clan, another name for the Minamoto clan, prior to the establishment of the Kamakura shogunate.

This park is a haven for locals who stroll through to enjoy the changes of the seasons, and is a relay point along the hiking course that connects Kita-Kamakura to Kamakura Station's west exit and the Great Buddha. With amenities such as vending machines, two public restrooms, and picnic areas, the park provides a good resting spot for hikers, where one can enjoy the views and natural surroundings.

Statue of Minamoto Yoritomo

This statue was built using donations from volunteers. The shogun figure appears to still be protecting the town of Kamakura.

Hino Toshimoto Tomb

In the final year of the Kamakura shogunate, loyal retainer of Emperor Godaigo, Hino Toshimoto was captured for his role as a central figure in a plot to overthrow the shogunate and was executed by decapitation in 1332 on Mt. Genji, where he is now enshrined.

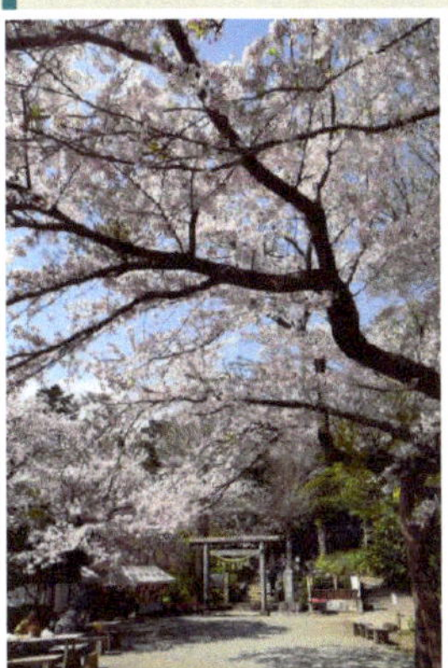

Kuzuharagaoka Shrine

This shrine was dedicated to imperial loyalist Hino Toshimoto under the instruction of Emperor Meiji, the highly regarded pioneer of the Meiji Restoration. Since Daikokuten, the god of wealth and match-making, is also enshrined here, the male and female rocks were deified in 2010. When approached, sensors around the rocks will set off music, making this quite a high tech place of worship.

Kanazawa-Kaido Area

Once an important road in ancient times, the Kanazawa-Kaido Road still serves as a commercial road that runs from Kamakura to Tokyo Bay. Here, one can find traces of the activity of the first shogunate, Minamoto Yoritomo, and remains of the temple of the Ashikaga clan who ruled over Kamakura after the demise of the Kamakura Shogunate.

Mon-Peche-Mignon

Bergfeld

Alter Stadt

Hokai-ji Temple

Okura Shirahata Shrine & Yoritomo's Tomb

Sugimoto-dera Temple

Kakuon-ji Temple

Zuisen-ji Temple

Jomyo-ji Temple

Hokoku-ji Temple

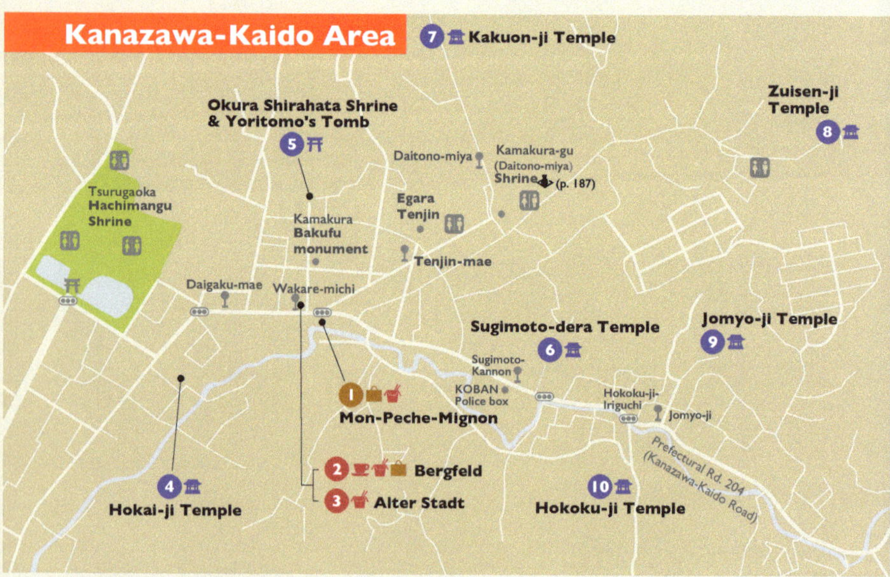

Bus Information (Bus terminal map is provided on p. 197)

1 2 3 5—Take any bus that departs from 4 and 5 at the East Exit of Kamakura Station

6 9 10——Take any bus that departs from 5 at the East Exit of Kamakura Station

5 7 8——Take any bus that departs from 4 at the East Exit of Kamakura Station

Mon-Peche-Mignon

- **Genuine French bakery**
- **Opens at 7:00 am**
- **Eat-in cafe space**

Owner Jiro Fujimori learned the ropes of bread baking under Philippe Bigot, who is accredited as the bread master who introduced French bread to Japan. After 10 years of apprenticeship, he was qualified to open a bakery under his own name.
You will find a variety of offerings, from standard bread to pastries such as pizza, sandwiches, and apple pie. All ingredients are carefully selected and made without additives or preservatives.

One particularly recommended item is their casse-croûte—a very simple sandwich of ham and cheese stuffed inside a buttered baguette; the satisfying flavor of the wheat and salty ham fills your mouth with each bite. The sandwich of the day made with fresh vegetables and egg is also filling and delicious, and can be made vegetarian or vegan on request. For a quick snack or a casual but quality lunch, enjoy your purchases seated at a table out in front sof the bakery or on the second floor of the bakery. There is a very nice large parking area, a convenience rare in Kamakura.

Kamakura Sta. East Exit, 20 mins. or Wakare-michi bus stop 0 min.

🏠 4-3-17 Yukinoshita
📞 0467-53-7805
🕐 7:00am-7:00pm
Mon

(Bread) Baguette ¥388
Casse-croûte ¥378~
(Cafe) Cafe au lait ¥432
Soft-serve ice cream ¥410

2  Bergfeld

- *Authentic German bakery*
- *Eat-in cafe next door*
- *Sister bakery in Hase*

Inspired by the desire to create hearty and healthy bread and goodies for children, the founder of Bergfeld apprenticed under a German baker and opened a bakery here in Yukinoshita, not far from Hachimangu Shrine in 1980. Today, he and his son run two bakeries—this shop and a sister shop in Hase area.

The wide variety of German bread made using rye flour leavened with raisin yeast have a simple, but naturally rich sour flavor with a wonderful aroma filling each bite. Also available are German baked items including cake and cookies.

In 2001, Bergfeld opened up a cafe next door. The plaster-finished interior has the feeling of an old church with its recycled rusted beams and wood furnishings. Choose bread or pastry items from the bakery or order from the menu. During lunch hour from 11:00am to 3:00pm, they offer curry or a sandwich set that comes with salad and soup. The sandwiches feature their artisan bread. If it's a nice day and you prefer to have lunch out on a hike, get your sandwich to go!

<Main Store>
Kamakura Sta.
East Exit, 20 mins.
or Wakare-michi
bus stop 0 min.
🏠 3-9-24 Yukinoshita
📞 0467-24-2706
🕐 Bakery:
9:00am-6:30pm
Cafe:
10:30am-6:30pm
❌ 1st & 3rd Mon

<Hase Store>
Map p.122
Hase Sta. 3 mins.
🏠 2-13-47 Hase
📞 0467-24-9843
🕐 11:00am-6:30pm
❌ 1st & 3rd Tue

(Bread) Rye/Loaf ¥464
Meat pie ¥216
(Cafe) Lunch set ¥1,296~
Black Forest sandwich ¥1,188
BLT ¥972
German coffee: ¥540

③  Alte Stadt

- *Artisan ham and sausage*
- *High-quality domestic meat*
- *Natural ingredients*

Kamakura Sta. East Exit, 20 mins. or **Wakare-michi bus stop 0 min.**

🏠 3-9-24 Yukinoshita
📞 0467-22-6181
🕙 10:00am-6:30pm
Open 7 days/wk

Smoked ham ¥540/100g
Roasted ham ¥604/100g
Frankfurt sausages ¥420/100g
Hot dogs ¥183/piece
Coarsely ground pork sausages ¥496/100g
Freshly fried croquettes ¥172~

A local favorite, this ham and sausage shop has even earned a reputation from German customers as the real deal. To ensure the very best quality, Alte Stadt does not use any frozen meat, preservatives, or antioxidants in their products, and use only the bare minimal amount of additives and phosphates. Instead, the experienced chefs take the time and effort to smoke the meat with cherry wood or salt-cure in lieu of using any chemicals, maintaining the same familiar taste for over 30 years.

Since all items are pre-cooked, they can be consumed as-is, but a little heat may help enhance or release the aromas and flavors of the sausages. In addition to the standard sausages and cold cuts, seaweed is also sold here as if to remind the customers of the ocean nearby.

4   Hokai-ji Temple 宝戒寺

The Hokai-ji Temple was built on the same grounds where the Hojo clan both resided and met their tragic end, marking the end of the Kamakura Shogunate. Hojo Takatoki and his 870 retainers shut themselves up inside the temple and lit it on fire to save themselves from the dishonor of being killed by their rivals. This temple was built to placate their spirits. When the garden is in bloom, it appears to be healing the sorrows of the temple's sad history.

Kamakura Sta. East Exit, 13 mins.
3-5-22 Komachi
0467-22-5512
8:00am-4:30pm
Open 7 days/wk
¥200, Ele ¥100

5   Okura Shirahata Shrine & Yoritomo's Tomb 大蔵・白旗神社

Shirahata Shrine lies directly to the north of the site of the first shogunate government led by Minamoto Yoritomo, the Okura Bakufu, where his palace used to stand and from where he ruled. Yoritomo also enshrined the Kannon, Bodhisattva of Mercy here. North of the shrine is the tomb of Yoritomo marked with a very modest stone stupa.

Kamakura Sta. East Exit, 20 mins. or Wakare-michi bus stop 2 mins.
2-1-24 Nishi-Gomon
Sunrise-Sunset
Open 7 days/wk
Free

6  Sugimoto-dera Temple 杉本寺

Although its main hall was rebuilt in 1678, Sugimoto-dera Temple is in fact one of the oldest temples in Kamakura, founded in 734.

At one point, a castle occupied the site behind this temple to control the area between Kamakura and Mutsuura Port by Tokyo Bay. After the Kamakura Shogunate was overthrown, a battle raged here at the cost of the lives of 300 samurai; here, you can find their lives immortalized among the cluster of mysterious *gorinto* stone stupas.

Kamakura Sta. East Exit, 25 mins. or Sugimoto-Kannon bus stop 1 min.
903 Nikaido
0467-22-3463
8:00am-4:30pm (D/C 4:15pm)
Open 7 days/wk
¥200, Ele ¥100

7 🏛 Kakuon-ji Temple 覚園寺

- *Tranquil temple of old*
- *Guided tours*
- *Captivating Buddhist sculptures*

This temple dates back to the Okura-Yakushido prayer hall built by Hojo Yoshitoki, the second regent of the Kamakura Shogunate in 1218. After battling in the second Mongol invasion, Hojo Sadatoki, the ninth regent (who had succeeded his father, Hojo Tokimune), founded this temple in 1296 in hopes of avoiding a third invasion. Generation after generation, this temple served as a training hall for four different Buddhist sects to members of the Hojo clan, as well as a place to sustain the hearts of many others, through their appeal for national peace and peace of mind and body.

Enshrined in the main hall is the Yakushi Sanzon (Yakushi Triad), consisting of three sculptures that represent the Yakushi Buddha and two bodhisattvas—Nikko (Bodhisattva of Sunlight) and Gekko (Bodhisattva of Moonlight)—surrounding it are the twelve protective deities. Each of the many sculptures here and around the temple grounds has a fascinating story, which one can hear while touring the old structures that include a relocated traditional farmhouse.

In order to preserve this temple as a place of tranquility and prayer, and its distinguishing character that has been maintained since medieval times, the temple is only open for guided viewing. Tours around the temple are organized at specific times (no reservations necessary) and last for about 50 minutes. The tours are only in Japanese, so it might be best to come with a Japanese speaker who can assist you, but a visit is well worth the effort. (No photography is allowed on the temple grounds.)

Kamakura Sta. East Exit, 30 mins. 🚶 or Daitono-miya bus stop 10mins. 🚶

🏠 421 Nikaido

📞 0467-22-1195

🕓 **Time schedule of guided tours (no reservations necessary) (In Japanese only):** 10:00am, 11:00am, 1:00pm, 2:00pm, 3:00pm (7 days/wk), 12:00pm (Sat, Sun, Holidays)

Rainy days, Apr 27, Aug 1-31, Dec 20-Jan 7

¥ **¥500, Ele/Mid ¥200**

8  Zuisen-ji Temple 瑞泉寺

www.kamakura-zuisenji.or.jp/en/index.html

- *Rock garden created by Muso Kokushi*
- *Gorgeous autumn leaves*
- *Hiking trail starting point*

Zuisen-ji Temple was founded in 1327 by Muso Soseki, the chief priest of Engaku-ji Temple and Jochi-ji Temple, also well known as the creator of the temple gardens of Tenryu-ji and Saiho-ji in Kyoto. Surrounded by the mountains known as "Momiji-ga-"yatsu" ("momiji" = "maple," "ga" = "of, " and "yatsu" = "valley") that transforms into gorgeous scenery in the fall season, the temple grounds are vast, extending to the summit, but are unfortunately not entirely open to the public; even still, it is enjoyable to stroll the garden of flowers and bamboo in such serenity.

Kamakura Sta. East Exit, 36 mins. or Daitono-miya bus stop 15 mins.

🏠 **710 Nikaido**
📞 **0467-22-1191**
🕘 **9:00am-5:00pm (D/C 4:30pm)**
📅 **Open 7 days/wk**
💴 **¥200, Ele/Mid ¥100**

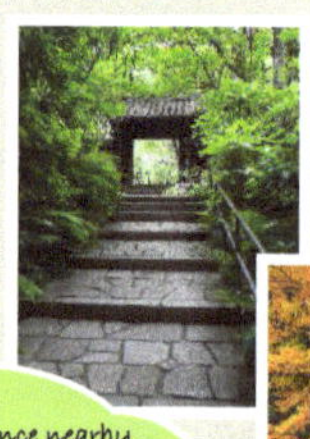

There is the entrance nearby to the Ten-en Hiking trail that goes toward to the back entrance of Kencho-ji Temple

Main Hall

Senju-Kannon, the Buddhist Goddess of Mercy with one thousand arms, is enshrined with the statue of the Seated Shaka-Nyorai, the principle image of Zuisen-ji Temple.

Garden

The garden of Zuisen-ji Temple may be better referred to as a rock garden, but not in the usual sense of the term…its cavernous landscape is carved out of a cliff, producing a sublime atmosphere. Muso Soseki is known to have sat in Zen meditation in the cave gazing at the moon reflected on the surface of the pond. Moon gazing is one of the essential themes of Japanese gardens, and ponds are the symbol of the reflection of one's true self and mind, making this garden a perfect place for the Zen practice of becoming one with nature.

9  Jomyo-ji Temple 浄妙寺

- **Kamakura's fifth-ranked temple**
- **Ashikaga clan's funerary temple**
- **Tea house overlooking a rock garden**

Kamakura Sta.
East Exit, 30 mins.
or Jomyo-ji
bus stop 1 min.

🏠 3-8-31 Jomyoji
📞 0467-22-2818
🕐 9:00am-4:30pm
Open 7 days/wk
¥ ¥100, Ele ¥50

<Kisen-an Tea House>
A set with matcha green tea and a dry confectionery decorated with the Ashikaga family crest ¥600
A set with matcha green tea and beautiful "wagashi" ¥1,000

The temple served as the family funerary temple for the Ashikaga clan, and its grounds extend on a vast area that includes a former residence of the Ashikaga clan next to the temple.

The roof is a distinguishing feature of the main hall, which was reconstructed in 1756. It is made of sheet copper and has a convex *mukuri*-shaped roof. While a majority of the shrines and temples have concave roof shapes that originated in China expressing dignity and strength, the *mukuri* shape is authentically Japanese, and is said to signify modesty and gentleness.

To the left of the main hall is Kisen-an, a traditional Japanese tea houses rebuilt by the monks of the Kamakura Gozan in the 1500s. There, you can enjoy matcha green tea and *wagashi* while looking out at the serene rock garden, as well as experience the *sui-kin-kutsu* garden feature.

Located on the ruins of a sub-temple is a Western-style house built by a wealthy man in the early 1900s that operates as a bakery and restaurant.

While many may be surprised at the thought of a Western restaurant on the premises of a Zen temple, it is historically common for a temple to change with the times.

Sui-kin-kutsu

A bamboo pole that extends from the veranda of the tea house is part of a traditional garden feature called *sui-kin-kustu* (*sui*=water, *kin*=koto [Japanese harp], and *kutsu*=cave) that also serves as a draining device. When water drains into the jug through the small hole, it produces tiny drips into the water that mimic the sound of a *koto* harp.

⑩ Hokoku-ji Temple 報国寺

www.houkokuji.or.jp/english.html

- *Beautiful bamboo grove*
- *Moss and rock garden*
- *Historical site of the Ashikaga clan*

Kamakura Sta.
East Exit, 30 mins.
or Jomyo-ji
bus stop 3 mins.

🏠 2-7-4 Jomyoji
📞 0467-22-0762
🕐 9:00am-4:00pm
Dec 29-Jan 3
¥ Free
Entry to bamboo
garden: ¥300
Matcha green tea
¥500

Known more commonly as the "Bamboo Temple," Hokoku-ji Temple was founded by the Ashikaga clan in 1334, the year following the fall of the Kamakura Shogunate. In 1439, when Ashikaga Mochiuji was defeated in a rebellion he led against the Ashikaga shogunate, he performed *harakiri* (ritual suicide by disembowelment) at the Zuisen-ji Temple nearby, inciting his son Yoshihisa, who was only 10 years old, to also perform *harakiri* here at the Hokoku-ji Temple.

Yagura tombs

Dug horizontally into the cliff, the *yagura* tombs contain the ashes of Ashikaga Ietoki and Yoshihisa, making this temple one of the shogunate branch of Kanto region's most significant sites associated with the tragic history of the demise of the Ashikaga shogunate.

The main hall

The main hall was built in the mid-1300s and to its right is the Kashodo Hall, built in 1978. Near the bell tower, there is a memorial of stone pagodas dedicated to the lives that were lost on both sides of the 1333 siege in Kamakura that overthrew the shogunate.

Bamboo grove

To visit the bamboo grove, you are charged an entrance fee at the ticket stand to the left of the main hall. Matcha green tea is served in a tea house alongside the grove, which sits upon the remains of Kyuko-an, a hermitage where the founder of this temple and Zen monk, Tengan Eko, trained.

Garden

The garden between the bell tower and main hall is a restoration of the *karesansui* rock garden initially created by Tengan Eko, where you can experience the refined world view of this literary figure.

Zaimoku-za Area

Extending from central Kamakura towards Wakae Island (the old   port site), the Zaimoku-za area retains the colorful flavor of its past as a lively merchant town with some traditional Japanese vendors remaining.

- Bonzo
- Bento Bunny
- Yorozu-ya Shoten
- Shimizu-yu
- Okuda Style Surfing
- Good Morning Zaimokuza
- Kamejikan
- Komyo-ji Temple

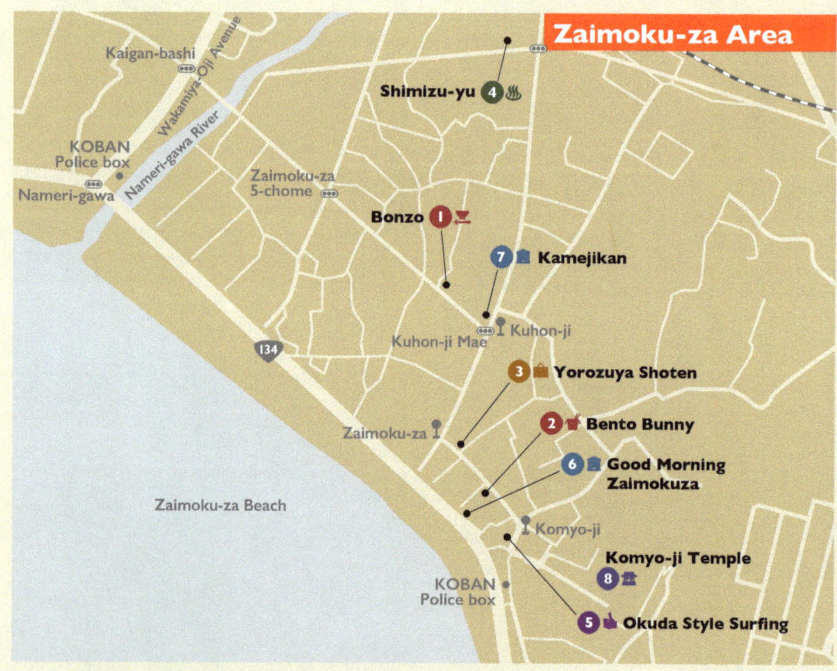

Bus Information (Bus terminal map is provided on p. 197)

1-**8** — Take Bus No. 40 for Zushi Station or Bus No. 41 for Kotsubo that depart from **17** at the East Exit of Kamakura Station

1 🍵 Bonzo 梵蔵

bonzo.shopinfo.jp

- *Fresh homemade soba noodles*
- *Owner with a passion for homemade soba*
- *Delicious à la carte and course meals*

**Kamakura Sta.
East Exit, 18 mins. 🚶
or Kuhon-ji bus stop
2 mins. 🚶**

🏠 **3-17-33 Zaimokuza**
📞 **0467-73-7315**
🕐 **<Lunch>
11:30am-2:30pm (L.O.)
<Dinner> Res. only
6:00pm-8:30pm (L.O.)**
▧ **Wed, IR**

Homemade sesame tofu
¥300
Cold soba with Kamakura
vegetables and "shirasu"
(whitebait) ¥1,550
Ten-zaru (cold soba with
tempura) ¥1,900
Shochu ¥800~
Sake ¥1,000~
<Course meals/Res. only>
Lunch ¥3,500
Dinner ¥5,000, ¥8,000

The name "Bonzo" refers to the Hindu word "Brahma," meaning "the ultimate reality of the universe." Owner and soba master, Ippei Hayashimoto, opened this shop after returning from backpacking around the world. From the millstone located in the corner of his shop, Ippei grinds buckwheat for the noodles several times a day. Through such meticulous labor, he aims to draw out the vital energy of buckwheat to connect people with nature.

While waiting for your noodles, snack on some dishes with a cup of sake or *shochu* (distilled liquor). Specialties include homemade sesame tofu tempura, a delicacy made from ground sesame paste and Japanese arrowroot, and deep fried in tempura batter. The nutty sesame flavor and creamy texture that melts in your mouth is a different experience all together from regular tofu. No reservations are required for à la carte items during lunch, but you may have to wait for a seat or to fill your order, since it tends to be a popular lunch spot. Reservations are only accepted for those ordering course meals for lunch. Dinner is by reservation only and only course meals are served with soba noodles complemented by dishes with vegetables, seafood, duck, and tofu. We recommend ordering a course meal for full enjoyment of the delightful homemade cuisine.

Reservations are taken by phone in English..

②  **Bento Bunny**　手作り弁当バニー

- *A bento shop loved by locals*
- *Use of organic and natural ingredients*
- *Just a block from the beach*

The owners of this shop, a local favorite since its opening over 30 years ago, are long-time Kamakuraites. ased on their motto of "love, security, and peace of mind," Bento Bunny offers nutritious food choices that give people highly vital energy. To the extent possible, they use products and seasonings made without the use of additives and grown with zero or minimal use of pesticides; their meat products are also carefully selected.

The menu offers a wide variety of items such as daily specials, Japanese bento, Chinese bento, or special bento with your choice of white or brown domestically grown rice, sandwiches, rice balls or deli items.

The prices are also quite reasonable considering the quality and taste; it's no wonder this shop is so well loved by locals and hungry surfers. Normally it takes about 5 minutes to make each bento after placing an order, but it may take longer between 11:30am-1:00pm, when there is a crowd. If visiting around this time, be prepared to wait a while.

Kamakura Sta. East Exit, 25 mins. or Zaimoku-za bus stop 1 min.

🏠 **6-5-26 Zaimokuza**

📞 **0467-22-1188**

🕐 **Weekdays 8:00am-2:00pm Sat, Sun & Holidays 8:00am-4:00pm**

Open 7days/wk

"Yamato-buta Tonkatsu" (Pork cutlet) Bento ¥1,000
Special "Momo-karaage" (fried chicken) Bento ¥700
Locomoco Bowl ¥800
Jumbo "katsu" (pork cutlet) curry ¥1,050
Rice balls ¥140~

There are some tables and seats outside the store where you can enjoy bento.

Hungry surfers' favorite!

3  **Yorozuya Shoten** 萬屋商店

· *General store combined with a local bar*

Yorozuya boasts a history of over 100 years as a general store, and the current owner, Kazuo Habuta, is the fourth generation to succeed its operations. Here, the traditional custom of "kaku-uchi," allowing the customer to drink their liquor in the store after making their purchase, continues. (In earlier times, this was customary for all liquor stores in Japan.) At the end of the day, many neighbors gather in Yorozuya to drink canned beer or sake with snacks. The owners and regulars are friendly and always welcome new faces, so don't hesitate to step outside the tourist zone and buy a drink and join in to experience the local life on the backstreets!

Kamakura Sta. East Exit, 22 mins. or Zaimoku-za bus stop 1 min.

🏠 6-3-25 Zaimokuza
📞 0467-22-0214
🕐 8:30am-10:00pm
Tue

4  **Shimizu-yu** 清水湯

· *Mom-and-Pop Public Bath*

In former times, *sento*, or public baths, could be found in any town in Japan as a place of community where one could recover after a hard day, but they have since disappeared with the passage of time. Shimizu-yu is now the only *sento* left in central Kamakura.

When Mr. Shimizu, the son of the former owners, lost his parents, he was a businessman who commuted to Yokohama daily, with no plan to keep the bathhouse in operation. In response to local pleas to keep it going, however, his family joined forces, and now, his sister and wife run the operation on weekdays, and he takes over on the weekends.

To intimately experience the local community, enjoy a dip; be sure to observe proper bathing etiquette. (Either purchase or bring your own soap/shampoo/towel.)

Kamakura Sta. East Exit, 13 mins.

🏠 1-10-24 Zaimokuza
📞 0467-22-4697
🕐 3:00pm-9:00pm
Mon(*), Wed(*), Fri(*)
💰 ¥470,
   Ele ¥200, Child ¥100

5  Okuda Style Surfing

- *Surf shop offering lessons and rental gear*
- *Reliable local information*
- *Located right near the beach*

This surf shop located along Zaimoku-za Beach has surfboards, body boards, SUP (stand up paddle) boards, and wet suits for both rental and sale, and offers private lessons for various levels of skill with professional instructors.

Walk-in rentals are possible; advanced reservations are recommended since wet suit sizes are limited. When renting gear, be sure to confirm the local rules, which iincludes restricted SUP areas and surfing hours (between 9am to 5pm from July to August).

If you are living nearby and can visit often, the shop offers memberships that provide access to their facilities, such as board lockers, showers, and locker rooms.

Kamakura Sta.
East Exit, 27 mins. or Komyo-ji bus stop 0 min.
6-14-2 Zaimokuza
0467-23-8284
10:00am-7:00pm
Open 7 days/wk

Rental fee:
Surf board (+leash):
¥2,160/1hour~
Body board (+leash & fin):
¥1,080/1hour~
SUP board (+le sh & dp e)a
¥3,240/1hour~
Wet suits: ¥2,160/1day

Lesson fee: ¥6,480/3 hours includes insurance, use of shower

They have basic English skills for e-mail correspondence and lessons:
info@padobo.com

Lessons may be canceled due to unfavorable weather conditions on day of reservation.

Manager Toshihiro Harada, a native of Zushi, a neighboring town, was recognized as the Japan representative at SUP world tournament. He and other staff members can give reliable information on local marine sports.

Okuda Style also has surfboards and surf gear for sale, and you can custom-order wet suits. Japanese custom-made wet suits have a fabulous reputation for their high quality. Orders take a few weeks, so are only recommended for locals or long-term travelers.

6  Good Morning Zaimokuza

good-morning-zaimokuza-jp.book.direct/en-us

- *A homey, beachfront B & B*
- *Reasonable rates*
- *Dining hall open for breakfast and dinner*

Opened in 2016, Good Morning Zaimokuza is a comfortable B & B overlooking the ocean. From sunrise to sunset, visitors can experience the wind and the sound of the waves while gazing at the changing scenery. The four private rooms host simple white wall interiors accented with natural wood. The three rooms on the second floor have a shared balcony with a communal bath and toilets. Guests are provided with clean, comfortable futons. As if the staff's hospitable service itself isn't appealing enough, you are sure to be charmed by the proprietress and her tasty Japanese-style breakfast. Set meals are made with local, seasonal ingredients, and since the dining hall is open to the public, you are sure to find a few regulars. At night, the space is transformed into a bar where local fishers or wave riders gather, fresh out of the water.

Guests can try long board surfing, SUPing, or other water sports. If you are interested in rentals or lessons, the staff will provide you with information on nearby surf shops.

Kamakura Sta. East Exit, 28 mins. 🚶 **or Komyo-ji bus stop 2 mins.** 🚶

🏠 **6-5-19 Zaimokuza**
📞 **0467-38-5544**
🕐 **C/I 4:00pm**
   C/O 10:00am

<Rate>
¥5,400~ (w/ breakfast)
Shower & Toilets: Shared
*Reservations: Book on their English website
<Dining hall> (Open to the public)
Breakfast (¥900):
8:00am-10:00am (L.O. 9:30am)
Bar:
5:00pm-9:00pm (L.O. 8:30pm)

7  Kamejikan 亀時間

kamejikan.com/en

- *Pioneer of Kamakura guesthouses*
- *A 5-minute walk from the beach*
- *Cafe & bar open on weekends*

**Kamakura Sta.
East Exit, 20 mins. 🚶
or Kuhon-ji bus stop
1 min. 🚶**
🏠 **3-17-21 Zaimokuza**
📞 **0467-25-1166**
🕐 **C/I 3:00pm
C/O 10:00am**

While backpacking around the world, owner Masa Sakurai became familiar with interesting styles of guesthouses where cheapness wasn't the only allure. This inspired him to open Kamakura's first guesthouse in 2011. In his search for a suitable place and renovation of the 90-year-old house, he was supported by members of "Transition Town Kamakura (p. 032) and Hayama," a non-profit group, to create this guesthouse. Both the owner and staff members are key figures within the local community. Inside the front door adorned with the turtle logo ("kame" means "turtle" and "jikan" means "time"), you'll find a lounge area that is used as a cafe & bar on weekends, which is open to the public. The guesthouse is furnished with secondhand furniture and fittings made from driftwood, creating a relaxing atmosphere where time can be spent like slow turtle. Guestrooms are partitioned by "shoji," or traditional paper sliding doors, which means it is easy to hear the activities of other guests—but allow that to be part of your authentic Japan experience. The refined features of Japanese residential architecture remain here and there. Enhance your appreciation of the Japanese way of life by sleeping on futon spread over soft tatami mats.

<Rate>
Private room (tatami mat)
2 rooms: ¥9,000
(room charge)~
Domitory (co-ed):
1 room (6 persons)
¥3.200 (p/p)~
Breakfast (¥500) is available upon request.

<Cafe>
(noon-5:00pm on weekends)
Brown sugar & ginger spice soy milk ¥600
Danish panckae (aebleskiver) ¥890
Lunch set ¥1,180

8  Komyo-ji Temple 光明寺

- *Temple with largest main gate in the Kanto region*
- *Faces the ocean and Mt. Fuji*
- *Largest wooden building in Kamakura*

Kamakura Sta.
East Exit, 30 mins.
or Kuhon-ji bus stop
1 min.
🏠 6-17-19 Zaimokuza
📞 0467-22-0603
🕐 Apr-Oct.14:
   6:00am-5:00pm
   Oct.15-Mar:
   7:00am-4:00pm
   Open 7 days/wk
¥ Free

Established around 1243, Komyo-ji Temple served as the main training center of the Jodo (Pure Land) sect. In its time, it brought relief to ommoners with its strong emphasis on sutra readings over practice or study. As a large temple patronized by members of the Hojo clan, it developed as the center for Buddhist prayers, and prospered as a place for education, training, and prayer for national welfare. It has the largest main gate of a temple in the Kanto area (Greater Tokyo and surrounding regions), reflecting its past grandeur. The current main hall, constructed in 1698, escaped damage in the Great Kanto Earthquake, and is the largest wooden architectural structure existing in Kamakura.

Take off your shoes and step into the main hall to view the many interesting displays, such as the various Buddha statues and a large wooden rosary carved with sutras.

Around July, many lotus flowers bloom in the pond, some even from cultivations of 2000-year-old ancient lotus seeds. Walk around the back of the main hall to the right and go up the hill to get to the observatory, which commands a view of Mt. Fuji on clear days. Near the temple's gates are the ruins of Wakae-jima—part of one of the oldest surviving artificial harbors in Japan, and at one time was the city's main port. Standing here, you can get a feeling of the significance of Komyo-ji in its age of glory.

Path to the observatory.

Hase & Yuigahama Area

The Yuigahama Coast that spreads out directly in front of the
Tsurugaoka Hachima-gu Shrine once served as a site for samurai to
train and compete in martial arts and also served as their burial ground,
but now is bustling with surfers and sea bathers.
Yuigahama Street leading from Central Kamakura to the Great Buddha
is a popular place for stores owned by young entrepreneurs who
relocated to the area.

CASA. Kamakura Espresso. PUB & BED

HOUSE YUIGAHAMA

ESSELUNGA NATUDECO

Beau Temps

Kaseiro

Tsuruya

WOOF CURRY

Oltrevino

HANABI

Ichikanjin

SAIRAM

Magokoro

Matsubara-an & Cafe

Pizzeria GG

Totoyamichi

Namihei

Chikaramochi-ya

Second Hands Sosuke

hotel aiaoi

Hostel YUIGAHAMA+SOBA BAR

WeBase Hostel Kamakura

Kaihinsou Kamakura

Kamakura Noh Butai
(Noh Theater & Museum)

Kamakura Museum of Literature

Kotoku-in Temple

Hase-dera Temple

Yagura caves were created by hollowing out cliffs
for tombs for people of high stature and where
Buddhist statues are enshrined (since flat land was
limited).

Yato are valleys created by the folds in hills or mountains.
The town of Kamakura developed along *yato* landforms,
and many temples were built by cutting vertically into the
rock walls with the valley floor stretching out below.

Hase & Yuigahama Area

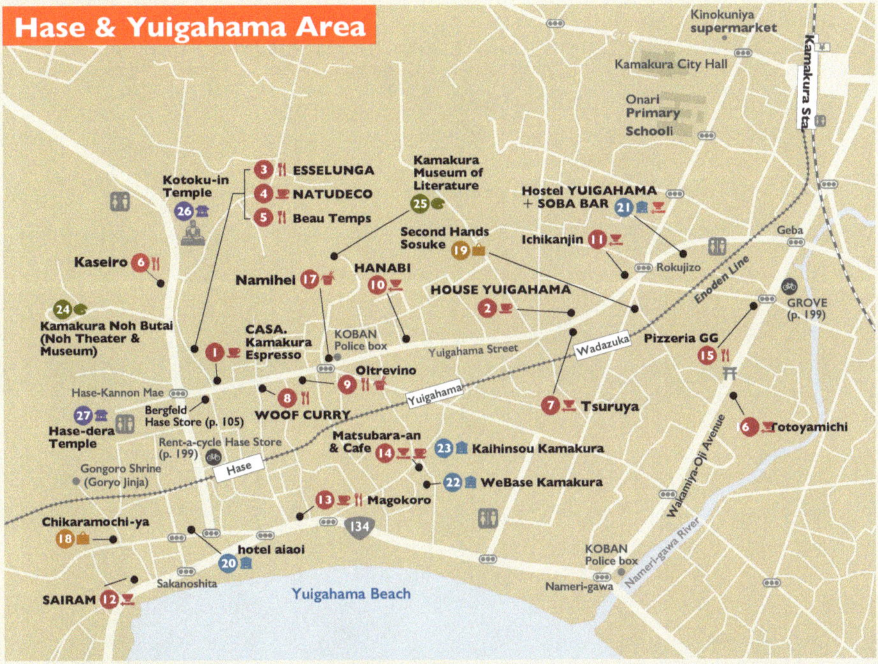

Bus Information (Bus terminal map is provided on p. 197)

1 – 27 — Take any bus that departs from 6 at the East Exit of Kamakura Station

 CASA. Kamakura Espresso. PUB & BED

- *Espresso cafe & pub*
- *Linked to a guest house*
- *Managed by an architect*

Hase Sta. 3 mins.
1-15-5 Hase
0467-55-9077
8:00am-8:00pm
Mon

<Menu>
Espresso ¥320~
Beer ¥540~
Sandwiches ¥600~
Salada (S)¥350 (M)¥600
Affogato ¥500

<B&B>
Twin (2 single beds)
¥11,400 for 2 persons
¥5,700 for 1 person
Twin (Bunk bed)
¥13,400 for 2 persons
¥9,000 for 1 person
<Reservations>
Book on booking.com

Details that distinguish this small establishment include exterior walls of rusted zinc and a sharp interior of black and white. Customers can order an authentic espresso, coffee, or alcoholic beverages along with a snack while seated at the cozy counter or lounging on a sofa.

The owner, an architect who had been commuting to Kamakura for surfing opened his architectural office and café in this town because he wanted more people to experience uniquely designed spaces as part of their daily lives and because the "Allpress" coffee of his former hometown made a big impression on him. Customers can enjoy a simple baguette sandwich lunch along with their espresso or cappuccino or rest their feet after a long walk with craft beer or wine and a snack of cheese or pickles.

CASA also operates a white-washed B&B with tidy private rooms with bunkbeds in the back and or with twin beds on the second floor. CASA is conveniently located near tourist spots including the Great Buddha and Hase-dera temple, and is just a five-minutes walk from the beach.

2 ☕ HOUSE YUIGAHAMA

- *Bright and sunny cafe*
- *Library of interior design books*
- *Renovation material gallery*

Filling the need for a hub for the local community, a local realtor renovated this former fish store into a unique multi-use space consisting of a cafe, library, gallery, and office.

The cafe walls are lined with books in both English and Japanese on lifestyle, such as interior design and gardening, so feel free to browse while you enjoy a glass of kombucha with a sandwich or a homemade muffin.

Playfulness and stylishness go hand in hand here; on display in the gallery of interior renovation materials are such items as European wallpaper and re-appropriated lights originally used on squid fishing boats. There is also an office in the back, serving as a collective workspace for interior designers and realtors.

Whether you just want to take a break from your stroll around town, or are looking for interaction with the locals, come inside and see what it's all about.

Wadazuka Sta.
5 mins. 🚶
🏠 1-12-8 Yuigahama
📞 0467-53-8589
🕙 11:00am-6:00pm
(L.O. 5:30pm)
▨ Wed

Plain hot dogs ¥480
Veggie sandwich ¥500
Muffins ¥300
Coffee ¥400~
Kombucha ¥500~

Toilet renovated inside the freezer of the former fish store!

 3 🍴 ESSELUNGA

- *Toscana-style Italian restaurant*
- *Organic and all-natural ingredients*
- *Vegan full-course menu available*

Trained in Tuscany, Chef Tanaka makes every effort to procure the finest ingredients, including organic vegetables grown with care, and fresh, local seafood; but he takes it even further than that. In his restaurant garden, over 10 kinds of herbs and vegetables are grown from organic seed, and restaurant employees roll up their sleeves between lunch and dinner hours to tend them. That's how passionate he is about the quality and standard of his cuisine.

The menu features local Toscana dishes that are rich with flavors of just-harvested ingredients. For lunch, choose from among the 3 course options—each a combination of an appetizer plate and your choice of a variety of pasta or main dishes.
For dinner, enjoy tasty items from the à la carte menu, or on special occasions, why not try a special dinner course (requires reservations a day in advance)? Vegetarians or vegans rejoice! There is also a beautiful vegan full-course menu, still quite a rare find in Japan.

Hase Sta. 4 mins. 🚶
🏠 1-14-26 Hase
📞 0467-24-3007
🕐 11:30am-3:30pm
(L.O. 2:00pm)
5:30pm-10:00pm
(L.O. 9:00pm)
Mon, 2nd & 4th Tue
(Open on holidays)

Lunch course ¥2,160
Terrine with 12 kinds of vegetables ¥2,430
Seafood pasta with fresh tomatoes in aglio e olio ¥2,700
Grilled "wagyu" beef with aged balsamico vinegar ¥4,104
Dinner course ¥7,560
Vegetable course (vegan available upon request) ¥6,264
Wine by the glass ¥864~

ESSELUNGA, NATUDECO, and Beau Temps

A one hundred-year-old Japanese house, the former home of the owner's relative, is located on a quiet back street and is the pioneer of restaurants set in vintage Japanese-style houses in Kamakura, a setting with increased popularity. The owner maintained the traditional design while adding new touches in the renovation, which he undertook himself. Today, there is a main Italian restaurant, Esselunga, and a wine bistro, Beau Temps, and a cafe Natudeco, added on both sides surrounding the courtyard.

Inspired by the restored health of his wife through a macrobiotic diet, and his daughter's healthy response to food without additives after experiencing food sensitivities, the restaurant focuses on high-quality organic food. The chefs and staff took over and successfully created these three eateries with the aim to revive the holistic life style of Kamakura with a modern sensibility.

4 ☕ NATUDECO

- *Charming organic cafe*
- *Microbiotic, vegan, gluten-free menu*
- *Serves healthy breakfasts from 8:00am*

Hase Sta. 4 mins. 🚶
🏠 1-14-26 Hase
📞 0467-40-6973
🕗 8:00am-8:00pm
(L.O. 7:00pm)
(close at 6pm on Sun)
▨ Open 7 days/wk, IR

Morning Plate ¥960
Veggie burger ¥1,300
Microbiotic plate ¥1,600
Organic Matcha drink ¥700
Soy cafe au lait ¥640
Organic matcha tiramisu
(vegan) ¥640

This quaint organic cafe is an oasis not only for locals who are particular about organic or all natural food, but also for tourists who seek respite from the crowds. Originally a garage, this cafe was converted into a comfortable cafe using natural materials and filled with sunlight.

Natudeco shares the same policy as Esselunga, the Italian restaurant next door: to the extent possible, use only organic ingredients. They also use unique food products not often found in Japanese restaurants, such as "super food" items like quinoa and chia seeds. Their "Macrobiotic Plate" has a variety of side dishes with brown rice, and they also serve gluten-free "Veggie Curry." The vegan style veggie burger is so delicious and filling that it's a favorite even with meat lovers. Be sure to order from their fancy dessert and drink menu; they have matcha green tea, and cake or smoothies made with organic powdered green tea from Kyoto. Wine can be ordered from Esselunga's wine list, so drop in and enjoy organic wine by the glass and healthful food.

5 🍴 Beau Temps

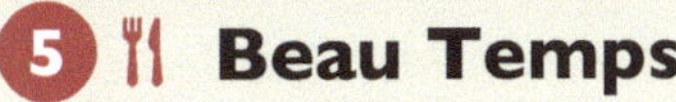

- *Organic bistro wine bar*
- *Casual interior with outdoor terrace seating*
- *Open until 11pm*

Hase Sta. 4 mins. 🚶
🏠 1-14-26 Hase
📞 0467-40-6172
🕐 12:00pm-3:00pm
(L.O. 2:00pm)
6:00pm-11:00pm
(Food L.O. 10:00pm)
📋 Open 7 days/wk, IR

Lunch course ¥1,945
Fresh fish carpaccio ¥1,400
Assorted charcuterie (ham, salami, paté, etc.) for one ¥1,080
Side dishes ¥540~
¥Main dishes (meat, fish) ¥2,160~
Wine by the glass ¥760~

This casual bistro offers a selection of fine organic wines that reflect the care of wine makers who use sustainable agricultural methods, such as biodynamics and organic farming.

For lunch, there is a course menu that includes a salad of freshly harvested local vegetables with a main dish choice of either meat or fish, complemented with homemade pain de campagne made using raisin-based natural yeast, and a cup of their specialty coffee.

For dinner, enjoy a variety of appetizers, hearty main dishes, and satisfying desserts that go perfectly with natural wine.

You'll be nourished not only by the food, but also by the atmosphere; natural light floods the restaurant from a large skylight, and unpainted wood and diatomaceous earth finishes create a comfortable interior. There is also outdoor terrace seating, presenting romantic dining options.

The friendly and casual service balances nicely with high-quality food and wine, making this a very popular eating venue, so reservations are recommended for both lunch and dinner.

The menu is hand-written on a blackboard only in Japanese, but the friendly servers speak basic-level English so don't hesitate to ask them recommendations. Bon appetite!

6 🍴 Kaseiro 華正楼

- *Authentic Chinese cuisine*
- *The former home of a nobleman*
- *Film director Yasujiro Ozu was a regular*

Hase Sta. 5 mins. 🚶
🏠 3-1-14 Hase
📞 0467-22-0280
🕐 11:00am-9:30pm
   (L.O. 8:00pm)
▨ Open 7 days/wk

<Lunch>
Weekdays: ¥3,240~¥7,560
Weekends and holidays:
¥5400~
<Dinner>
¥5,400~¥12,960
*A 10% service fee will be added.
*To make reservations, parties need to be 2 or more persons on weekdays and 3 or more for weekends or holidays.

In days of old, this three-story traditional Japanese house was surrounded by a pine forest and served as the vacation home of a nobleman. Today, the street it sits along, which connects Hase-dera Temple to the Great Buddha, is very busy, but the elegance of old-time Kamakura as a vacation home town still remains.

After removing your shoes, step into the *ryokan*-style (a "*ryokan*" is a Japanese style inn) lobby, and you will be guided to a guest table upstairs.

There are many private rooms with *tatami* mats partitioned by *shoji* screens and *fusuma* sliding doors. Convenient for Chinese-style dining the tables are round, since most of the food is served on large platters for sharing. The relaxed dining experience overlooking the garden and ocean makes this restaurant popular for special occasions with family and friends.

The cuisine is authentic Beijing fare, and most items are served as course-style menus for both lunch and dinner. Each dish is prepared with care and refined flavors. You can also order from the à la carte menu, but very often the restaurant is full—especially on weekends and holidays—so it may take time to fill your request.

There are very few vegetarian/vegan items on the menu, but with advance reservations, they will be happy to make special accommodations.

7  Tsuruya つるや

- *Well-established grilled eel restaurant*
- *Time-honored 1-hour grilling time*
- *Frequented by famous local authors*

Given the local adage, "If you say grilled eel, it must be Tsuruya," you know this is the place for eel in Kamakura.

Founded in 1929, third-generation owner Yoshihide Kawai still preserves the original grilling method in which the eel is prepared fresh after the order is taken; first, the raw eel is cleaned, then gently steamed, and finally, after it is juicy and plump, grilled over a charcoal fire for approximately an hour. While the wait isn't for everyone, the gourmand-style of eel dining is to kill time with a *tokkuri* carafe of Japanese sake while snacking on eel bone crackers. If you prefer to avoid the wait, advance reservations are also an option. Or, in place of grilled eel, you could order a rice bowl with chicken, egg, or shrimp. On the first floor, there are two tables that seat four. The second floor offers more spacious surroundings with 5 tables and tatami mat seating, but you must remove your shoes before going upstairs.

Since this is a popular eatery, we recommend making reservations (only in Japanese) before your visit.

Wadazuka Sta. 2 mins.
🏠 3-3-27 Yuigahama
📞 0467-22-0727
🕐 11:30am-7:00pm
Tue

"Una-ju" (Grilled eel over rice) served in a Kamakura-bori lacquerware box
¥2,970~¥5,346
(*Prices vary depending on the size of the eel)
"Ebi-tama-don" (Egg and shrimp over rice) served in a bowl ¥1,620
Sake ¥540~

For an authentic eel experience, try the "Una-ju" (¥3,564)

8 🍴 WOOF CURRY

- *Slow-cooked curry roux*
- *Stylish interior*
- *Open until 9:00pm*

Hase Sta. 4 mins. 🚶
🏠 **2-10-39 Hase**
📞 **0467-25-6916**
🕐 **11:00am-9:00pm**
▨ **Wed**

Vegetable curry ¥900
Chicken curry ¥900
Special curry (curry with
vegetables, boiled egg, and
a choice of chicken, beef
or pork) ¥1,250
Coffee ¥500, Juice ¥550
Beer ¥700

Although the history of curry in Japan has followed a unique path, it is now eaten to such an extent that it has been assimilated into Japanese cuisine. Woof Curry concocts a deep-colored curry that resembles a demi-glace sauce, also known in Japan as "European-style curry." Simmered over several days with sautéed onions, vegetable purée, and over 10 spices, the curry has a mellow and well-defined taste that isn't overpowered by the spices.

The menu is simple: the same curry roux is used in every dish, but you can select from among the feature ingredients, namely vegetables, beef, or chicken. Curry set meals come with a salad and a drink, but you can add a side of rice or more spice with an additional charge. The drinks are also served with care. Enjoy a cup of scrupulously prepared andlocally roasted coffee or quench your thirst with a glass of 100% fruit juice.

Solo diners are also very welcome, while the spacious second floor is convenient for families or large groups. In a town where late dining options are limited, Woof Curry operates until 9:00pm, making it perfect for a casual dinner choice.

9 Oltrevino

- *Italian deli fare*
- *Fine selection of wine*
- *Take-out or eat-in*

Hase Sta. 4 mins.
2-5-40 Hase
0467-33-4872
<Eat-in>
12:00pm-6:30pm
(L.O.)
<Shop>
12:00pm-7:00pm
Wed

Chef-owner Kazuki Furusawa is a full-fledged Kamakuraite, and subsequent to his culinary training in Japan, his food experiences ranged from cultivating grapes at a winery to working as a chef and sommelier in a top-ranking restaurant in Florence.

He operates Oltrevino with his wife, Chie, a prolific author of books on Italian food and culture.

The elegant interior coordinated by Chie has a vintage flair, with carefully selected and imported antique furniture and a wine cellar. The display cases stocked with ingredients, deli foods, and desserts are a feast for the eyes as well as the tummy. Eat-in or take-out, the choice is yours. All you need to do is decide what pasta you want with what sauce. Particular about fresh, seasonal ingredients, Chef Kazuki believes in using local vegetables, seafood, and meat. He describes the concept of his restaurant as a place to enjoy the essence of dining, and, of course, to experience the luxuries of delicious food and quality living.

Simply put, the sophisticated cuisine, reasonable prices, and fine quality wine make this a must-try dining experience.

Florence-style spaghetti with tomato sauce and ricotta cheese, and homemade bread ¥1,950
Pasta lunch set comes with an appetizer, dessert, and coffee or tea ¥3,240

10 HANABI

http://www.ramen-hanabi-en.com/

- *Well-balanced Japanese ramen*
- *Additive-free ingredients*
- *Choice of noodle thickness and broth*

Donning a stylish sleek black apron, Hanabi's owner was born and bred in Kamakura. Following an urge to respond the lack of a tasty local ramen shop, he quit his job as a company employee and opened his own shop in 2005.

Since ramen has the image of being tasty but unhealthy, as a father, Hanabi's owner/chef wanted to create a ramen dish that was healthy enough for his children. Accordingly, he carefully selects his ingredients to ensure their quality and safety, and makes the noodles by hand every morning. For the broth, he makes no exceptions in avoiding synthetic food products, such as additives or preservatives.

Choose between "thick noodles" or "thin noodles" for the popular *Tsuke-men* (dipping noodles) dishes, with a hot broth that has a gentle "*dashi*" (bonito-based Japanese soup stock) flavor. If you are craving something rich-tasting, try the "*Wafu* (Japanese-style) Ramen" made with a soy-sauce and bonito *dashi*. If it's a simple taste you're after, go for the "*Shio* (salt) Ramen," made with three different varieties of natural salt. Depending on how hungry you are, for either dish, there is a choice on the quantity of noodles.

With a modest style, the owner simply seeks to have a perfect balance of flavors in each bowl. No matter how many visits, one can never tire of this ramen. That explains why it is always crowded with locals— families and solo customers alike.

Yuigahama Sta.
3 mins. 🚶
🏠 1-2-5 Hase
📞 0467-23-9005
🕐 Mon-Fri:
 11:30am-3:00pm
 6:00pm-10:00pm
 Sat:
 11:30am-4:00pm
 6:00pm-10:00pm
 Sun, Holidays:
 11:30am-4:00pm
 6:00pm-9:00pm
📝 Tue(*)

"Wafu" (Japanese-style) Ramen (soy-based broth) ¥750
"Shio" Ramen (salt-based ramen) ¥800, Cold "Tsuke-men" ¥850
Ebisu draft beer ¥420~
Organic grape soda ¥360
*Free "extra noodle" service during lunch time on weekdays.

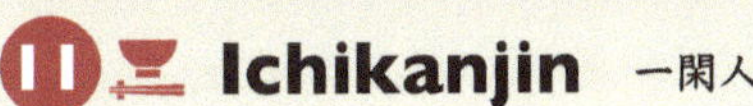

Ichikanjin 一閑人

- **Unique ramen dishes**
- **Bright, clean interior**
- **Delicious side dishes**

Ichikanjin is an unusual ramen shop: not only does it stand out with its pastel green façade and pig signage, it also has a unique menu to match.

While the standard *Shio* (salt) Ramen and *Shoyu* (soy sauce) Ramen are delicious, the *Tsuke-men* (dipping noodles) are a must-try. Their custom-made flat noodles resembling fettuccini mixed with whole grain flour come with fresh Kamakura vegetables, melt-in-your-mouth homemade roasted pork fillets, and a variety of wood ear mushrooms. To eat *tsuke-men*, squeeze lime or lemon juice over the chilled noodles, then dip them in the warm, rich, and spicy soup served in a separate bowl. The richness and tanginess provide a perfectly balanced flavor unlike anything you have ever tasted. Aside from the searingly hot "Habanero Pepper Tsuke-men," the gentle-flavored "Soy Milk *Shio* Ramen," and the seasonal ramen, other options are boiled *gyoza* (potstickers) and a fresh Kamakura veggie salad. Every dish, including side dishes, are made without synthetic seasonings. Shingo Umezawa, the owner whose dishes have many loyal fans, is committed to his standard of creating distinctive, rich, and complex flavors.

Wadazuka Sta. 5 mins.
🏠 1-10-3 Yuigahama
📞 0467-33-4559
🕐 11:30am-3:30pm, 6:00pm-8:30pm (L.O)
Mon

"Tsuke-men" ¥850~
"Shio" (salt-based soup) ramen ¥750
Soy Milk "Shio" ramen ¥780
Habanero Pepper "Tsuke-men" ¥950~
Kamakura Salad ¥250~
Draft beer ¥450~

12 SAIRAM

www.sairam-kamakura-en.link/

- *Organic vegan restaurant*
- *Vegetables grown using natural farming methods*
- *Smoke-free terrace with an ocean view*

Hase Sta. 6 mins.
20-11 Sakanoshita
0467-61-1831
11:30am-5:00pm
Mar-Jun: Wed,
Apr-July: Open 7
days/wk

<Spring-Fall menu>
(Picture) Lunch/deli style
¥1,944
Deli ¥550/100g
Chocolate parfait ¥1,080
<Winter menu>
Pasta set ¥2,376
"Blessings of Nature" set
¥3,024

Sairam is a vegan restaurant run by a contracting firm that builds houses from natural materials. As with their buildings, their food also is prepared with carefully selected all-natural ingredients. Vegetables are grown using natural farming, known for its no-till, no-fertilizer, no-pesticide methods; you can even taste the life energy in the food.

From spring through fall, lunch is served on large deli platters; you can choose as much or as little as you like and pay accordingly. Accompanying these platters is a bowl of fermented brown rice with red beans (cooked in a pressure cooker then matured for a few days in a rice cooker)—a popular Japanese super food—with warming miso soup.

During the winter months, the selection is limited to set lunches with main dishes, such as pasta, curry, or lasagna combined with soup and vegetables. Vegan parfait and cake are among the variety of tasty sweets on the dessert menu—all enjoyable for vegans and non-vegans alike!

⑬ ☕ 🍴 Magokoro 麻心

- *Organic cafe featuring hemp cuisine*
- *Ocean view*
- *Dogs welcome*

Hase Sta. 4 mins. 🚶
🏠 2-8-11 Hase
📞 0467-38-7355
🕐 10:00am–11:00pm
 (Food L.O 8:00pm)
▨ Mon

Plate of the day (fish or vegetarian) ¥1,800 Hemp curry plate ¥1,300
French fries with garlic seasoning ¥720
Microbiotic cake ¥650~
Vegan hemp ice cream ¥320~
Homemade ginger ale ¥750

Situated on the 2nd floor of a building facing Yuigahama beach, Magokoro is where you can relax with a meal at the counter and enjoy the serene ocean view. Run by Shinji Morishita, a key Kamakuraite who organizes music events and parties, this organic cafe creates dishes that introduce the health benefits of hemp. In fact, before WWII, hemp was widely used in Japan as a source of food, natural fiber, tools for Shinto rituals, and other daily needs. Here, the plaster on the walls is mixed with the crushed stems of hemp plants, giving the interior a natural finish. Their menu is made up entirely of dishes that use hemp seed, hemp oil, and hemp charcoal powder.

For lunch, try the lunch plate—a choice of either a fish or vegetarian dish as your main item, accompanied by soup, salad, and rice mixed with hemp charcoal. Popular with vegetarians is the vegetable curry, cooked with 7 spices and hemp powder and adjusted to your desired level of spiciness.

In the daytime, enjoy a cup of organic hemp coffee and a plate of macrobiotic sweets while gazing out over the sea, and in the evening, choose from the à la carte menu. To wash down your meal at lunch or dinner, try a glass of their organic wine or specialty sake.

The entrance can be a bit tricky to spot, but look out for a signboard at the bottom of the steps leading up to the second floor.

14 Matsubara-an & Cafe 松原庵

- *Soba noodle shop and cafe*
- *Offers a full à la carte menu*
- *Terrace seats surrounded by greenery*

Yuigahama Sta.
1 min. 🚶
🏠 **4-10-3 Yuigahama**
📞 **0467-61-3838**
0467-61-2299 (Cafe)
🕐 **11:00am-9:00pm**
(L.O.)
Open 7 days/wk

Lunch course ¥3,456
"Ten seiro" (cold soba with tempura) ¥1,998
Japanese Beef Steak ¥2,484

Located in a quiet residential district that once was lined with vacation homes, this soba shop occupies an old private dwelling surrounded by ancient pine trees. Tastefully refurbished, the house gently blends into its surroundings.

At this stylish eatery, soba noodles are made fresh daily. In addition to a variety of hot and cold soba items, there are also seasonal noodle items such as *yuzu* (Chinese citron) or *shiso* (Japanese basil). Since the concept of the shop is to enjoy soba and sake, there are plenty of beautiful and tasty à-la-carte items with vegetables, fish, or meat that go well with their wide variety of sake and *shochu* (Japanese distilled liquor). You have a choice of seating either on *tatami* mats, regular chairs, or on the outdoor terrace. In any case, the Japanese style of this eatery will not disappoint. Enjoy the view out over the garden. If the wait for the soba shop is long or if you have a craving for homemade scones after your meal, enjoy a cup of deep-roasted coffee at the cafe next door.

It's no wonder this is one of the most popular restaurants in the area; the authentic Kamakura sensibility is reflected in the tableware and interior, and locals often dine here with visitors from afar. If you are looking for a blend of old beauty and modern style, be sure to stop by for a bowl of noodles!

15 🍴 Pizzeria GG

- *Genuine Napoli-style pizza*
- *Bright and spacious ambiance*
- *Take-out pizza also available*

Wadazuka Sta.
6 mins. 🚶
🏠 2-9-62 Yuigahama
📞 0467-33-5286
🕐 <Lunch>
11:30am-4:00pm
<Dinner>
Mon-Fri
5:30pm-10:30pm
Sat 5:30pm-10:30pm
Sun: 5:30pm-9:30pm
(L.O. 40 min before
closing time)
Open 7 days/wk

Antipasto items ¥302~
Al Filetto (pizza with mozzarela,
basil & cherry tomatoes) ¥1,728
GG (pizza with mozzarela, basil,
eggplant, ricotta & salami) & after
ricotta ¥1,998
Italian beer ¥918

If the bright and spacious interior doesn't make you feel you have gone to Naples, the pizza surely will. The Napoli-trained chefs here bake the pizzas in an oven constructed by Italian craftspeople who were flown in on request. The high standards of both ingredients and baking have garnered them the approval from the maestro of the Associazione Verace Pizza Napoletana.

Experience the delightful combination of fresh, local vegetables and seafood with imported Italian ingredients. The menus hosts nearly 10 varieties of rossa and bianca pizza, a wide selection of antipasto items, and classic Italian dolce.

If you are in town on weekdays, don't miss their popular pizza lunch that comes with a drink and a dolce. The reasonable prices and genuine Napoli flavors explain why local Italians in the area dine here. Although Kamakura is known for its small-scale eateries, this pizzeria serves large groups of people and is also kid-friendly. We recommend making reservations for dinner, especially if you are planning on visiting with a large group or during the summer season. Because there aren't many staff members who speak English fluently, we suggest that you have a Japanese-speaking friend place the reservation for you.

16 Totoyamichi 魚屋路

- *"Sushi go round" restaurant*
- *Casual and reasonably priced*
- *A 5-minute walk from the beach*

Wadazuka Sta.
6 mins. 🚶
🏠 **2-13-8 Yuigahama**
📞 **0467-60-1047**
🕐 **11:00am-11:00pm**
Open 7 days/wk

Sushi: ¥129/plate~
Lunch set (Sushi & miso soup/
weekdays only): ¥745~

Prices are coded according to the color or pattern on the plates. To pay your bill, signal any server; they'll tally your bill using the stack of plates, then give you a numbered tag which you should bring to the register to make your payment.

If you're looking for reasonably priced sushi in Kamakura, this is the place. Considering its convenient location along Wakamiya-Oji Avenue, the dishes are affordable and the atmosphere is casual. A nation-wide franchise but local favorite, Totoyamichi is known for its use of quality ingredients, Japanese rice (many inexpensive eateries use imported rice), and fresh, local seafood.

If this is your first time at a "sushi go round," there are a few things you must know before stepping inside: small platters of sushi are transported in front of the counter on a conveyer belt and you are free to take whatever items suit your fancy. Stack up the plates as you finish each one, and after you are done eating, a shop attendant will come around to count your plates at the counter and tally your bill. You can also order from a menu with photos.

Although traditional sushi restaurants are the ultimate luxury with lively counter seating where you can observe the sushi chef carefully preparing each order, dining at one can be expensive (often prices are not even listed on the menu!), and they sometimes refuse first-timers, are often too small for groups, and can't accommodate children. This is why even Japanese natives save them only for special occasions. On the other hand, "sushi go round" eateries are affordable and the billing method is transparent, making it possible for anyone to enjoy sushi.

The special menu features a selection of locally caught fish in season.

17 Namihei　なみへい

- **An all-natural snack store**
- **"Tai-yaki" grilled in wrought iron molds**
- **Eat-in lounge on tatami floor**

Yuigahama Sta.
3 mins. 🚶
🏠 1-8-10 Hase
📞 0467-24-7900
🕙 10:00am-6:00pm
Mon(*), IR

"Tai-yaki" ("an") ¥180
"Tai-yaki" (matcha) ¥220
Shaved ice ¥600~
Baked piroshki ¥220
Yaki-soba ¥430
Organic coffee ¥250
Tapioka drink ¥400

Sensitive to food additives, owner Shingo Hamada opened a snack store to sell safe snacks affordable enough for children to purchase with their pocket money.

The feature item is a popular Japanese sweet snack called *tai-yaki*, a waffle in the shape of a red snapper (symbolizing good fortune) filled with *an*, a sweet adzuki red bean paste. Yet unlike any other store (in Japan, you can commonly find stands selling mass-produced *tai-yaki*), they grill each *tai-yaki* one-by-one in old-fashioned heavy wrought iron molds. The difference is vast—Hamada's *tai-yaki* have crisp waffle exteriors and fluffy *an* interiors.

Other offerings include *yaki-soba* (fried noodles) and piroshki (Russian stuffed rolls), and in the summer, in place of the *tai-yaki* grill, Hamada breaks out the shaved ice machine for the staple heat remedy, *kaki-gori* shaved ice, sweetened with naturally flavored syrup. All items are homemade and do not contain any chemical additives or preservatives, and butter- and dairy-free bread items made with natural yeast are also available.

If you have a bit of time to rest your feet, enjoy your snack at the eat-in counter or on the *tatami* mats inside. A perfect stop for those not only with children, but hungry adults looking for a quality snack.

18 Chikaramochi-ya 力餅家

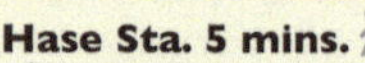

- **Well-known Japanese confectioner**
- **300-year-plus history**
- **Specializing in mochi rice cakes**

Hase Sta. 5 mins. 🚶
🏠 18-18 Sakanoshita
📞 0467-22-0513
🕘 9:00am-6:00pm
Wed,
3rd Tue of the
month

"Gongoro Chikaramochi"
<Nama-mochi>
A box of 10 pieces ¥670
<Gyuhi>
A box of 9 pieces ¥930
1 piece ¥95

Chikaramochi-ya is a Kamakura confectioner with a history of over 300 years specializing in *mochi* (pounded glutinous rice) rice cakes topped with *anko* (sweet adzuki bean paste).

Dip under the shop's *noren* curtain entrance that says "Chikaramochi-ya" in bold Chinese characters, and you will find delightful, old-fashioned presentation of display cases filled with *mochi* rice cakes, *manju* sweet buns, dried candy, steamed *mochi* rice with adzuki beans, and *sembei* rice crackers.

The shop's current proprietor is the 9th-generation descendant of the original founder. Their famous "Gongoro Chikaramochi" confection is named after Gongoro Kagemasa, a samurai who was the first recorded strength-stone lifter in a sport of lifting stones to demonstrate one's strength. (The stone Gongoro lifted is purportedly kept at the nearby Gongoro Jinja Shrine.) The elegant taste of freshly prepared *mochi* rice cake spread with smooth *anko* is a time-honored favorite.

Additive-free, homemade manufacturing methods used here are unchanged since the shop first started producing these classic Kamakura confections, favorites with tourists and locals alike.

The *nama-mochi* ("raw *mochi*") items have a 1-day expiry date and the *gyuhi* type (steamed rice flour and sugar) have a 3-day expiry date.

We recommend a visit early in the day since their sweets sell out quickly—especially during the early-May "Golden Week" holidays, hydrangea viewing season and many weekends during the April-through-October tourist season.

Take-out only.

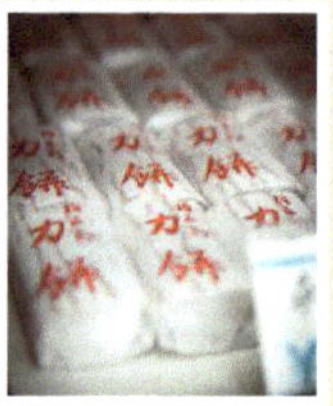

19 Second Hands Sosuke そうすけ

- *Sells curios and antiques*
- *Features furnishings from the 1950s*
- *Repaired and sold in a serviceable condition*

Wadazuka Sta.
1 min. 🚶
3-1-2 Yuigahama
0467-22-8781
11:00am-6:00pm
Mon

Quaint old chairs lining the storefront serve as the signage for this small vintage furniture shop.
With a passion for mid-century Japanese furniture, owner and furniture restoration expert Toru Yonekura selected and restored all of the furnishings that are packed into this store. Chosen not only for their vintage value, but also their practical value, each item has been carefully repaired and refinished to service-able condition.
Tastefully designed Japanese furnishings were mostly made of solid wood up until the late 1950s.
Although they have largely fallen out of use by the older generations who tend to have a preference for modern materials, some people of the younger generations seek out the nostalgia and beauty in function that can only be found in this kind of shop.
Filled with roughly 300 reasonably priced items from furniture to accessories such as chairs, desks, bookshelves, glass shelves, and lamps, if you are in need of quality second hand furnishing,
this is the place for you.

Just the place to find one-off compact wooden furnishings suited for Japanese-scale homes.

20 🏛️   hotel aiaoi

aiaoi.net/english

- *Small hotel run by a young couple*
- *Captures the serene ambience of Kamakura*
- *Ocean views*

Hase St. 3 mins. 🚶
🏠 2-16-15 3F Hase
📞 0467-22-6789
🕐 C/I 4:00pm-9:00pm
    C/O 12:00pm
IR

<Rate>
¥10,600～¥14,500 (w/ breakfast)
Showers & Toilets are shared
<Lounge>
Guests only:
9:00am-12:00pm
Open to public:
6:00pm-10:00pm
<Menu>
Beer ¥800～
Coffee ¥400, Cake ¥450～
<Reservations>
Book on the English website

Go and Yuko Komuro, the young owners of this small boutique hotel, began operation in 2016 out of this single story of a building with 6 guest rooms and a lounge. They created a small gem in Kamakura to offer their guests the experience of nestling close to nature, appreciating the timeless value of things from the past, and the joy of community particular to the area.

The interior is stylish and overflows with a sense of beauty and warmth hand-finished by the owners together with friends. They tastefully incorporated material they salvaged from old houses that were being demolished in the area.

With a choice among single, double, or twin, there are 6 guest rooms—each with a different layout and interior design concept. The linen used for the sheets and towels, and fabric of the custom-made pajamas were carefully selected using the standards of what the owners themselves prefer to use.
For breakfast, enjoy freshly cooked meals lovingly prepared by Yuko in the lounge. Organic rice grown by her father is cooked in an earthen pot every morning, and a bucket of fresh seafood caught a stone's throw from the hotel is delivered by a young local fisherman. If stormy weather continues for days, they may wind up empty-handed, but they are able to improvise, dovetailing nicely with their concept of living in accordance to nature.

As an off-the-beaten-path experience, it is certain that this exposure to daily Kamakura life at aiaoi will be long lasting and become deeply ingrained in your travel memories.

The meaning behind the hotel name "aiaoi" (crafted from a play on the words meaning "meet" ["ai"] and "blue" ["aoi"]) is "to meet Kamakura's blue sky and sea." Each day, the expression of the sky and sea continuously change from moment to moment, each one is special and beautiful. While these expressions may always exist, if one doesn't attempt to see or experience them, they will pass unnoticed.

21 Hostel YUIGAHAMA + SOBA BAR

hostelyuigahama.com/en/

- *Hostel with a twist*
- *Dormitory-style bunks and single rooms*
- *Soba bar on the first floor*

**Kamakura Sta.
West Exit 8 mins.**
🏠 2-5-16 Yuigahama
📞 0467-81-4242
🕐 C/I 3:00pm
   C/O 11:00am
▨ Open 7 days/wk

<Hostel>
Dormitory (mixed) ¥3,500
Double ¥13,000~
Twin ¥14,000~

<Soba bar> (Cash only)
Lunch: 11:30am-3:00pm
Bar 6:00pm-10:00pm
"Niku" Soba (buckwheat
noodle with chicken) ¥918
Grilled chicken with miso ¥648
Sake ¥756~

A local real state company that manages the cafe "House Yuigahama" down the street opened this hostel in 2016. With the help of local designers and artists, the owners renovated a rickshaw storehouse with a balanced blend of vintage flair and ad-hoc wood furnishings to suit their concept of creating a unique place for exchange between locals and tourists.

Along with unisex dormitory-style lodging on the first floor is a soba bar run by Kamakura's popular soba restaurant "Fukuya." The menu features Japanese traditional dishes from the Tohoku region (the north-eastern region of Japan). As Yamagata Prefecture's regional classic dish, soba is served during the day, while at night, finger foods that go well with sake from that area and other alcoholic beverages are offered. On the second floor is a lounge and 5 single rooms that have either twin or double-sized beds. Shower and bathroom facilities are communal.
Full of cheerful ambience and convenient amenities with reasonably priced lodging, relaxing private single rooms, and a soba bar where you can interact with locals, Hostel Yuigahama's hostel has much to offer.

22 🏢 WeBase Kamakura

we-base.jp/kamakura/en/

- *Multi-use hostel complex*
- *Solo or group travelers welcome*
- *Yoga studio and other cultural offerings*

Yuigahama Sta.
4 mins. 🚶
🏠 4-10-7 Yuigahama
📞 0467-22-1221
🕐 C/I 4:00pm
   C/O 11:00am

Bed in a dormitory-style room
¥3,500~
Private double room ¥9,600~
Family room for 1~6 persons
¥30,000 (P/R)
Japanese futon room for 1~12
fpersons ¥33,600~
<Reservations>
Book on the English website

This multi-use community hostel has a wide range of room types to suit different travel styles and needs. There are shared dormitory-style rooms (co-ed and single-sex) with pods, private rooms with beds, and tatami mat rooms with futons for groups. While some room types have their own toilets and baths, the large, communal bath and private shower rooms are clean and convenient.

A casual French bistro, Brasserie Gent, operates inside the hostel, and serves meals with fresh, seasonal ingredients that include seafood from off the coast of Sagami Bay and local vegetables.

The yoga studio adjacent to the hostel offers discounts for hostel guests and also holds culture workshops, outdoor activities such as hiking, and parties and other events.

As suggested by their concept "community hostel," the hospitality and facilities at WeBase Kamakura catalyze interaction between their guests and the local community. Bicycles and lockers are also available for rental.

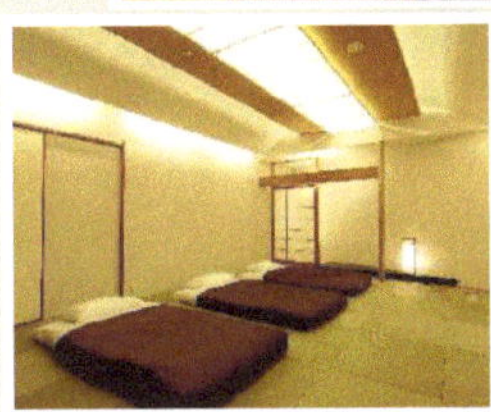

23 Kaihinsou Kamakura かいひん荘 鎌倉

- **"Ryokan" serving Japanese-style food**
- **Complete renovation of an old villa**
- **Enjoy "kaiseki" cuisine in your own room**

Yuigahama Sta.
2 mins. 🚶
🏠 4-8-14 Yuigahama
📞 0467-22-0960
🕐 C/I 3:00pm
   C/O 10:00am

This inn's original structure was built in 1924 as one of the many unique country villas of the affluent class, in a style that blends both Japanese and Western architecture. Kaihinsou is the only remaining *ryokan* (traditional Japanese inn)-style inn in Kamakura that serves *kaiseki* traditional multi-course Japanese cuisine in its guest's rooms (service not available in the Western-style room).

There are various sizes of rooms; each has its own unique charm and character. There is one Western-style room on the 2nd floor, and 12 Japanese-style *tatami* mat rooms, and one Japanese-Western style room in the extension.

After taking a relaxing bath, slip into a *yukata* cotton kimono and dine on the exquisite *kaiseki* meal that uses only the freshest seasonal produce. Unwind and enjoy the bona fide experience of a traditional Japanese resort.

In the words of the proprietor, Mr. Inoue, "Long ago, you could see the sea from here, but now the views have been obstructed by tall buildings. The town, however, remains very much unchanged. Since a single day trip to Kamakura can be too limiting, we offer visitors a chance to stay overnight to appreciate a greater depth and genuine Kamakura experience."

<Rooms>
*Japanese room: 12
Japanese-Western room: 1
Western room: 1
<Room rate>
* Japanese "tatami" room
(w/out meal ¥11,340~
 w/ breakfast ¥13,500~
 w/ dinner and breakfast
¥19,980)~
Japanese-Western room
(beds and "tatami" room)
¥15,660~
Western room ¥15,660~

*All rooms have a private bath/toilet
*Rate is per person

<Reservations>
Book on
www.japanican.com
www.jalan.net

24  Kamakura Noh Butai (Noh Theater & Museum)　鎌倉能舞台

www.nohbutai.com/english.htm

· *Traditional Japanese performing art*

Noh is said to have originated from popular entertainment imported from China in the 700s, and the current form was perfected into a sophisticated theatrical art in the late 1300s. Noh is considered to be the world's oldest continuous theatrical art because its original style of performance has remained almost unchanged since its inception. Noh performances are held regularly here, but when not in use, visitors can visit the theater and the exhibitions of Noh masks, costumes, and instruments. (We recommend bringing someone who speaks Japanese for assistance since there are no English explanations.)

Hase Sta. 7 mins.
🏠 3-5-13 Hase
📞 0467-22-5557
　(Noh Museum)
🕙 10:00am-4:00pm
　Sun & Holidays
💴 ¥500, Students ¥300

25  Kamakura Museum of Literature　鎌倉文学館

· *Museum of Kamakura-related Literature*

One of Kamakura's three famous Western buildings still in existence, this museum used to be the villa of a former marquis and was built in 1936. Located close to the former residence of Yasunari Kawabata, who wrote "The Sound of the Mountain," this villa also served as the model for a residence that appears in Yukio Mishima's novel, "Spring Snow."
As part of the rotating displays, in addition to manuscripts, letters, and personal items of such Kamakura- loving literary figures as Kawabata and Soseki Natsu-me, there is also documentation from Japanese classics, such as the Manyoshu and *waka* poetry to modern literature. Most explanations are in Japanese, but you will be sure to enjoy the splendor of the villa and the cultural ambience of Kamakura's literati of a former age.

Yuigahama Sta.
7 mins.
🏠 1-5-3 Hase
📞 0467-23-3911
🕙 Mar-Sep:
　9:00am-5:00pm
　(D/C 4:30pm)
　Oct-Feb:
　9:00am-4:30pm
　(D/C 4:00pm)
　D/C 30 mins. prior
　Mon(*), IR
💴 Varies depending on
　the exhibition

26 Kotoku-in Temple 鎌倉大仏殿高徳院

www.kotoku-in.jp/en/

- *Kamakura Daibutsu (Great Buddha)*
- *Seated in the same position since 1252*
- *13.35m high and 121 tons*

Hase Sta. 7 mins.
4-2-28 Hase
0467-22-0703
Apr-Sep:
8:00am-5:15pm
Oct-Mar:
8:00am-4:45pm
Open 7 days/wk
¥200, Ele ¥150

This statue is referred to as the Kamakura Daibutsu (Great Buddha), to distinguish him from the "Great Buddha" of Todai-ji Temple in Nara (the former ancient capital to the west of Kyoto). Although recorded as being built in 1252, there is a lot of mystery behind the circumstances and details of its creation and creator. The Buddha's stooped shoulders and proportionately large head are characteristic of sculptures made in the Song Dynasty.

The name of the Buddha of the Western Pure Land, Amitabha Nyorai, means "infinite light," and accordingly, the statue was initially covered in gold leaf that is still visible on the Buddha's right cheek. No doubt, when the statue was built, the Buddha's resplendent form gave hope to people, and even now, after sitting in the same position for over 760 years, his gold leaf worn from centuries of weathering, he still emits an air of peacefulness.

With a small fee, you can explore the inside of the Great Buddha from a low entrance on the side. For deeper appreciation, we recommend visiting the temple's English website, where there is a detailed description of the features and casting process.

Rahotsu (Spiral hair)

The Great Buddha's head is covered in small spiral *rahotsu*, or "snail-like" curls, which is one of the symbols of enlightenment. In most images of Buddha, the spirals locks of hair are clockwise, but on Kamakura Daibutsu, they are counterclockwise. There is a theory that the shogunate of Kamakura made them counter-clockwise as a symbol of opposition to power in Kyoto, where the capital was located at the time.

Renben (Lotus petals)

In middle of the Edo Period, there was a plan for 32 *renben*, or lotus petals, to be cast for the Buddha's seat, but only four petals were completed.

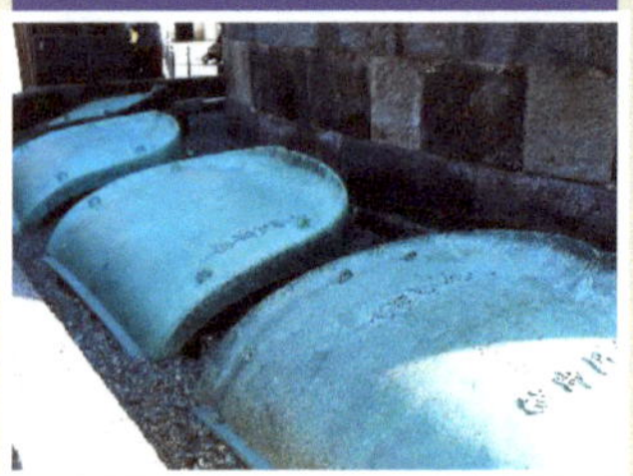

Soseki (Stone base)

When the Great Buddha was built, it was protected and sheltered by a Great Buddha Hall, but this was destroyed by strong winds in the 1400s, and since then the Great Buddha has been braving the storms without shelter. The 53 stones set around the Buddha are the remaining *soseki*, or stone base, of the Great Buddha Hall.

27  **Hase-dera Temple** 長谷寺

www.hasedera.jp/en/

- *Gorgeous statue of Kannon displayed inside*
- *Wide ocean view*
- *Popular for hydrangeas and fall colors*

Hase Sta. 5 mins.
3-11-2 Hase
0467-22-6300
Mar-Sep:
8:00am-5:30pm
(D/C 5:00pm)
Oct-Feb:
8:00am-5:00pm
(D/C 4:30pm)
Open 7 days/wk
¥400, Ele ¥200

<Teraya Cafe>
Coffee ¥350
Soft-serve ice cream ¥350
<Kaikoan Restaurant (next to the observation platform)>
Vegan curry rice with salad and soup ¥1,200
Matcha green tea ¥600

As the legend goes, two eleven-faced statues of Kannon (the "goddess of mercy") were made from a large camphor tree at the earnest wish of a monk in Nara in 721. One became the principal image of Hase-dera Temple in Nara and the other was set adrift in the ocean with a prayer for salvation for the people. Fifteen years later, in 736, it washed up on the shore of Nagai, Yokosuka, south of Kamakura, and was made the principal image of Hase-dera Temple in Kamakura.

Near the main gate, there are two small ponds surrounded by flowers and a cave where Kobo Daishi (also known as Kukai) practiced asceticism, moving towards the hillside, highlights include the main hall featuring the Kannon statue, a lookout over the ocean, and a path along a sea of hydrangeas. The Kannon statue has a gleaming gold finish and is strikingly gorgeous.

Hase Kannon

Hase Kannon is the name of the eleven-faced Kannon, a 9.18-meter-tall statue made of wood in the image of the bodhisattva believed to bring salvation to those who are suffering. Adorning the crown of its head is the head of Buddha with 10 faces surrounding it, each with a different expression—some calm and some angry—in response to different circumstances. Ashikaga Takauji, the first shogun of the Ashikaga shogunate, had the Kannon statue gilded, and Yoshimitsu, his grandson who built Kinkaku-ji temple, the Golden Pavilion in Kyoto, dedicated the halo.

Kannon Museum

This museum is not only about Kannon statues—you can also see unique Buddhist statues and other treasures including mesmerizing mandalas. An introductory video with English subtitles is shown and there are English explanations for each exhibited item. Allow 15 to 30 minutes for viewing.

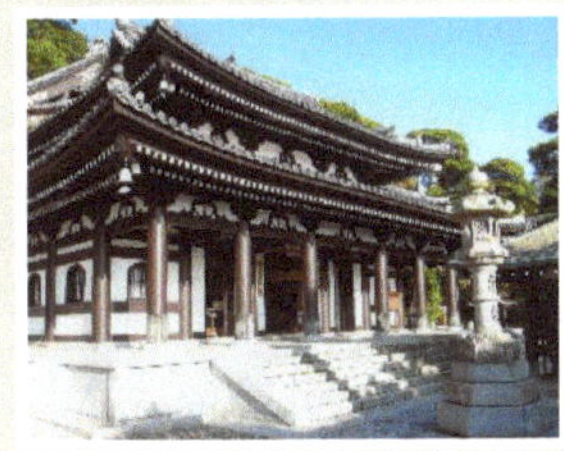

Kyozo

This is the scripture house (kyozo) that contains a prayer wheel. Turning this large wheel full of scriptures while praying is said to be the equivalent of reading all the sutras. Since its designation as a cultural property, the wheel can only be turned during the first three days of the year, or on the 18th of each month.

Observation Platform

The wide view from the observation platform reveals a rare view of both sides of Sagami Bay and the Miura Peninsula. At the restaurant next to the platform, enjoy vegan curry, pasta, or sweets along with a cup of matcha green tea or other refreshments while taking in the view.

Prospect Road

Hydrangeas completely cover the mountain slope in June. At this time of year, the temple is crowded even on weekdays and admission might be restricted.

Maple leaves

When the maple leaves change color at the end of November to early December, the temple complex stays open until after sunset and the trees are illuminated for enhanced enjoyment.

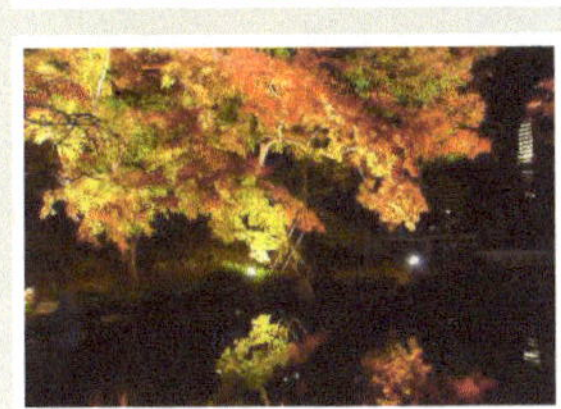

Information on Shakyo
(Hand copying the sutras)

Inside Shoin Hall, copy the scriptures by hand or trace images of the Buddha while seated with a view of the serene rock garden. You must be accompanied by someone who speaks Japanese.

Inamuragasaki & Shichirigahama Area

The streets running between Hase to Gokuraku-ji are sprinkled with small temples and stores and are perfect for strolling.
A beach popular among surfers spreads from Inamuragasaki Park —a park with a view of Mt. Fuji—to Shichirigahama.

- yoridocoro KAMAKURA
- SICILIANA
- R OLD FURNITURE
- JONAS GLASS VISION
- Gokuraku-ji Temple
- Joju-in Temple

 yoridocoro KAMAKURA

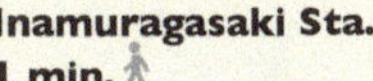
yoridocoro.com/en

- *Japanese home-cooked meals*
- *Serves dried fish from the Gulf of Suruga*
- *Cafe service after 2:00pm*

**Inamuragasaki Sta.
1 min.** 🚶

🏠 **1-12-16
Inamuragasaki**
📞 **0467-40-5737**
🕐 **7:00am-9:00am,
11:00am-6:00pm**
▧ **Open 7 days/wk**

Morning Set:
(Served with white rice/15-grain rice, miso soup, and "tsukemono" pickles)
Dried fish set menu ¥600~
Raw egg over rice ¥500
Lunch Set:
(Served with white rice/15-grain rice, miso soup, "tsukemono" pickles and a small side dish)
Dried fish set menu ¥1,000~

Owner Takeshi Megumi grew up enjoying holidays and leisure in Kamakura, and in his travels abroad, he realized that wherever he went, the freshest and most exciting moments were spent in activities with local people. Inspired by that idea, Takeshi opened up a shop to serve Kamakura visitors the most basic and authentic Japanese home cooked breakfasts—from morning until closing time—of rice, miso soup, and dried fish that introduce unique regional character. A fish connoisseur, Takeshi takes pride in his selection of dried fish. Also popular on the menu is a raw egg dish—*Tamago kage-gohan*. With eggs specially ordered and delivered directly from a farmyard in Kanagawa, the rice is served with the egg whites beaten to a froth and then topped with the yolk. The fluffy texture makes it extra delicious. Standing on a triangular lot along the Enoden railway, this shop has a casual and relaxing ambiance created through the cooperative handiwork of the owner and his friends. Right outside, the Enoden passes close at hand.

Cafe time begins from 2:00 pm until closing, so you can pop in for after-lunch refreshment. Their freshly brewed coffee is roasted locally, and there is also a choice of beer, wine, or sake.

2 🍴 SICILIANA

- *Welcoming ambience*
- *Natural wine and slow food*
- *Ocean view*

Italian restaurant Siciliana is located in a perfect spot directly overlooking Shichirigahama Beach. With 30 years of experience cooking Italian cuisine, ownerchef Keiji Ikeda's dishes are popular, and the restaurant is always bustling with locals like a veritable "kitchen of of the community."

As a surfer, Ikeda is highly tuned into nature, so he designed his concept on using ingredients and cooking methods that are as natural as possible. He mainly uses vegetables purchased at the local vegetable market and local fish caught nearby, but also selects choice ingredients from all over in Japan such as raw oysters, which are served year-round. Other specialties are free-range chicken from Miyazaki Prefecture in Kyushu or goat from Okinawa. Locals tend to favor the dishes cooked on a charcoal grill, which enhances the flavors of the fresh ingredients. The wine selections at Siciliana are mostly natural wines since the owner is a self-described wine lover and says they are gentler on the body even when you over-imbibe.

Shichirigahama Sta.
3 mins. 🚶
🏠 1-3-12
  Shichirigahama
📞 0467-81-4880
🕐 12:00pm-3:00pm (L.O.)
  6:00pm-9:00pm (L.O.)
▨ **Wed, Thu**

Raw oysters ¥200~
Colorful "Bagna càuda" ¥1,000
Lunch set (appetizer, choice of charcoal-grilled fish or meat, pasta, salada, and bread)
¥1,580~ --- a real value !
(available noon-3pm)

3 🛍 R OLD FURNITURE

- *Japanese-style used furniture and antiques*
- *Inside a century-old Japanese house*
- *Revolution, relax, and recycle theme*

**Inamuragasaki Sta.
3 mins.** 🚶
🏠 **3-7-14
Inamuragasaki**
📞 **0467-23-6172**
🕐 **12:00pm-Sunset**
▨ **Mon, Tue**

Reasonably priced and selected for their timeless beauty, the items here are well-suited for modern interiors.

Located inside a traditional Japanese house built before the Enoden Line began operation, this shop has a collection of Japanese-style antique furniture, folk art, and antiques. Almost like a small gallery, you are sure to encounter unique one-of-a-kind finds. The owner of the shop, Junya Yoshikawa, believes the time has come take a critical look at the mass production and mass consumption of the present age. The store name, "R" was taken from the three words, "revolution," "relax," and "recycle," which are the shop's theme. The items sold here have simple Japanese taste, without over stylization, making them versatile and fresh. Yoshikawa's philosophy is that he is not simply selling objects, but is promoting an approach to quality living with well made furnishings. Despite their old age, the selections here possess a consciously produced aesthetic sensibility, and their universal beauty has been carefully preserved, retaining an air of timeless modernity.

There is a small sister store called "R No. 2" near Inamuragasaki Station where you can stop by on a stroll along the railway.

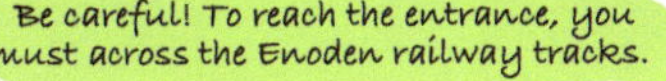
Be careful! To reach the entrance, you must across the Enoden railway tracks.

4 JONAS GLASS VISION

- *Glass artist's studio & gallery*
- *Glass blowing workshops*
- *Minutes from Shichirigahama Station*

**Shichirigahama Sta.
6 mins.**
🏠 **2-28-10
Shichirigahama-
higashi**
📞 **070-6573-7526**
🕐 **10:00am-6:00pm**
▨ **IR**

If you wish to visit,
please first confirm by phone.
Applications for hands-on
courses must be sent by
E-mail.
Jonas is fluent in English,
Japanese, and Swedish.
www.jonasglass.com/contact

Jonas Kaku, who is of Japanese-Swish heritafe has had a career of more than 20 years in glass production. His studio is located on an elevated terrain exposed to the sea and the breeze of Shichirigahama. Alongside producing his own glass art works, he teaches hands-on workshops to convey the charm of glass blowing, an art in which each piece expresses the unique individuality of its creator.

His studio also has a gallery shop where his visionary and original glass bowls and other wares are sold. In addition to being an artist, Jonas is also a surfer, and his work incorporates photos and other inspirations from nature. He also deals antiques from Northern Europe, and among them, some items from Scandinavia, as Sweden is his mother's home.

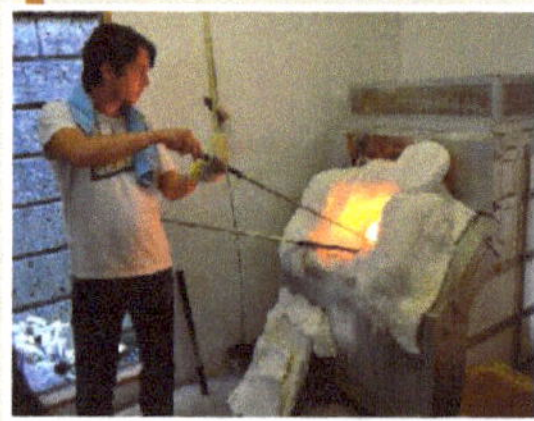

The hands-on glass blowing course takes 30 minutes, but Jonas recommends participants arrive 20 minutes before the course begins to decide on a design. Courses run from ¥6,000, with rates varying depending on the size of the piece and the number of colors used. Bookings can be made for parties of 2 to 4 participants. Be sure to give yourself plenty of time to get the creative juices flowing!

The freshly blown glass must be left overnight to cool, but they can be picked up or delivered by post the following day.

5   Gokuraku-ji Temple 極楽寺

· *History of social action*

Established by the Hojo clan in 1259, Gokuraku-ji Temple was formerly a vast temple under clan protection with many branch temples extended over an area that includes the elementary school site behind it today. The founding abbot, Ninsho Ryokan (1217–1303), carried out such social welfare programs as road building—including digging a road to the temple out of the mountain—and curing people afflicted with leprosy. On display at the temple is a stone mortar where Ryokan reportedly prepared tea as a medicine.

At one time, Gokuraku-ji Temple also managed the port on Wakae Island, including its tax revenues. (No photography is allowed on the temple grounds.)

Gokuraku-ji Sta.
2 mins. 🚶

🏠 3-6-7 Gokurakuji
📞 0467-22-3402
🕘 9:00am-4:30pm
📅 Open 7 days/wk
¥ Free

6  Joju-in Temple 成就院

www.jojuin.com/engish.html

· *Temple with a bird's-eye view of the sea*

Joju-in Temple was founded in 1219 by the third Hojo regent of the Kamakura shogunate, Hojo Yasutoki. A follower of the Shingon sect of Buddhism, Yasutoki established this temple at this location, because it was where the founder of the sect, Kobo Daishi (also known as Kukai), had trained. The site was also a citadel of defense for both land and sea, due to its situation along one of the seven *kiridoshi* excavated roads that lead to Kyoto, and bird's eye view of both Wakae Island, which was a port, and Sagami Bay. Within the modest temple grounds, there are some statues that include those of Kobo Daishi and Fudo Myo-o, the God of Fire. The stairs leading up to the temple are very steep, however, the wonderful scenery from the temple gate that overlooks the sea is well worth the trip.

Gokuraku-ji Sta.
3 mins. 🚶

🏠 1-1-5 Gokurakuji
📞 0467-22-3401
🕘 Mar 2-Oct:
   8:00am-5:00pm,
   Nov-Mar 1:
   8:00am-4:30pm
📅 Open 7 days/wk
¥ Free

Kamakura-yama Area

This quiet residential area that extends over hills to the west of backstreets of the Great Buddha is dotted with stores and views that spread across the landscape. Since access is tricky from the station, this area is recommended for those traveling by car or those who have already been to the main tourist attractions of Kamakura.

- **Kamakura 24sekki**
- **Raitei**
- **Le Milieu**

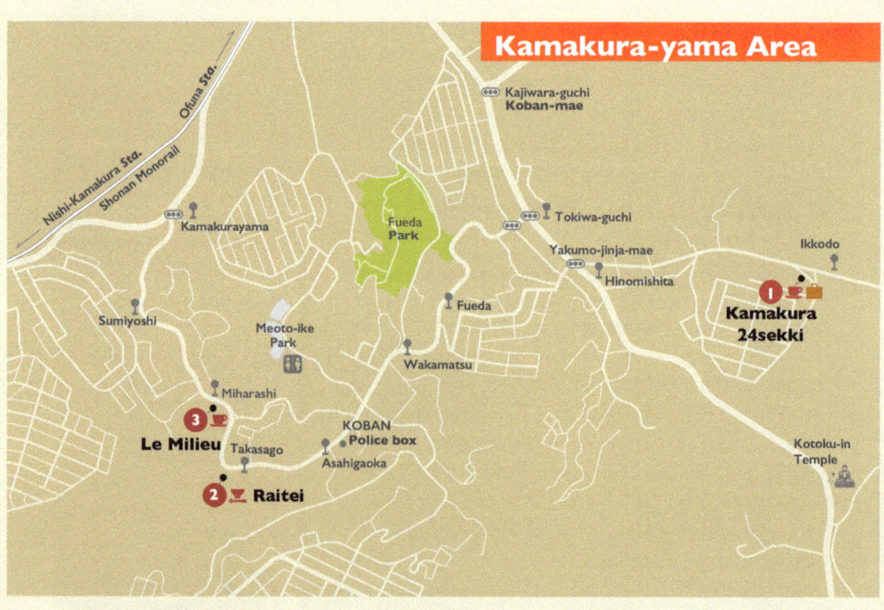

Bus Information (Bus terminal map is provided on p. 197)

❶——Take Bus No. 50 or 51 departing from **8** at the West Exit of Kamakura Station

❷❸—Take Bus No. 4, 5, 6 or 9 departing from **6** at the East Exit of Kamakura Station

Kamakura 24sekki

- *Vegan bakery cafe*
- *All-natural sandwiches and soup*
- *Naturally leavened bread*

The name of the cafe, 24sekki, means "24 divisions of the solar year," an idea that originated in China to accurately identify the transitions of the seasons that came to Japan in the 6th century. Used to determine optimal times for seed sowing and harvest, the calendar is an important measure for living in harmony with nature and awareness of the seasons. Owner Tomomi Takizawa uses leaven made from natural yeast to make the bread and relies on the 24 *sekki* calendar to gauge her baking activities.

Concerned about her health after working for many years in Tokyo, Tomomi became aware of the effects of food on the body and the mind. She therefore uses only safe and reliable ingredients produced in Japan that do not contain any agricultural chemicals or additives; items on her bread and cafe menu do not use any meat, fish, dairy products, eggs, or sugar. Allowing customers to appreciate the food as a blessing of nature, teaching the true potential for good flavor and energy, 24sekki is popular despite its distance from the nearest train station.
Here, you can enjoy the slow passage of time and subtle changes throughout the year.

Kamakura Sta. West Exit, 20 mins. or Ikkodo bus stop 30 secs.

🏠 923-8 Tokiwa
📞 0467-81-5004
🕐 <Shop>
　11:00am-4:30pm
　<Cafe>
　11:30am-2:30pm (L.O.)
　Mon, Tue, Wed, Thu
　IR

Vegetable sandwich & soup made with vegetables grown with natural farming methods ¥1,210~

2 Raitei 檑亭

www.raitei.com/index_en.html

- *Vast garden with soba restaurant*
- *Magnificent hilltop view*
- *Traditional tea room experience*

This sprawling 50,000-square-meter Japanese garden covers the terrain of Mount Kamakura on property formerly owned by a railroad businessman. The current owner bought the property and opened a restaurant inside the existing villa 50 years ago.

In the 1800s and early 1900s, there was a trend for wealthy people to relocate historic buildings to use as their vacation homes. The original villa structure is one such example as a *minka* (traditional Japanese folk house) formerly owned by an affluent farmer in Yokohama that was relocated in 1929. The entrance gate, too, was once part of a local temple.

In preparing for the restaurant, the new owner remodeled the first floor, maintaining the old *minka* style. The dining tables and seating are made from the trunks of pine trees on the property that had died of pine wilt disease. Casual dining options include à la carte items like hot and cold soba, *sashimi,* and tempura, as well as set menus and rice bowls with various toppings. Enjoy a meal with a view of the spacious garden through the large glass windows.

Kamakura Sta. West Exit, 50 mins. or Takasago bus stop 1 min.

🏠 3-1-1 Kamakurayama
📞 0467-32-5656
🕐 <1F Soba restaurant>
11:00am-sunset
< 2F "Kaiseki-ryori" restaurant >
By reservation only
11:00am-8:30pm
Open 7 days/wk except last Mon-Thu of July
<Tea House>
🕐 Sat, Sun & Holidays
11:30am-4:00pm

Entrance (San-mon Gate): Small hut to pay admission fee ¥500 is located on the right-hand side of gate.

The second-floor lounge is a reservation-only dining spot serving traditional course-based Japanese meals. Light floods the space through Japan's first stained-glass windows. Views of the garden with Sagami Bay and Mt. Fuji in the distance through the old window panels add a new dimension to the experience. The antique chandelier and hybrid Japanese and Western furnishings give a timeless ambience.

The large tatami room in the rear is partitioned with *shoji* sliding screens into three spaces. There, customers can experience traditional, full-course Japanese meals in private and at leisure; 5-course meals are offered at lunch and 4-course meals for dinner. Reservations must be made at least 10 days in advance through the form on their English website.

The strolling garden features a *sukiya*-style tea room, stone Buddha statues, and a bamboo grove. Here too, time seems eternal as you walk through the garden and admire the flowers that change with the seasons.

If you need to rest your feet, we recommend a tea break at Ro-an, the tea house. (Only open on weekends and holidays.)

Enjoy your tea outdoors under bright, Japanese-style red umbrellas, or inside the tea house. They also serve coffee, matcha green tea and *umeshu* plum liquor, as well as Japanese sweets including *mitsumame*, *mochi* dumplings, and particularly popular rich buckwheat flour cheesecakes. On hot summer days, cool off with a bowl of shaved ice amidst the thick greenery.

To get there, you will need to take a bus or cab from the station. No matter the season, we recommend a visit to this garden, restaurant, and tea house for a quiet get-away from the crowds. Admittance to the garden is ¥500, but if you eat or drink at one of their establishments, the entrance fee will be subtracted from your bill.

<Tea house "Ro-an">
Soba flour cheese cake ¥550
Matcha ¥750
Sake,Beer ¥700~
(Credit cards are not accepted)

3 ☕ Le Milieu

- *Authentic French sweets*
- *Ocean view*
- *Large, open terrace seating*

Le Milieu is a patisserie and cafe that opened in 2016 on a hillside overlooking the ocean. It is owned by pastry chef Takahiro Yamakawa, who also operates a popular patisserie in Tokyo.

Taking advantage of the steep slope of the site, there are two buildings located on two levels: a rooftop terrace with a parking area and a cafe space at the bottom of a large staircase. At the top of the summit of Mt. Kamakura, views from the wide terrace seating are spectacular.

Displayed inside the cafe are rows of dainty, delicious cakes, danishes, and other baked goodies for eat-in or take out. They all are created with orthodox delectability with a touch of Kamakura class.

For eating inside or on one of the terraces, order at the cash register before being seated.

During lunchtime, 10:00am to 2:00pm, they serve sandwiches (choice of white or rye bread) and croque monsieur. During wintertime, lunch sets are served with stew. For teatime, enjoy a cup of coffee or tea and choose from among the wide selection of cakes. Or, a glass of sparkling wine might be a nice way to unwind while taking in the view.

All in all, Le Milieu is the perfect place to spoil yourself when you need a break from your busy daily routine.

Kamakura Sta. West Exit, 50 mins. 🚶 **or Miharashi bus stop 0 min.** 🚶

🏠 **3-2-31 kamakurayama**

📞 **0467-50-0226**

🕘 **9:00am-6:00pm**

IR

Lunch set (quiche, hamburger, gratin) ¥1,750~¥2,200
Sandwich plate (choice of sandwich w/small salad) ¥670
Cake set (choice of cake and drink) ¥1,100
Afternoon tea stand set for two ¥4,000
Coffee ¥620
Sparkling wine ¥600

Kita-Kamakura Area

Of the Kamakura Gozan, or "Five Mountains" (five great Zen temples),
three are dotted among other Zen temples sheltered in deep greenery.
One can experience the atmosphere of the ancient capital of Kamakura
particularly in these quiet locations bathed in a sacred ambience.

- Hanalei
- Hachinoki
- Kousen
- Engaku-ji Temple
- Tokei-ji Temple
- Jochi-ji Temple

- Meigetsu-in Temple
- Kencho-ji Temple

> **Kamakura Gozan** is the temple system in which the shogunate rated the temples of the Rinzai sect, one of the schools of Zen Buddhism.

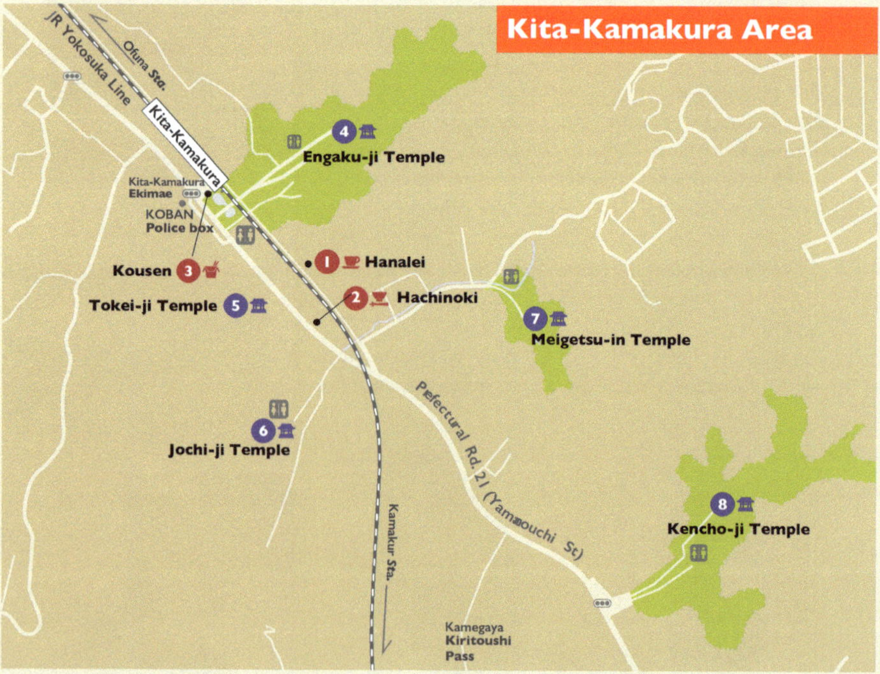

I 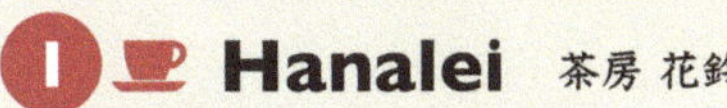 **Hanalei** 茶房 花鈴

- *An elegant Japanese-style cafe*
- *Japanese sweets and matcha drinks*
- *A 3 minte walk from Kita-Kamakura Station*

Kita-Kamakura Sta. East Exit, 3 mins.
⌂ **395 Yamanouchi**
☎ **0467-24-9737**
⏱ **10:30am-5:00pm (L.O. 4:30pm)**
▨ **IR**

"Uji kintoki" milk (shaved ice with matcha, served in summer) ¥900
"An-mitsu" ¥650
Bento lunch ¥1,200 (not available in summer)
"Amazake" ¥500 (Only available in winter)

A convenient 3-minute walk from Kita-Kamakura Station, this Japanese style cafe is easy to miss because it is hidden behind a small Japanese garden. Once visitors pass through the *noren* entrance curtain bearing the cafe's name, whose Chinese characters mean "flower" and "bell," they will find a large space where they can relax.

The menu mainly offers Japanese-style sweets such as *an-mitsu* (*an*=red bean paste, *mitsu*=raw black sugar syrup), which is a vegan dessert with agar, *an*, *mitsu*, and fruit, but they also serve bento (except in the summer), *udon* noodles, and other lunch items. In the summer, *kaki-gori* shaved ice or matcha floats (vanilla ice cream floating in a cold matcha drink) are popular, and in the winter, *amazake* might be interesting to try. *Amazake* is a traditional hot fermented rice drink that is high in nutritional value, which gives it its reputation as a "drinkable IV drip." (Though the name *amazake* contains the word "sake," the drink has no alcohol.)

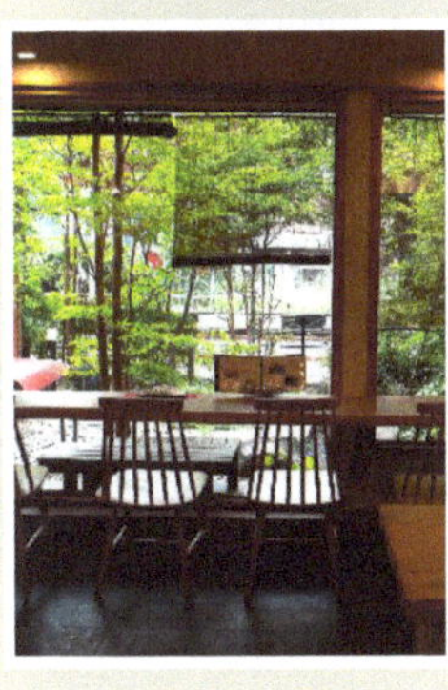

② Hachinoki 鉢の木

www.hachinoki.co.jp/english

- *Kamakura's landmark establishment*
- *Buddhist vegan and "kaiseki" cuisine*
- *In close proximity to one another*

Founded in 1964 by the mother of the current owner, Joji Fujikawa (p. 027), Hachinoki began as a small restaurant near Kencho-ji Temple that served rice balls and simple home cooked meals. Since then, Hachinoki has grown to become Kamakura's landmark establishment, with two formal, grand branch restaurants—Kita-Kamakura-ten and Shinkan—located within 5 minutes of Kita-Kamakura Station on foot.

The Kita-Kamakura-ten branch serves traditional *shojin-ryori* and the Shinkan branch serves *kaiseki-ryori*. Their menus are prepared with fresh seasonal ingredients by talented chefs who beautifully and delicately reflect the seasons. The dishes are served on lacquer ware and trays that have carefully been used and treasured over the years.

Both restaurants are introduced by small gardens that are modest but elegant, and have a variety of dining options with tables and chairs, *tatami* mat rooms, and private rooms on both first and second floors. Although they have a formal ambience, the staff is friendly and accommodating even for solo travelers or large groups. Experience the essence of Japanese culture through their food and you will understand why Hachinoki has long been the prime dining choice for locals, tourists, and VIPs from abroad.

<Kita-Kamakura-ten>
Kita-Kamakura Sta. West Exit, 5 mins. 🚶
🏠 350 Yamanouchi
📞 0467-23-3723
🕐 <Lunch>
Weekdays:
11:30am-2:30pm (L.O.)
Sat, Sun & Holidays:
11:00am-3:00pm (L.O.)
<Dinner>
Res. only
5:00pm-7:00pm (L.O.)
▨ Wed

<Shinkan Branch>
Kita-Kamakura Sta. West Exit, 5 mins. 🚶
🏠 350 Yamanouchi
📞 0467-23-3723
🕐 <Lunch>
Weekdays:
11:30am-2:30pm (L.O.)
Sat, Sun & Holidays:
11:00am-3:00pm (L.O.)
<Dinner>
Res. only
5:00pm-7:00pm (L.O.)
▨ Open 7 days/wk

 Kita-Kamakura-ten (*Shojin-ryori*)

The Kita-kamakura-ten branch specializes in *shojin-ryori*, which is Buddhist vegan cuisine that does not use any animal products, even for soup stock. The basics of *shojin-ryori* were developed through Zen Buddhism in Kamakura, and thus, Hachinoki's dishes have always reflected the Zen spirit of Kamakura. Even today, they provide catering services for events at various temples around the area. The refined dishes are made with seasonal vegetables, tofu, and other soy-based items. If you would like to experience a day of serenity, enjoy their meals between visits to Kita-Kamakura's famous Zen temples.

<Lunch courses>
¥3,888, ¥4,860, ¥6,156

<Dinner courses>
¥8,640~
Refer to the website below for reservations.
www.hachinoki.co.jp/english/

 Shinkan

The Shinkan branch specializes in *kaiseki-ryori*, or traditional Japanese course meals. Hachinoki serves fresh seafood from nearby Sagami Bay and the finest meats in addition to vegetables and tofu. Shinkan is recommended for those who are not vegetarian, but who would like to enjoy traditional Japanese cuisine in a truly Kamakura-like atmosphere.

<Lunch courses>
¥2,592 ¥3,888 or ¥4,536

<Dinner courses>
¥7,020~¥10,800
Refer to the website below for reservations.
www.hachinoki.co.jp/english/

3  **Kousen** 光泉

- *Boxed sushi takeout*
- *Time-honored "Inari sushi"*
- *Patronized by filmmaker Yasujiro Ozu*

Kita-Kamakura Sta.
West Exit, 0 min. 🚶
🏠 **501 Yamanouchi**
📞 **0467-22-1719**
🕙 **10:00am-2:30pm**
🚫 **Tue**

"Inari-zushi" only ¥680
"Inari-zushi" & "nori-maki"
¥680   *Take-out only

The current owner and her son have taken over her mother's small operation of packing take-out boxes with sushi—a business that has been running for close to 50 years.

There are only two items on the menu: "*Inari-zushi* Box" (fried bean curd pouches stuffed with sushi rice), and a "Boxed Set with *Inari-zushi* and *nori-maki*" (*nori* seaweed rolls)."

The fried bean curd pouches for the *Inari-zushi* are thin and juicy *abura-age* that are seasoned and then stuffed with *sumeshi*, or vinegared rice. At Kousen, no additives or preservatives are used, and they take the time and effort to season their *abura-age* by simmering them in a savory sweet *dashi* stock of sugar, soy sauce, and sake.

The *nori-maki* rolls included in the boxed set are 3 *kappa-maki* (cucumber rolls) and 3 *kampyo-maki* (gourd strip rolls). *Kampyo* is dried gourd stewed in a sweet soy-sauce based sauce.

This sushi, well-loved in the past by such notable historic residents of Kita-Kamakura as Rosanjin and Yasujiro Ozu, is often sold out early on, so we recommend dropping in around opening time, or else having someone who speaks Japanese place your orders in advance.

Since preservatives are not used in preparing these boxed meals, to fully enjoy the flavor, they should be consumed as soon as possible.

Although there are tables inside, the meals are take-out only.

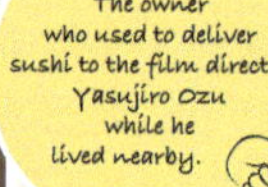

Kitakamakura sta.
Kenchoji

4  Engaku-ji Temple 円覚寺

- *Kamakura's second-ranking temple*
- *D. T. Suzuki's Zen base*
- *Two national treasures on view*

Hojo Tokimune, the 8th regent of Kamakura Shogunate who ruled the shogunate from 1268 to 1284, invited his Chinese Zen master, Mugaku Sogen, to found Engaku-ji Temple in 1282.

A prominent historical figure, Tokimune succeeded the Shogunate when he was only eighteen years old, and led the battles against two Mongolian invasions. Just like his father, Hojo Tokiyori, who established Kencho-ji Temple nearby, Tokimune was also a Zen enthusiast, and founded Engaku-ji Temple to mourn for the war dead, without distinction between allies and enemies.

The current temple buildings are all reconstructions, since the original structures were damaged in repeated fires and earthquakes. Architectural high-lights are the two-storied Sanmon Gate (the main gate), Butsu-den (the main hall), and the Shariden (reliquary hall)—the only national treasure in the region—with its grand roof typical of the traditional style of Zen Buddhist temples adopted from China in the Kamakura period.

One of the most important Zen Buddhist complexes in Japan, Engaku-ji Temple is known as the first temple to introduce Zen to the common people (it had previously been only for nobles). It is also well known as the place of practice for many intellectuals inclu-ding the eminent Buddhist Scolar D. T. Suzuki (p. 022) and the authors Soseki Natsume. The vast temple precinct has a few tea houses if you'd like to relax with a bowl of matcha green tea and find a peaceful moment within the Zen atmosphere.

Kita-Kamakura Sta. East Exit, 1 min. 🚶
🏠 **409 Yamanouchi**
📞 **0467-22-0478**
🕐 **Mar-Nov:**
   8:00am-4:30pm
   Dec-Feb:
   8:00am-4:00pm
📅 **Open 7 days/wk**
💴 **¥300,**
   Ele/Mid ¥100

<Kosho Benten Chaya>
Vegan curry ¥800
Matcha green tea ¥650
Soft serve ice cream ¥350
(vanilla/matcha green tea)

<Butsunichi-an Temple>
Admission ¥100
Matcha green tea ¥500

<Annei at Nyoi-an Temple >
Matcha green tea ¥600
(¥1,200 w/ Japanese sweet)
Coffee ¥500

A — Byakuro-chi Pond

The approach along Prefectural Road No. 21 and the Byakuro-chi ("White Heron Pond") crossed by a small bridge possess traces of the original entrance of the temple complex. In 1889, the Yokosuka Line divided the site to serve the Yokosuka Naval Arsenal and related Imperial Japanese Navy facilities at Yokosuka.

B — So-mon Entrance Gate

C — Sanmon Main Gate

This impressive gate was built in 1785 and is known as the model for Japanese author Soseki Natsume's novel "The Gate," a story based on his Zen practice at Engaku-ji Temple.

D — Butsu-den Main Hall

The Butsu-den (*butsu*=Buddha, *den*=hall) is the main building among the many temple structures and is where Engaku-ji's most valuable object of worship is enshrined. Large-scale events and morning zazen meditations are also held inside the hall. The original hall collapsed in the Great Kanto Earthquake, but was rebuilt in 1964. Be sure to go inside to see the dynamic painting of a white dragon on the ceiling.

E — Koji-an Training Hall

Koji-an (*koji*=lay people, *an*=hermitage) is where various Zen meditation meetings are held for the public. The design is based on a training hall built for commoners by Zen abbot Imakita Kozen, the master of D. T. Suzuki's master.

F — Dai Hojo

Dai Hojo (*dai*=big, *hojo*=3 square meters) was originally the abbot's residence, but currently serves as the space for Buddhist services and Zen meditation meetings. The grand Chinese juniper trees in the front garden was planted by the founder, Mugaku Sogen.

G — Myoko-chi Pond

The Myoko-chi ("Pond of Exquisite Fragrance") is considered to have been created when the temple was founded, but details are unknown. The pond behind Dai-Hojo is the source for the Myoko-chi.

L — Benten-do (Hall of Benten)

Benten-do takes requests for prayers with a ritual drumming on a "kito-daiko" ("prayer drum"). If you would like to experience this, and have Japanese language assistance, inquire at the office. Depending on the priest's availability, they may be able to perform the ritual for you during your visit. With a donation of ¥3,000, ¥5,000, or ¥10,000, you can request prayers for the health and well being of your family, an answer to your prayers, etc.

H — Annei Cafe

The main hall of Nyoi-an, one of the sub-temples not generally open to the public, functions as a cafe on certain days of the week. Here, you can enjoy matcha, coffee, and Japanese sweets while looking at the garden. Open on Wed, Thu & Fri 10:00am-4:00pm,

I — Butsunichi-an Mausoleum

The mausoleum of the founder of Engaku-ji Temple, Hojo Tokimune, and other associated historical figures. Admission is ¥100. Enjoy a bowl of matcha green tea (¥500) in the garden.

J — Shari-den Reliquary Hall (Designated National Treasure)

The original building was destroyed and the current structure was moved from a nunnery in Kamakura. Believed to have been built in the 1500s, the Shari-den is the only designated national treasure in the entire prefectural area and is representative of authentic Zen Buddhism-style architecture with its grand curved eaves and the *kato-mado* (*ka*=flower, *to*=head, *mado*=window) window design.
It allegedly enshrines the relics of Buddha—a bone and one of his right molars—the latter, an offering from a temple of the Song Dynasty in the 13th century. This hall is only open to the public around New Year's holidays and special opening days in November, but is viewable from the exterior.

K — O-gane Great Bell

After climbing a steep set of stairs, you will find O-gane ("Great Bell") on top of the hill. It was built in 1301 by Tokimune's son, Sadatoki, as a symbol of his hope for the people of the nation. It is a designated national treasure and is the largest temple bell in the Kanto area.

M — Kosho Benten Chaya Cafe

Next to Benten-do is an outdoor tea house with a nice view from the mountain top. Enjoy a nice break with their vegan curry, matcha green tea, or other refreshments.

5 Tokei-ji Temple 東慶寺

www.tokeiji.com/english/about

- *Long history as a nunnery*
- *Refuge for women seeking a divorce*
- *Global base of Zen thought*

**Kita-Kamakura Sta.
West Exit, 4 mins.**
🏠 **1367 Yamanouchi**
📞 **0467-22-1663**
🕐 **Apr-Sep:
8:30am-4:30pm
Oct-Mar:
8:30am-4:00pm**
📅 **Open 7 days/wk**
💴 **¥200,
Ele/Mid ¥100**

Tokei-ji was founded in 1285 by Kakusan Shido-ni, the widow of Hojo Tokimune (founder of Engaku-ji Temple across the street). Her son Hojo Sadatoki, then top regent of the Shogunate, granted her request for a law for temples to serve as refuge for women suffering from spousal abuse, since at the time, women could not file for divorce. For close to six hundred years, Tokei-ji protected many married women who sought divorce through their women-only policy, and assisted them with *en-kiri*, or divorce code, which nullified their marriage after three years at the nunnery.

In its day, it had been given high temple ranking and had many chief nuns from noble families, that included a daughter of Emperor Godaigo and women from the Hojo and Ashikaga clans. Later, the *en-kiri* code was abandoned due to the *Haibutsu-kishaku* movement, the movement to abolish Buddhism during the Meiji Revolution, and it was closed as a nunnery in 1902. Through its first male Zen priest, Shaku Soyen, and his lay follower D. T. Suzuki (p. 022), who was a scholar of Zen Buddhism, this temple became the base for spreading Zen thought to the rest of the world.

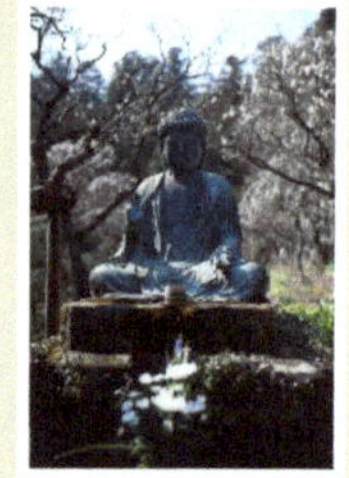

At this temple, you can find the graves of Shaku Soyen, D. T. Suzuki, and Kitaro Nishida, Japan's foremost modern philosopher, and Suzuki's friend who also studied Zen Buddhism. You will also find the graves of nuns in the hill to the right of the main path. While strolling the grounds, sense the gentle atmosphere of a temple that had provided sanctuary for women for the bulk of its history.

6  **Jochi-ji Temple** 浄智寺

- *The fourth-ranking Kamakura temple*
- *Wild, rocky ancient rear garden*
- *The entrance of the hiking trail*

**Kita-Kamakura Sta.
West Exit, 7 mins.**
🏠 1403 Yamanouchi
📞 0467-22-3943
🕘 9:00am-4:30pm
📅 Open 7 days/wk
💴 ¥200,
   Ele/Mid ¥100

To pray for the soul of the premature death of Hojo Munemasa (1253-1281), Jochi-ji Temple was built in 1281 by his wife, children, and his elder brother, Tokimune, who was also the founder of Engaku-ji Temple. Munemasa was the third son of Hojo Tokiyori, who established Kencho-ji Temple.
As regent of the Kamakura shogunate, Tokimune was the de facto ruler of Japan and his younger brother Munemasa was his most trusted right hand man. Consequently, Munemasa's death brought him deep sorrow and lead him to establish a sub-temple on equal scale with Engaku-ji. Over time, it fell into disrepair and most of the buildings were destroyed in the Great Kanto Earthquake. Although the current temple buildings are not the original structures, they still have plenty of character, and together with the worn stone steps leading to the main gate, have historic charm.

The road on the left side of the temple is the hiking path toward Mt. Genji.

The Sanmon main gate with a *kato-mado* "flower head" window is unusual in that it also functions as a belfry. The main hall features three wooden sculptures of the Buddha (Amida, Shaka, and Miroku) representing the past, present, and future. Behind the temple you will find a peaceful bamboo grove, and among the *yagura* cave tombs, you will find a statue of Hotei, one of the seven Buddhist gods of good fortune. Give his shiny, black tummy a rub for happiness and good health——at the very least, it will make you smile.

Lacking large temple structures, this temple is one of Kamakura's more modest spots, but the quiet atmosphere surrounded by lush greenery is a perfect place for finding peace.

7  Meigetsu-in Temple 明月院

- *Iconic round window with garden view*
- *Theme of the rabbit in the moon*
- *Beautiful hydrangeas and fall colors*

Kita-Kamakura Sta. East Exit, 8 mins.
🏠 189 Yamanouchi
📞 0467-24-3437
🕐 July-May:
9:00am-4:00pm
June:
8:30am-5:00pm
Open 7 days/wk
¥500

<Gessho-ken Tea house>
The tea house next to the entrance.
Matcha green tea ¥700
Coffee w/ cookies ¥600

In 1256, Hojo Tokiyori, the fifth regent of the Kamakura Shogunate who built Kencho-ji Temple, became a Buddhist priest and established Saimyo-ji Temple on the site of a small local temple. His premature death, however, from illness at the age of 37, resulted in its abandonment. Subsequently, Tokiyori's son, Tokimune (founder of Engaku-ji Temple) invited Rankei Doryu (1213–1278), the founding priest of Kencho-ji Temple, to build a new temple, which led first to a period of expansion, then eventual decline. Initially one of many sub-temples, Meigetsu-in is now the only temple left standing, however, the original precinct still penetrates deep into the hills and connects to the grounds of Kencho-ji Temple.

The icon of Meigetsu-in Temple, the round window of the Hojo (Main Hall) often referred to as the "Window of Enlightenment," is said to symbolically express enlightenment, truth, and the universe. The captured view of the inner garden beyond is like a picture of ever-changing beauty throughout the seasons. Meigetsu-in means "Bright Moon Temple," and its round window also signifies the moon. You will also find motifs of bunnies here and there for their folkloric connection to the image seen in the shadows of the moon—a rabbit pounding *mochi* rice. You are welcome to take photos, but also be sure to appreciate the world beyond the window of enlightenment with your mind and heart.

During the season of hydrangeas and irises in June, and the fall foliage season in late November to early December, the back garden is open to the public with an extra ¥500 admission. Pay admission at the window located to the left of the Hojo Main Hall.

Entry here is permitted with a donation when not in use.

A **Entrance Gate**

B **The Approach**

The temple path in mid June to early July is packed full of hydrangeas with many people coming to visit.

C **Main Hall**

Constructed after WWII, details regarding the architect who designed the round window are unknown. Access to the garden is normally not permitted, but it is open to the public in June when the irises are in bloom, and in fall when the autumn colors are at their finest.

D **"Karesansui" Garden behind the Hojo Main Hall**

E **Kaizan (Founder's) Hall**

Built in honor of the samurai, Uesugi Norimasa, who extended the temple grounds in the 14th century. Among the buildings still standing, this is the oldest, with records dating back to 1719.

F **"Yagura" Tomb**

Said to be the tomb of Uesugi Norimasa, who is enshrined in the Kaizan Hall commemorating its founder. The inside of the cave is decorated with many Buddhist statues including that of the Buddha.

G **Grave of Hojo Tokiyori**

The grave of the founder, Hojo Tokiyori, who met his final fate at this temple.

H **Tea house "Gessho-ken"**

Seating is provided either inside the tea house or outside on the red carpet. Green tea is served with Japanese sweets, but coffee or juice are also available. Whether seated inside or out, enjoy a peaceful moment admiring the beautiful garden.

8  Kencho-ji Temple 建長寺

- *Ranks No. 1 among Kamakura's Zen temples*
- *The oldest Zen training monastery*
- *Panoramic city view*

Kita-Kamakura Sta. East Exit, 15 mins. 🚶
🏠 8 Yamanouchi
📞 0467-22-0981
🕐 8:30am-4:30pm
▧ Open 7 days/wk
💴 ¥500, Ele/Mid ¥200

Not only is Kencho-ji Kamakura's oldest Zen training monastery, it is ranked the number one temple among Kamakura's five greatest Zen temples (the *Kamakura Gozan*). Deeply devoted to Buddhism, Hojo Tokiyori (1227-63), the fifth ruling regent of the Kamakura shogunate and patron of the temple, invited Rankei Doryu (1213-78), a Chinese Zen master of the Song Dynasty, to found Kencho-ji Temple in 1253 under the orders of Emperor Go-Fukakusa. When initially built, it consisted of a *shichidou garan* (the seven principle buildings necessary for a Buddhist temple) with 49 sub-temples built in the Zen sect style.

The oldest Zen training monastery in Japan, Kencho-ji allegedly once served over 1,000 monks-in-training.

Due to disasters both intentional and natural, most of the original *garan* buildings no longer remain, but because of the temple's protection under the Tokugawa clan in the Edo period (1603 to 1868), Kencho-ji consists of many temple buildings and sub-temples that were relocated from other locations related to the clan. The *shichidou garan* layout remains in which the central buildings are aligned north to south—also remaining are its ancient temple bell, symbolic great Chinese junipers, and strict Zen training.

The temple's precincts are vast—it takes fifteen minutes or so just to climb the approximately 250 steps leading into the inner complex from Hojo. In the very back, you will find a Shinto shrine called Hanso-bo.

The observation deck at the top of the stairs commands a panoramic view of the entire Kencho-ji Temple complex and the city of Kamakura. On a clear day, you can even see Mt. Fuji, so, if you have the stamina, it can be worth the climb.

A Somon (Outer Gate)

This gate was built in 1783 for a temple in Kyoto, and was then moved to Kencho-ji Temple in 1940.

B Sanmon (Main Gate)

The current Sanmon was rebuilt in 1754, and is about 20 meters tall. Its magnificent design features the *zenshuyo* Zen sect style, imported from China in the Song Dynasty, as seen in its *tsume-gumi*, or complex bracketing arrangement.

C Binzuru

The small wooden statue sitting under Sanmon Gate is one of Buddha's disciples, "Binzuru." Binzuru had strong psychic powers, but since he misused them, Buddha told him to remain in the world to spread the Buddhist law to help others. It is believed that people with health troubles can be cured by rubbing Binzuru's equivalent body part that is in need of healing.

D Bonsho (Temple Bell)

Cast under commission by Hojo Tokiyori in 1255, this bell is now a National Treasure.

E Butsu-den (Buddha Hall)

The Butsu-den enshrines a principal deity, a seated statue of Jizo Bodhisattva (Kshitigarbha Bodhisattva). The current hall once served as a mausoleum at Zojo-ji Temple (the family temple of the Tokugawa clan, located right next to Tokyo Tower). This history is what makes its gorgeous coffered and painted ceiling unique from other Buddha Halls of Zen temples. Although the paintings are faded, they depict birds and flowers of the four seasons. The old juniper trees in front of the hall are over 760 years old and were planted from seed by the founding priest, Rankei Doryu.

F Hatto (Dharma Hall)

Rebuilt in 1814, the Hatto is the largest wooden Buddhist structure in Eastern Japan. It houses a statue of the thousand-armed Kannon who is enshrined as the principal deity.

The painting of a dragon among clouds on the ceiling took its Kamakura painter three years to complete.

G Mushi-zuka (Monument for insects)

A local anatomist also known as an insect collector made a place to pray for insects that have to sacrifice their lives for human. It is designed to give an impression of insect cages spiraling into the sky; its creator, architect Kengo Kuma, is currently overseeing the design of the main stadium for the 2020 Tokyo Olympics.

H Hojo (Main Hall)

The Hojo originally served as the chief priest's residence, but is now used for rituals and religious services. The image enshrined here is "Shaka Nyorai" (Shakyamuni Buddha).
In a corner of the Hojo are foldable blue seat cushions for practicing zazen. In the rear is a garden designed by Zen master Muso Kokushi. When viewed from above, the pond shows the shape of the Chinese character *kokoro* (spirit) to allow people to visually experience the spirit of Zen.

I Hanso-bo

Hanso-bo is the *chinju*(*) of Kencho-ji Temple. ("*han*" means "half", and "*so*" and "*bo*" refer to a Buddhist monk or priest, so "*hanso-bo*" means "half priest.") The name came from the legend of an old man who devotedly served as a monk. After the old man died, he appeared in the dream of a sculptor of Buddhist statues as half priest, half ordinary man with a red face and big nose like the *Tengu*, a legendary goblin depicted as half-crow, half-man, believed to be a protector from fires, thus the row of *Tengu* statues along the path. *Hanso-bo* was originally located at a temple in Shizuoka Prefecture, but was brought by request of the Zen master of Kencho-ji in 1890. The stones along the path reveal the names of those who made donations to build this shrine. Since many of the temple's buildings were repeatedly lost to fire, it is no wonder this tutelary shrine was located here.

There is an observation deck above the shrine that overlooks the entire temple complex and town of Kamakura. The narrow dirt path beside the platform leads to a hiking course. To enter Kencho-ji Temple from the hiking course, pay an entry fee at the reception at *Hanso-bo* next to the vending machine.

Shutto-gutsu

The shoe rack on the side of the hall holds special shoes that monks wear when they dress up for rituals and other formal occasions.

(*)Chinju "Chin" means "tranquillize" and "ju" means "protect." *Chinju* is a tutelary god or spirit that makes the area tranquil and gives it protection.

Enoshima Area

Enoshima, an island connected by a bridge from the town directly west of Kamakura, is popular among tourists for both its sacred and scenic value. It was a training sanctuary for the ascetic practices of renowned religious figures and highly protected by shoguns as a holy place.

At the beginning of the Edo period, common folk were permitted access to the shrines, and Enoshima became such a popular tourist spot that it became the subject of Ukiyoe silkscreen prints and Kabuki plays. Despite its seemingly close proximity, the island offered experiences that were slightly out of the ordinary, and even today, people visit the island throughout the year for the same reason.

For the 1964 Tokyo Olympics, Enoshima Island served as the venue for sailing competitions, and is currently being prepared for the 2020 Tokyo Olympics.

The Market SE1
Iglu Hyouka
iL-CHIANTI CAFE ENOSHIMA
Eno-maru
NAKAMURAYA YOKAN

Enoshima Area
Katase Nishihama Beach
Odakyu Enoshima Line
Shonan Monorail Line
Shonan Enoshima
Enoshima
Ryuko-ji Temple (p. 187)
Enoden Line
Enoshima Aquarium
Katase Enoshima
The Market SE 1
Iglu Hyouka
Koshigoe
Fujisawa City Tourist Center
Katase-Enoshima Tourist Information
Enoshima-iriguchi
Katase Higashihama Beach
Koyurugi-Jinja Shrine
Koyurugi Misaki
Enoshima Ohashi/ Benten-Bashi Bridge
Benten-maru Passenger Boat
Enoshima Shrine, Hetsu-no-miya
Enoshima Yacht Harbor
"Sea Candle" Observation Lighthouse
Enoshima Island
A
B
O
1
2

Bronze "Torii" Gate and Nakamise Street
Enoshima Tourist Information Center
Enospa
Nishi-ura
Ebisuya
Enoshima Shrine, Hetsu-no-miya
Iwamoto Honkan
Police Station
Hoan-den
"Escar" Escalator
Shita-michi
Benten-maru Passenger Boat
"Sea Candle" Observation Lighthouse
Samuel Cocking Garden
Okutsu-no-miya, Wadatsumi-no-miya
Nakatsu-no-miya
NAKAMURAYA YOKAN
Eno-maru
Yama Futatsu
Enoshima Yacht Harbor
Kanagawa Gender Equality Center KANA TERRACE
Chigo-ga-fuchi, Iwaya Cave
iL-CHIANTI CAFE ENOSHIMA
C
D
E
F
G
H
I
J
K
L
M
N
O
P
3
4
5

Enoshima sightseeing spots

A Fujisawa City Tourist Center

🕐 8:30am-5:00pm 📶 Eng Eng 🚻

B Katase Enoshima Tourist Information

🕐 8:30am-5:00pm 📶 Eng Eng

C Enoshima Tourist Information

🕐 9:00am-5:00pm Eng Eng

D Bronze "Torii" Gate and Benzaiten Nakamise St.

The narrow street to Enoshima Shrine is lined with retail shops, restaurants, and inns. The inn to the right of the approach, Iwamoto Honkan, was established as a lodge for pilgrims and has a history of over 700 years.

E Nishi-ura

A small beach from where Mt. Fuji can be seen on clear days.

F Enoshima **"Escar" Escalator**

🕐 9:00am-7:05pm

💴 Full rate (for 3 sections)
Adult ¥360, Ele ¥180
Partial rate (for 1 section):
¥100-¥200, Ele ¥50-¥100

To the left of the vermillion *torii* gate is a three-section escalator that will take you up to the top of the hill. Hiking up to the summit on foot takes approximately 20 minutes, but Enoshima Escar will deliver you there in four minutes. Combination tickets (the full rate ticket for Enoshima "Escar" and access to the "Enoshima Sea Candle" Observation Lighthouse) are available at the ticket booth located at the first section of Enoshima Escar, and will save you ¥110 (Ele: ¥60) per ticket.

G Enoshima Shrine, Hetsu-no-miya

Initially, Enoshima temples and shrines known collectively as Yogan-ji had co-existed for over 1,000 years until the Meiji government imposed the policy of separating Shinto and Buddhism (See p. 013), leaving only Enoshima Shrine, which now enshrines three sister goddess: Hetsu-no-miya, Nakatsu-no-miya, and Okutsu-no-miya. Passage through the vermillion *torii*, the two-storied gate, and up the stairs will bring you to Hetsu-no-miya. The original shrine was erected in 1206 by Minamoto Sanetomo.

H Hoan-den

🕐 8:30am-4:30pm

💴 ¥200, Mid/HS ¥100, Ele ¥50

Next to Hetsu-no-miya is the octagonal Hoan-den, and enshrined within is the eight-armed Happi-Benzaiten guardian deity commissioned by Minamoto Yoritomo.
In its arms are weapons among other symbols of strength. Another deity is the Myoon-Benzaiten, the goddess of the arts. Both are said to be products of the Kamakura era and are the two Benzaiten that were venerated by the shogun and worshippers in the Edo era (1603–1867).

I Nakatsu-no-miya

This shrine was established in 853 by priest Jikaku Daishi in response to a divine message he received from the goddess Benten while training at the Iwaya Caves. Since originally the goddess of the arts, Myoon-Benzaiten, was worshiped here, stone lanterns have been donated by Kabuki actors who also left behind their handprints.

J Samuel Cocking Garden

🕐 9:00am-8:00pm D/C 7:30pm

💴 Adults ¥200, Ele ¥100

This garden is all that remains of the villa and greenhouse that was the former property of a British trader who lived in Japan during the Meiji era.

K "Sea Candle" Observation Lighthouse

🕐 9:00am-8:00pm D/C 7:30pm

💴 Adult ¥300, Ele ¥150

This 60m-high lighthouse is located within the garden. Ride the elevator to the top of this 60m-high lighthouse to enjoy a full panoramic view from either the observation floor or the open wood deck. In the Fujisawa City Museum on the first floor, you will find an interesting display of old photos of Enoshima and records from the old lighthouse.

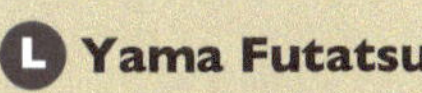

L Yama Futatsu

Yama Futatsu (meaning "two mountains") is the name of the valley between Enoshima's two highlands. Here, you can sense the forces at work, visible in the volcanic strata along the sheer edge of the cliffs.

M Okutsu-no-miya and Wadatsumi-no-miya

The first goddess, the eldest of the three sister goddesses of Enoshima, was enshrined here, closest to the Iwaya Caves. Built as a respite for the goddess when the waves flooded the caves, it is where you can pay respects the first goddess. The "torii" gate was dedicated by Minamoto Yoritomo

when Benzaiten was transferred to the Iwaya Caves in 1182. Glaring down from atop a rock just beyond the "torii" gate is a large dragon, Wadatsumi-no-miya ("Palace of the Dragon King"). The dragon was installed right above the Iwaya Caves in 1994 as a tribute to the many legends of dragons connected to Enoshima.

N Chigo-ga-fuchi, Iwaya Caves

Go down the steep stairs beyond the ocean-view eateries and you will reach a flat rocky expanse—a wave-cut platform that rose by about a meter from the Great Kanto Earthquake of 1923. Within the cliff is a sea cave carved out through years of erosion from the waves. The interior of the cave maybe closed due to damage from the October 2017 typhoon.

O Benten-maru Passenger Boat

Capacity: 35 people

🕐 10:00am-Sunset

💴 Adults ¥400, 6-12 years old ¥200

This boat takes you from the island pier near the Iwaya Cave to the pier on Benten-Bashi Bridge in 10 minutes. It operates every 15 minutes, but operations may be suspended during critical weather conditions.

P Shita-michi

If you prefer to return on foot, take the left path at the fork in the road beyond Okutsu-no-miya, which is not only the quickest route, but is also serene and lush with greenery.

①  The Market SE1

· *Homemade gelato and Neapolitan pizza*

At this small, locally cherished shop, the owner serves fresh homemade gelato and pizza daily. The music-loving owner has a thing for London and has traveled the world as the chef of Honda's F1 racing team. After returning to Japan, he opened this shop in his favorite spot of Enoshima, serving gelato to bring joy to people. He prides himself on his high standards for preparation that bring out the original flavors of the ingredients—carefully selected colorful, seasonal vegetables and fruit; and the milk itself is from an organic farm that was the first to produce pasteurized milk in Japan. Both the gelato and pizzas are made with the freshest available ingredients. Ask the owner what his recommendations are for the day and enjoy savoring your Italian treats at the counter inside.

Enoshima Sta.
3 mins. 🚶
🏠 1-6-6 Katasekaigan, Fujisawa-shi
📞 0466-24-8499
🕐 11:30am-6:00pm
📅 Apr-Dec: Mon(*), Jan-Mar: Mon(*),Tue, IR

Gelato
Single ¥430, Double ¥540
Pizza ¥860~
Wine by the glass ¥470~

②  Iglu Hyouka   イグル氷菓

· *Takeout popsicles*

This is a popsicle shop run by the wife of the owner of SE1, offering popsicles children can easily buy at a more affordable price than gelato. These popsicles are made with the same carefully selected seasonal fruit and vegetables as the gelato at SE1.

Koshigoe Sta.
5 mins. 🚶
🏠 3-8-26 Koshigoe
📞 0467-32-3539
🕐 11:00am-4:00pm
📅 Mid Apr-Oct: IR, Nov-Mid-Apr: Closed

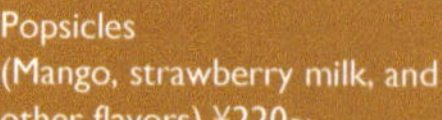

Popsicles
(Mango, strawberry milk, and other flavors) ¥220~

 ❸ iL-CHIANTI CAFE ENOSHIMA

- *Casual Italian cafe & restaurant*
- *Superb ocean view*
- *Kid-friendly*

This casual Italian cafe and restaurant at the base of a lighthouse is situated at the top of a precipitous cliff, with a large terrace seating area affording a sweeping view of the ocean. This is a perfect spot for gazing at the blue ocean on a clear day or at the colorful sunset beyond the sea.

The menu features about 100 items, including antipasto, pizza, pasta, and desserts. While the wine menu is in Italian and the dishes of the day explanations are in Japanese, the drink and food menu is available in English.
Popular dishes include pizza, pasta (of which there are over 10 selections from standard to those made using local vegetables and seafood), bagna càuda (with a piping hot dipping sauce in which to dip colorful vegetables and baguettes); and a soft shell crab burger set with a deep-fried whole soft-shell crab served in a bun.

Although there are many small Japanese seafood restaurants in Enoshima, we recommend this Italian restaurant for groups or those with children. When it is crowded, such as on weekends when the weather is clear, take a numbered ticket from the machine outside the restaurant and wait to be called.

To avoid crowds, after 2:00 pm is best, or if you can speak Japanese, make a reservation in advance.

Enoshima Sta.
20~25 mins. 🚶
🏠 **2-4-15 Enoshima, Fujisawa-shi**
📞 **0466-86-7758**
🕐 **11:00am-9:00pm (L.O. 8:00pm)**
▨ **Open 7 days/wk**

Bagna càuda ¥1,188
Pizza
(M) ¥1382~, (L) ¥1,836~
Pasta (M) ¥1,318, (L) ¥1,922
Soft-shell crab burger set ¥1,490
Italian gelato ¥432~

4 ☕ Eno-maru

- *Cafe in a renovated folk house*
- *Relaxed atmosphere for adults*
- *Rice bowl lunches*

Enoshima Sta.
25-30 mins. 🚶
🏠 **2-3-37 Enoshima,**
Fujisawa-shi
📞 **0466-47-6408**
🕐 **11:00am-Sunset**
📛 **Wed**

Matcha green tea bavarois
¥450
Chocolate sundae ¥600
Fondant au chocolat ¥550
Coffee, tea, or juice ¥400~
Beer ¥500~
Lunch options
(Rice bowl with a bowl of
miso soup and a drink)
¥1,300
Mini rice bowl (after 3pm)
¥600

Without its red big *noren* curtain hanging in the entryway, one would otherwise easily pass by this unassuming chic cafe without a glance.
With the inspiration to support artists acquired through his previous work handling art and crafts items at a department store in Tokyo, the owner opened this shop with a gallery annex in 2011.

Enter this renovated old folk house that is close to 100 years old, and you will find yourself inside a high-ceilinged space finished in charcoal-mixed plaster with modern interior décor. Furnished with traditional Japanese *chabudai* low tables and a tasteful blend of old and new, the result is a relaxing ambience perfect for adults.

For tea time, there are desserts including homemade cakes and bavarois prepared by the owner's wife, and drinks; then at lunch, you have a choice between two rice bowl sets that come with a bowl of miso soup and a drink; after 3 pm, they serve small sized portions of these rice bowls. The rice bowl options are kettle fried whitebait on rice, or *maguro* (raw tuna) and avocado on rice; for those who can't eat fish, we recommend ordering the latter without the *maguro*, and simply enjoy a topping of seasoned avocado on rice.

It's always fun to drop in at the gallery next door that displays works of art curated by the owner, tableware, or bric-a-brac.

5 ☕ 🛍 NAKAMURAYA YOKAN 中村屋羊羹店

www.noriyoukan.com/english/

- *116-year-old "yokan" shop*
- *Tasteful antique decor*
- *Trial-sized bites on menu*

This long-standing *yokan* shop is in a place called Yama-futatsu, a valley at the border of two geologic strata that divides Enoshima in two.

Yokan is traditional Japanese sweet made of pureed red-bean paste, sugar, and agar poured into a rectangular frame to set, then sliced and eaten. Founded initially in 1902 strictly to sell *yokan* as a

souvenir, the current shop was built in 1922, and still retains the charm of the Enoshima of yesterday. The fourth-generation owner, Noriaki Nakamura, and his family work together to carefully produce *yokan* in the method passed down to them through the family.

For those who visited Yama-futatsu over 100 years ago before there were escalators, sweet *yokan* and tea must surely have been a special treat after a tiring climb. *Yokan* is served with drinks in the cafe or at the storefront seating, so enjoy a break with this historical treat, and share in the delight of a time-honored experience. For people used to eating traditional Japanese sweets, we recommend the famous *nori* (seaweed) *yokan*; for novices we recommend, "cream tofu," a dessert made with fresh cream and tofu. *Yokan* keeps for several months at room temperature, so after sampling the bite-sized bits with your matcha, why not bring home a beautifully packaged mini-sized *yokan* to introduce this classic souvenir to your friends and family?

Enoshima Sta.
30~40 mins. 🚶
🏠 **2-5-25 Enoshima, Fujisawa-shi**
📞 **0466-22-4214**
🕐 **9:00am-6:00pm**
Open 7 days/wk, IR

Bite-size "yokan" ¥120
Cream tofu ¥250
"Meoto manju"
(Steamed bun with "an," or sweet adzuki bean paste)
white: smooth "an"
black: coarse "an"
with black sugar ¥120
Set of sweet and matcha green tea ¥600~
"Yokan" for take-out (mini-sized) ¥430

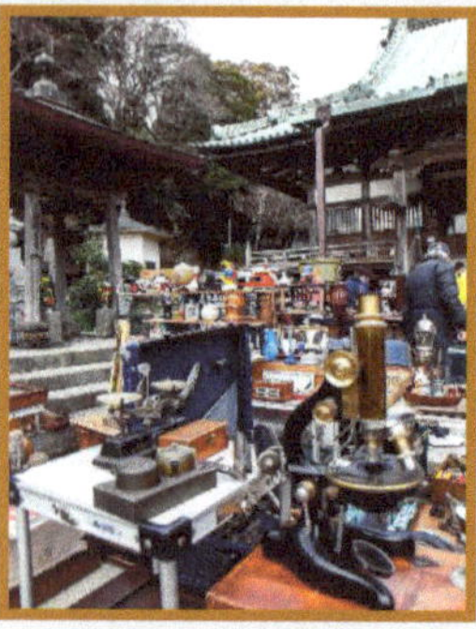

The town of Koshigoe is where the "Enoden" Railway runs along the road surface. If you walk toward Enoshima Station with the ocean to your back, you will come upon the towering Ryuko-ji Temple at the end of the road. Built upon the ruins of a former execution ground, this temple is where Nichiren, the founder of the Nichiren sect of Buddhism, was close to becoming executed in the late 13th century. It is said that one of his students erected this temple in the mid-14th century.

It is here that an antique fair takes place on the third Sunday of every month. There are approximately 40 participating vendors, which at times grows to close to 80. Antique wares are spread over three areas: among the open area right off the street; surrounding the temple gate at the top of the stairs; and in front of the main hall of the temple further up. You will find stalls lined with antique Imari plates and lacquered bowls, replicas of Japanese swords and Mid-century toys, and curios, and kimono. The wares are handled by professional antique dealers, and so you can be guaranteed of the quality, unlike at some of the hodge-podge flea markets.

Shonan Tatsunokuchi Antique Fair
(📍Map p. 180)

Date:	**3rd Sunday of the month**
Hours:	**7:00am~3:00pm (Rain or shine, except severe weather)**
Venue:	**Ryuko-ji Temple**
Address:	**3-13-37 Katase, Fujisawa City**

To find out how much the items are, you will need to inquire at the stalls. There may be a handful of vendors who speak English, but it might be easiest to communicate using a pen and paper. Very few vendors accept credit cards, so be sure to take along cash.

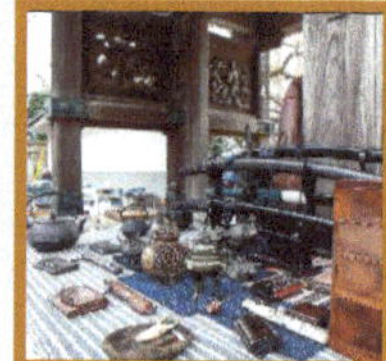

Kamakura-gu Temple Antique Fair
(📍Map p. 103)

An antique fair that takes place at Kamakura-gu Temple located east of Tsurugaoka Hachiman-gu Shrine on the second Sunday of the month.

Date:	**2nd Sunday of the month except October**
Hours:	**7:00am~4:00pm (Canceled if rainy)**
Venue:	**Kamakura-gu Shrine**
Address:	**154 Nidakido, Kamakura City**

Shichirigahama Parking Area Flea Market
(📍Map p. 153)

Flea market held at the large parking lot located directly off Route 134 that runs along the coast, overlooking Enoshima Island and Mt. Fuji.
Local people gather and enjoy selling and checking out used clothing, knick-knacks, hand-made items, and antiques.

Date:	**Jan-Mar: 2nd & 4th Sunday of the month, Apr-Dec (except Aug): 2nd & 4th Saturday & Sunday of the month**
Hours:	**9:00am~3:00pm (Canceled if rainy)**
Venue:	**Shichirigahama Kaigan Parking Area**
Address:	**2-1-12 Shichirigahama Higashi, Kamakura City**

FOUR-SEASONS CALENDAR

Annual Events & Flowers

Daffodils
suisen
Jan.-Feb.

Plum
ume
Jan.-Mar.

January

1st to 3rd: "Hatsumode"

The New Year's first worshiping at a shrine or temple.

2nd: "Funa-Oroshi" ritual at Zaimoku-za Beach

Local fishers' ritual to appeal to sea deities for the safety and abundance of the new year. Boats are decorated with special flags and gifts are tossed into the sea.

February

3rd: "Setsubun"

This ritual to expel evil spirits by throwing roasted soy beans at them are held at many temples and shrines.

Camellia
tsubaki
Jan.-Mar.

April

2nd Sunday to 3rd Sunday: Kamakura Festival

Various events including a procession along Wakamiya-Oji Avenue, *yabusame* (horseback archery), and a *shizuka-no-mai* dance are held at Tsurugaoka Hachiman-gu Shrine.

Magnolia
mokuren
Mar.-Apr.

June

2nd Sunday: Gosho Shrine Reisai Festival at Zaimoku-za Beach

Mikoshi (portable shrines) are taken on a procession parade through the town of Zaimoku-za to the beach. The *mikoshi* is carried into the water to pray for auspiciousness and safety.

Sweet daphne
jinchoge
Mar.

July

Early July to End of August: "Umi-biraki"

Beaches are open for swimming and other activities, and beach huts are in operation.

Late July: Kamakura Fireworks Festival

About 2,000 fireworks are launched on the water off Yuigahama Beach and Zaimoku-za Beach. +Ndp dnxud" I luhz r unv"p d| eh" f dqf hobg"duing"the Wn|r"R dp slf v in 2020.

Cherry blossoms
sakura
Mar.-Apr.

August

Early August: "Bonbori" ("Lantern") Festival

The precinct of Tsurugaoka Hachimangu Shrine is lined with about 400 *bonbori* paper lanterns.

Hydrangea
ajisai
May-Jun.

September

14th to 16th: Annual Grand Festival at Tsurugaoka Hachimangu Shrine

Mikoshi portable shrines procession along Wakamiya-Oji Avenue, *yabusame*, and other rituals are held at the shrine.

Lotus
hasu
Jul.-Aug.

October

Early October: "Kamakura *Takigi*-Noh"

Noh and *Kyogen*, traditional performing arts, are performed at Kamakura-gu Shrine in the evening. *Takigi* means "firewood." The outdoor stage is lit with bonfires. (For inquiries about ticket sales, contact the Kamakura City Tourist Association. Tel: 0467-23-3050)

Spider lilies
higanbana
Sep.

December

18th: "Toshi no Ichi" at Hase-dera Temple

At the market along the approach to Hase-dera Temple, auspicious items for the New Year such as *daruma* wishing dolls, calendars, and *kumade* rakes are sold.

31st: "O-omisoka" (New Year's Eve) & "Joya no Kane" ("New Year's Eve bell ringing")

People visit temples and shrines to pray for the New Year around midnight. Temples begin ringing the temple bell 108 times around 11:45pm, and at some, visitors get to ring the bell.
For details and other event information, contact the Kamakura City Tourist Association. Tel: 0467-23-3050

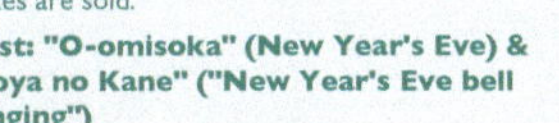
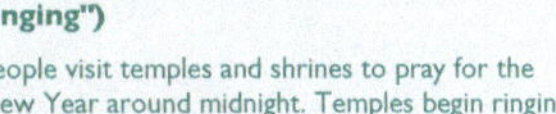

Autumn leaves
ko-yo
Nov.-Dec.

Photo: Nao Miyake (June), Kamakura City Tourist Association (April, July, September, December)

NATURE
Trails & Beaches

To some, the great charm of Kamakura lies in the natural environment surrounded by mountains and sea. Beautiful hiking trails are easily accessible from the city center, so you can even plan your sight-seeing around them.

The four trails introduced here are paths once roamed by samurai warriors. Since Kamakura was originally a rugged mountainous region, the leveled areas are thought to have been made in the time of the samurai. Due to the scarcity of land, caves were dug out into cliffs for use as tombs, and they remain to this day. The steep and rocky trails can be slippery at times, so we recommend wearing suitable clothing and shoes with enough traction.

At the seaside, you can enjoy marine sports while taking in the beautiful scenery. In summertime, particularly, beaches throng with people in a festival-like atmosphere. The map of the beach area on page p. 194 indicates the best spots for Mt. Fuji and sunset viewing on clear days.

Trail "A" Mt. Gion Trail

About 30 mins.
Highest Point: 60 m

This is the trail closest to the center of Kamakura.
It ends at the final resting place of the Kamakura Shogunate.

From the East Exit of Kamakura Station, cross Wakamiya-Oji Avenue, take a left at the post office then follow the sign to "Yagumo Shrine." It should take about 10 minutes to walk from the station to Yagumo Shrine.

1 At Yagumo Shrine, to the right of the main hall, there is a path flanked by red flags. The starting point of the trail is at the end of this path.

2 At the first fork, take a right towards Mt. Gion.

3 Enjoy the view at the top of Mt. Gion.

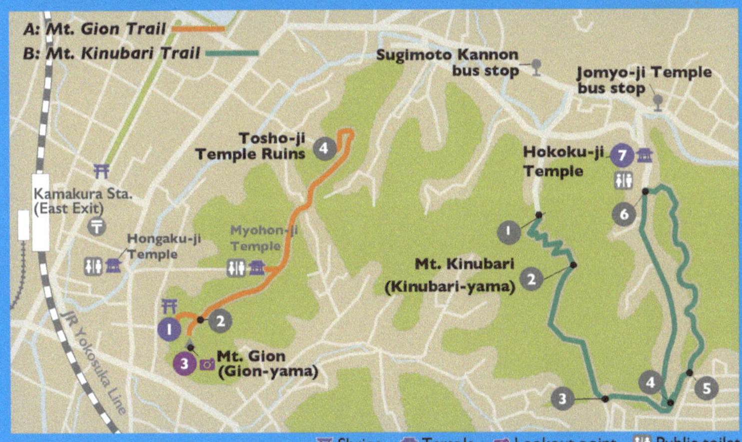

1 Yagumo Shrine

4 At the end of the trail are the ruins of the Tosho-ji Temple. Behind the fence lies a historic area—the *yagura* cave and ruins of the temple where the Hojo clan committed suicide, tragically marking the end of the Kamakura Shogunate.

Trail "B" Mt. Kinubari Trail

About 75 mins.,
Highest Point: 121 m

This is the originating point for
the historic Kannon pilgrimage route in the Kanto region.

From the East Exit of Kamakura Station, take a 10-minute bus ride to "Sugimoto Kannon," then cross the road and bridge and walk along the narrow residential road for about 5 minutes. For bus information, please see the section "Bound for Kanazawa-Kaido Area" on page p. 103.

1 Trail entrance.

2 At the fork in the road, take either path since both will arrive at Mt. Kinubari. Along the left path is an old stone quarry. At the top of Mt. Kunibari, views open out over the bay.

3 At the first fork, go straight through the park.

4 If you need a short cut to the trail end, take a left at the second fork (there is no signage).

5 Continue down to the end of the road, then take a right into the residential area. The entrance to the trail, an ancient pilgrimage route, is immediately on the left.

Trail "C" Mt. Genji Trail

This trail begins in Kita-Kamakura and leads up to Mt. Genji (Genji-yama). Discover the ancient shrines along the way until you reach the Great Buddha.

About 90 mins.
Highest Point: 93 m

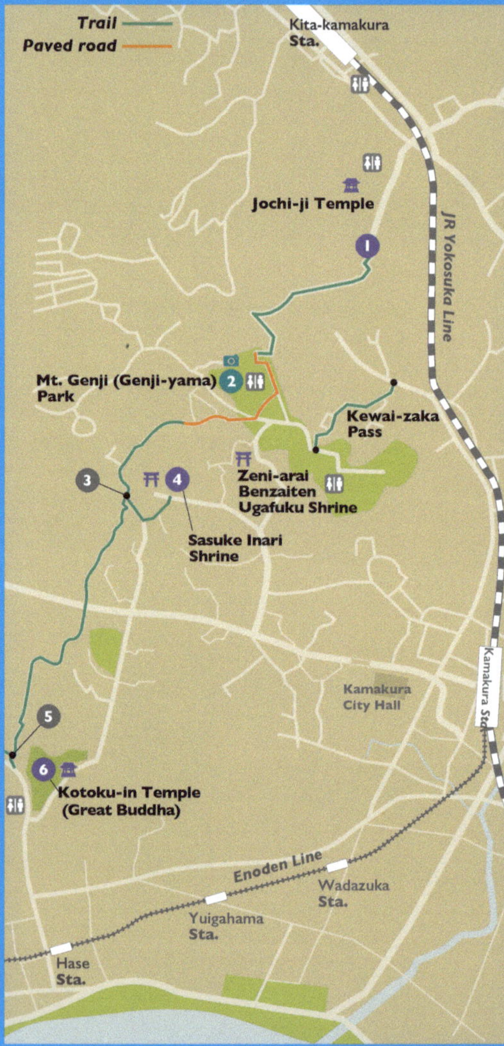

Walk about 7 minutes from Kita-Kamakura Station to Jochi-ji Temple, then take the side road and walk another minute or so.

1 Trail entrance.

2 Mt. Genji is a large, scenic park perfect for strolling. There are also picnic areas and toilets.

3 To get to Sasuke Inari Shrine, take the left path downhill. This will bring you to the rear of the shrine where you will see many red flags.

4 Sasuke Inari Shrine was once the main water source of the area. You could walk through to another old shrine, Zeni-arai Benzaiten Shrine. Go back to the fork then follow the sign to Hase Station.

5 If you have extra time, we recommend you take a right at the fork and walk 10 minutes to Daibutsu Kiridoshi Pass, an ancient road that once connected Kamakura to Kyoto.

6 After visiting the Great Buddha, take the Enoden Railway from Hase Station to Kamakura Station, or head to Enoshima.

If you prefer to take a short-cut, there are two ways: One is to take Kewai-zaka Pass (where fierce battles raged with the enemy, leading to the demise of the Kamakura Shogunate) from Genji-yama Park, and the other is to follow the sign to Zeni-arai Benzaiten Shrine from Genji-yama Park.

Trail "D" Ten-en Trail

About 110 mins.
Highest Point: 159 m

This route along the ridgeline allegedly played an important role for defense in the Kamakura era. Although the scenery to the right has been transformed by modernization, the land along the left is almost completely covered by temple grounds.

Take a bus from Kamakura Station to "Daitono-miya" bus stop, then walk to the trail entrance near Zuisen-ji Temple For bus information, please see the section "Bound for Kanazawa- Kaido Area" on page p. 103.

❶ The trail entrance is to the right just beyond the Sanmon gate of Zuisen-ji Temple.

❷ Here at Ten-en you will find a small teahouse where you can get some homemade tofu or vegetable dishes prepared by a friendly local couple.

❸ Mt. Ohira is the highest summit in Kamakura from where you can look out over the city of Yokohama. The large sloping rock face is fun to climb.

❹ Behind the raised area on the right side of the path, there is a stone called "Juo-iwa" into which three Buddhas are carved. Directly behind Tsurugaoka Hachiman-gu Shrine, there is a view that runs straight down the shrine complex and out to Wakamiya-Oji Avenue.

❺ At the observatory, weather permitting, you can overlook the vast temple grounds of Kencho-ji Temple, the city of Kamakura, and Mt. Fuji.

❻ At the bottom of the steps is the tutelary shrine of Kencho-ji Temple called Hansobo. If you pay an admission fee, you can walk down the steep stairway with over 250 steps to enter the grounds of Kencho-ji Temple, then return to Kita-Kamakura Station from there.

Beaches and Viewing Spots

Kamakura is known for its nice beaches, notably Zaimoku-za, Yuigahama, Shichirigahama, and Koshigoe Beach, where you can enjoy water sports like surfing, SUPing, wind surfing, or kayaking. Unless it's typhoon season, the water is relatively calm and safe for swimming. With the exception of Shichigahama, the beaches are open July through August for swimming and other activities. Beach huts operate during that time and provide food, drink, and toilet amenities, as well as showers for a fee. Lifeguards are on patrol from 9:00 am to 5:00 pm. Water sports are prohibited in the swimming area. Parking is available, but since spaces fill up quickly in the morning, we recommend using public transport. There are very few trash bins, so be prepared to take your trash home with you.

Zaimoku-za Beach: A beach in a calm inlet—at low tide, you can enjoy the tidal pools at Wakae Island on the east side of the beach.
<Access> A 20-min. 🚶 from JR Kamakura Station or 2-min. 🚶 from Zaimoku-za bus stop.

Yuigahama Beach: This beach is at the end of Wakamiya-Oji Avenue in the direction from Kamakura Station. It's an easily accessible beach and gets very crowded in the summer. In front of the beach is Kamakura Seaside Park with a lawn that's ideal for picnics.
<Access> A 15-min. 🚶 from the East Exit of JR Kamakura Station or a 5-min. 🚶 either from Wadazuka Station, Yuigahama Station, or Hase Station.

Kaihin Park Inamuragasaki: the small cape jutting out into the sea, has a grassy area and is popular for napping, yoga, or simply watching the sunset. The beach is accessible from the park by stairs.
<Access>A 5-min. 🚶 from either Inamuragasaki or Shichirigahama Station, or a 1-min. 🚶 from either Shichirigahama or Kamakura-koukomae Station.

Shichirigahama Beach: This long beach that extends from Inamuragasaki to Koyurugi-misaki is not officially a bathing beach, but there is access from the road down to the beach. There is a reef point with stronger currents than other shores, and the big waves make it an ideal surf spot. For convenience, there is a cafe, showers, and toilets and a large parking lot.

Koshigoe Beach: A great spot for viewing Enoshima from the beach. The west side of the bridge is called Koshigoe Beach and the east side is called Enoshima Higashi-hama Beach.
<Access> A 6-min. 🚶 from Koshigoe Station or a 16-min. 🚶 from Enoshima Station.

Depending on the beach, there may be regulations to follow. These may include instructions to keep your tattoos covered, or no smoking/drinking on the beach. We recommended checking the website below making plans to go to spend the day at the beach.
http://smart-beach-project.com/manner/

Sunrise and Sunset Times

	Sunrise / Sunset
Jan.	6:50am / 4:40pm
Feb.	6:41am / 5:09pm
Mar.	6:11am / 5:36pm
Apr.	5:28am / 6:02pm
May	4:50am / 6:27pm
Jun.	4:28am / 6:51pm
Jul.	4:30am / 7:00pm
Aug.	4:50am / 6:46pm
Sep.	5:14am / 6:09pm
Oct.	5:36am / 5:26pm
Nov.	6:03am / 4:47pm
Dec.	6:31am / 4:29pm

(2018)

* The first sunrise of the year, on Jan. 1st, is called "hatsu-hinode." Many people gather at the beaches from to welcome the sun for an auspicious start to their year.

* "Diamond Fuji" is when the sun sets right at the peak of Mt. Fuji. It can be seen around April 5th and September 8th.

- Sunset viewpoint
- Mt. Fuji viewpoint
- Beaches open during summer
- Surf spot
- Parking
- Public toilets

* Surf board rentals are available at "Okuda Style" surfboard shop (p. 117).

Safety flag signals for swimmers

- **Blue flag** : Swimming is allowed
- **Yellow flag** : Swim at your own risk
- **Red flag** : Swimming is not allowed
- **Orange flag** : Tsunami warning. Move to a higher elevation immediately.

Zushi

Zushi Station is one stop from Kamakura Station on the JR Yokosuka Line. The area surrounding the station itself is a quiet residential area with basic town amenities, but what makes the area special is Zushi Beach, only a 15-minute walk away. In summertime, the seafront throngs with crowds of sunbathers and is lined with beach huts. At other times of the year, it's a haven for wind surfers. Mt. Fuji can be seen from the south side of the beach (the area closest to Nagisa-bashi Bridge).

Access

Take the JR Yokosuka Line or the JR Shonan Shinjuku Line and get off at Zushi Station. Alternatively, you can take the Keikyu Line and get off at Shin-Zushi Station.

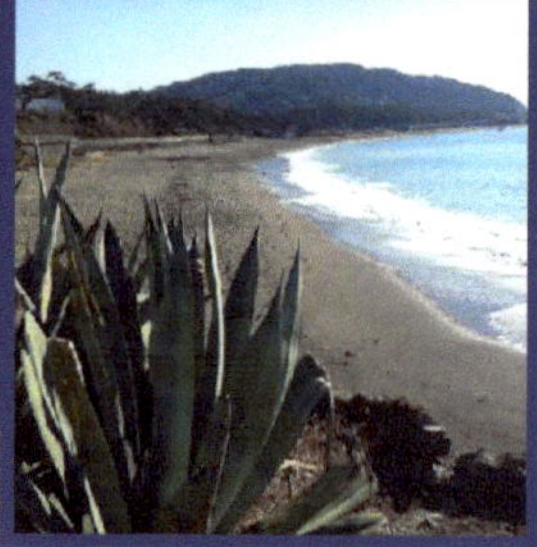

MIURA PENINSULA
A Brief Guide

| Zushi | Yokosuka |
| Hayama | Miura |

Hayama

This quiet residential area has a historic reputation as the high-status seaside holiday home resort. To get to the nearest beach, take a bus from Zushi Station and get off at "Morito Kaigan" bus stop. A few more minutes on the same bus will take you to "Isshiki Kaigan" bus stop, from where you go down a quiet alley for a minute before reaching the shore along which the Emperor has a summer villa. These beaches are both popular for paddle sports. Hiking trails along the seafront are also popular, with the hilly green backdrop of Hayama, stunning sunsets and views of Mt. Fuji.

Access

Take Bus No. 11 or No. 12 and ride for 10 to 20 minutes on the Keikyu Bus bound for Hayama-Isshiki ("Kaigan-mawari") from the East Exit of Zushi Station to get to Morito Beach, Isshiki Beach, or Hayama.

Yokosuka

Along Yokosuka's Sagami Bay lined with small fishing ports and beaches, there are places for swimming and marine sports. The entrance to a great hiking trail is near "Maeda-bashi" bus stop and runs along the creek. The Tokyo Bay side is lively with large commercial complexes and naval bases. On the southern end of Kannon-zaki Cape is a park perfect for a leisurely stroll.

Access

Sagami Bay side: Take the bus bound for "Sajima Island" or "Yokosuka City Hospital" from the East Exit of Zushi Station.
Tokyo Bay side: Accessed from Yokosuka Station on the JR Yokosuka Line , or Yokosuka Chuo Station on the Keikyu Line.

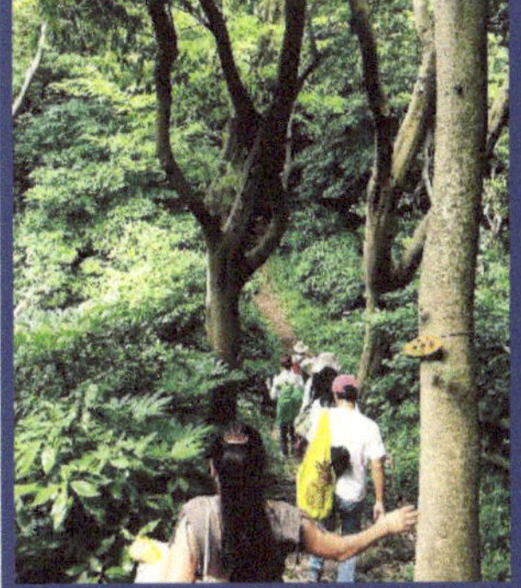

Located an hour to 1 and 1/2 hours from Tokyo by train, the Miura Peninsula is an ideal location for a day trip or a short stay. A beautiful region blessed with mountains and sea, you can forget the hustle and bustle of the city and enjoy trekking, cycling, or sea bathing.

Miura

Along the coastline of Sagami Bay, there are unique rocky shores, sandy beaches, and marinas. On the southern tip is a port town, and Joga-shima Island accessible by bridge from Misaki, and is popular for cycling. Farmland covers most of the inland region, with agricultural tourist spots and farm stands. There is also a forest where the natural ecosystem from river to ocean is conserved.

Access

Accessible from the Sagami Bay side to Misaki or Joga-shima by bus, or by rental bicycle from Keikyu Misaki-guchi Station.

Photos by Hiroichi Yanase

EXTRA INFO
Helpful Tidbits

Kamakura Station Map

Kamakura City Tourist Information Center 

Located right outside of the East Exit of JR Kamakura Station
📞 0467-22-3350
🕘 9:00am-7:00pm
    Open seven days a week except Dec. 29th through Dec. 31st
Free WiFi and two tablet computers are available for information searching.

ATM

There are ATMs for international bank cards and exchange machines at Mizuho Bank located at the East Exit near the Tourist Information Center.
🕘 Mon-Fri: 6:00am-2:00am
    Sat: 8:00am-10:00pm, Sun & Holidays: 8:00am-9:00pm
International bank cards can also be used at the ATMs in post offices and in Seven-Elevens (convenience stores).

WiFi

There are many free WiFi spots throughout Kamakura City. A free WiFi spot map is available at the Tourist Information Center.

Discount Passes

Kamakura-Enoshima Pass
💴 ¥700 (Ele ¥350)

Unlimited rides for one full day on local JR trains within a limited
area, and anywhere along the Enoden and the Shonan Monorail.
(If you extend beyond the valid station range, applicable fares will be
separately charged).
The Kamakura-Enoshima Pass is sold at JR Fujisawa Station, JR
Ofuna Station, JR Kita-Kamakura Station, and JR Kamakura Station.
Refer to details on the following website:
www.jreast.co.jp/e/pass/kamakura_enoshima.html?src=gnavi

Noriori-kun Enoden one-day discount pass
💴 ¥600 (Ele ¥300)

One-day pass for the Enoden Railway between Kamakura and
Fujisawa Station. Discounts are offered at restaurants, temples,
souvenir shops, and other establishments. Look out for the logo of
the pass at the entrance and show it to the cashier when paying.
The "Noriori-kun" Enoden one-day passes are available from the
ticket vending machines at all stations along Enoden line.
See details on the following website:
www.enoden.co.jp/en/tourism/ticket/noriorikun/

Kamakura Environmental Bill ("Kamakura Kankyo Tegata")
💴 ¥570 (Ele ¥290)

This pass allows you to ride as much as you like for one-day within
a specified area on five bus and train lines that run through the areas
with the most popular tourist attractions of Kamakura. Discounts
from participating shrines, temples, museums, or other shops or
services in the area are also offered. The list of participating
establishments is printed on the brochure that comes with the pass
(in Japanese only).
The "Kamakura Kankyo Tegata" pass is sold at Enoden Kamakura
Information Center, Enoden Kamakura Station, Hase Station and at
travel agencies. (Tickets are not sold for January 1st through 3rd).
For details see the following website:
www.enoden.co.jp/en/tourism/ticket/free/

Rental bike

Kamakura Rent-a-cycle Store   (🚲 Map p. 054)
🕐 8:30am-5:30pm (Weekends in Jul-Aug 8:30-6:00pm)
  Open seven days a week except Jan 1st -3rd
¥ Rental fee: ¥600/1hour~
*Insurance: ✕ Helmet rental: ○ English-speaking staff: △
*Picture ID required   *Returns can be made to their Hase branch

Rent-a-cycle Hase Store   (🚲 Map p. 122)
🕐 9:30am-5:30pm
  Open seven days a week except Jan.1st -3rd
¥ Rental fee: ¥600/1hour~
*Insurance: ✕ Helmet rental: ○ English-speaking staff: △
*Picture ID required   *Returns can be made to their Kamakura branch

GROVE   (🚲 Map p. 054)
🕐 10:00am-7:00pm   Closed on Wed, Thu
  *Mountain bikes only
¥ Rental fee: ¥2,310/1day~ (includes insurance)
  Helmet rental: ○ ¥500   English-speaking staff: △
 *Picture ID required

Yamamoto Shokai   (🚲 Map p. 054)
🕐 9:00am-6:00pm, Closed on Thu & 1st and 3rd Wed of the month
¥ Rental fee: ¥400/1hour~
*Insurance: ✕ Helmet rental: ○ English-speaking staff: △

Taxi

There is a taxi pool at both the East and West exits of Kamakura Station.
*The taxi company **KG GROUP** provides tours with an English-speaking driver to show visitors the tourist spots and recommend day plans.
¥ Regular taxi (up to 4 people) ¥5,980/1hour
  Jumbo taxi (up to 9 people) ¥6,640/1hour
*They require advanced booking by telephone (Japanese only) or e-mail (basic English only). Please provide them with your name, telephone no., date, time, and preferred size of car.
*Contact: KG GROUP
📞 0467-31-0101
e-mail: kggroup@gurin.co.jp

Rickshaw

Rickshaw company **EBISUYA** operates rickshaw tours.
*Location: Near Tsurugaoka Hachimangu Shrine on Wakamiya-Oji Ave.
🕤 9:30am-Sunset
¥ 30-min. tours: ¥7,000 (1 person), ¥9,000 (2 persons)~
*English-speaking staff available. See details on **ebisuya.com/en/branch**

LOCAL GUIDES

KAMAKURA WELCOME GUIDES

A volunteer guide group certified by Kamakura City Tourist Association provides free guided tours in foreign languages.
(Participants are required to pay for the transportation and admission fees for the guides.)
Friday regular tours (50 mins.): 10:30am/1:00pm (Apr-Oct)
Starts at the East Exit of Kamakura Station (No reservations required)
Arranged tours
See details on **kamakurawelcome.guide/en**

LOCAL FOCUS Production team staff (The Blue Co., Ltd)
See details on **www.the-blue.info**

Numbers to call in case of emergency

(Simply say "English, please," and you will be assisted immediately.)

📞 **119** to ask for an ambulance or rescue, report a fire, or contact an emergency call center at a local fire station.

📞 **110** to report an accident or crime to the police call center.

📞 **118** to report an accident or crime at sea to the Japan Coast Guard.

Lost and found

Kamakura Ekimae KOBAN (police box) (Map p. 197)
🏠 1-2-1 Komachi Kamakura
    (Located near the East Exit of JR Kamakura Station)

JR (Japan Railway) East Information Line
📞 050-2016-1603 (10:00am-6:00pm)

Visit **www.localfocus.info** for updates.

In planning your trip to the sites featured in the "Where to Go?" section (pp. 049-186), use this handy "at-a-glance chart" to meet your preferences and needs.

ICONS & SYMBOLS

P : Page number   C : Category   T : Take-out   BR : Breakfast   L : Lunch
CF : Cafe   D : Dinner   B : Bar   O/ 7 : Op en 7 days/w
[book icon] English website available   [instagram icon] Instagram account available

■ Restaurants, Cafes, Take-outs & Groceries

Area & Shop Name	P	C	T	BR	L	CF	D	B	Closed	Veg	Vegan	Eng	Eng	Wifi	Card	Group	Parking	Wheelchair	Website	Instagram
Kamakura Sta. East Exit Area																				
Narutoya+Tenzo	055	(bowl)			●		●		Tu, 2&4 W											
Tempura Hiromi	056	(bowl)			●		●		W*			●	●		●					
Kokuriko Komachi Store	085	(cup)	●			●			O/7	△		●	△			△		△		
RENDEZ-VOUS DES AMIS	057	(fork/knife)					●	●	Th	●		●	△	●	△	△				
COBAKABA	058	(bowl)		●	●				W	●		●	△					△		●
Kosuzu	059	(bowl)	●		●	△			M*	●		●	△			△		△		
Toshimaya	060	(bag)	●						W*				△		●	●		●		
floresta	061	(bag)	●						M*	●			●			●		△		
Kamkura Ham	062	(bag)	●						O/7				△		●	●		△		
Renbai	063	(bag)	●						O/7, IR				△			●		△		
Hideyoshi	064	(bowl)	●					●	Tu, IR			●	△					△		
PARADISE ALLEY	065	(bag)	●						IR				△	●				△		●
DAILY by LONG TRACK FOODS	066	(bag)	●						M				△		●			△		●
Kamakura Chiffon	066	(bag)	●						M			●	△		●	●		△		●
nugoo Cafe	071	(cup)				●			O/7											
Kamakurabori Museum Cafe	078	(cup)			●	●			M*	●	●	●	△	●	●	●			●	
Kamakura Sta. Weest Exit Area																				
Sông Bé Cafe	083	(cup)			●	●	●		Tu/W	●		●	△			●		△		
THE GOOD GOODIES	084	(cup)	●	△		●			W, L/Tu			●	●	●	●	△		△		●
Kokuriko Onaridori Store	085	(cup)	●		△	●			M	●		●	△			△		△		
BunBun Kochaten	086	(cup)	●		●	●			Tu			●	△			●	△	△		
Tsukui	087	(bowl)	●		●		●		IR	●		●	△		●	●			●	
Latteria Bebè	088	(fork/knife)	●		●		●		M				△			●		△		
Bistrot Orange	089	(fork/knife)			●		●	●	O/7						●	●				●
Katsuretsu-an	090	(bowl)	●		●		●		O/7			●	△	●	●	●		△		
Garden House	091	(fork/knife)		●	●	●	●	●	IR	△	△	●	●		●	●		△	●	●
HAPPY DELI Kamakura	092	(take-out)	●		●	●			Sun	●	△	●	●			△				
Sasuke Store	093	(take-out)	●						W, L/Tu			△	△							
Kanazaw a-Kaido Area																				
Mon-Peche-Mignon	104	(take-out)	●	●	●	●			M	△	△	△	△	●		△	●	△		
Bergfeld	105	(cup)	●		●	●			Tu/3M			●	●			●	△	△		
Alte Stadt	106	(bag)	●						O/7			△	●				△	●		

INDEX CHART

■ Restaurants, Cafes, Take-outs & Groceries

Legend columns: P = page; C = category icon; and the day-off / icon columns. (The category column "C" and the icon-column headers are printed as pictographs; the slash icon column gives the regular closing day, and the icon columns are shown here as: Veg (leaf), Vegan (two leaves), Eng menu, Eng staff, WiFi, Card, Group, Parking, Access, Review, Photo.)

Area & Shop Name	P	C	T	BR	L	CF	D	B	Closed
Zaimoku-za Area									
Bonzo	114				●		△		Th
Bento Bunny	115		●						O/7
Yorozuya Shoten	116		●					△	Tu
Yuigahama/Hase Area									
Casa. Kamakura Espresso	123		●		●	●			M
HOUSE YUIGAHAMA	124		●		●	●			W
ESSELUNGA	125				●		●		M,2&4Tu*
NATUDECO	127		●	●	●	●	△		IR
Beau Temps	128				●		●	●	IR
Kaseiro	129				●		●		O/7
Tsuruya	130				●		●		Tu(*)
WOOF CURRY	131				●		●		W
Oltrevino	132		●		●		●		W
HANABI	133				●		●		Tu*
Ichikanjin	134				●		●		M
SAIRAM	135				●	●			W,Th
Magokoro	136				●	●	●	●	M
Matsubara-an	137				●		●		O/7
Matsubara-an Cafe	137					●			O/7
Kosuzu Cafe	059					●			O/7
Pizzeria GG	138				●		●		O/7
Totoyamichi	139				●		●		O/7
Namihei	140								M*, IR
Chikaramochi-ya	141		●						W, 3Tu
Hostel YUIGAHAMA + SOBA BAR	145				●		●	●	O/7
Inamuragasaki & Shichirigahama Area									
yoridocoro KAMAKURA	154		●	●	●				O/7
SICILIANA	155				●		●		W, Th
Kamakura-yama Area									
24sekki	160		●		●	●			M,Tu,W,Th
Raitei	161				●		△		O/7
Raitei Tea House	161					●			Weekdays
le milieu	164		●		●	●			IR
Kita-Kamakura Area									
Hanalei	166				●	●			IR
Hachinoki Kitakamakuraten	167				●		△		W
Hachinoki Shinkan	168				●		△		O/7
Kousen	169		●						Tu
Enoshima Area									
The Market SEI	183		●	△	●				M*, Tu
Iglu Hyouka	183		●						M*, Winter

Area & Shop Name	Veg	Vegan	Eng (menu)	Eng (staff)	WiFi	Card	Group	Parking	Access	Review	Photo
Zaimoku-za Area											
Bonzo	●			△				△	△	●	●
Bento Bunny			△			●					
Yorozuya Shoten			△							△	
Yuigahama/Hase Area											
Casa. Kamakura Espresso	△	△	●	△	●			△			
HOUSE YUIGAHAMA	●	△	●	●	●			△		△	
ESSELUNGA	●	△	●	△	●	●					
NATUDECO	●	●	●	△				△		△	●
Beau Temps				△	●			△	△	△	●
Kaseiro	△	△	●	△				●	△	●	
Tsuruya			●							△	
WOOF CURRY	●		●	△						△	●
Oltrevino			●	△		●		△		△	
HANABI			●						△	●	●
Ichikanjin			●	△						●	●
SAIRAM	●	●	△	△				△			●
Magokoro	●	●	●	●	●	●	●				●
Matsubara-an			●	△				●	△		
Matsubara-an Cafe			●	△				●	△		
Kosuzu Cafe	●	●	●	△							
Pizzeria GG	●	△	●	△					△	△	△
Totoyamichi			●				●	●	●	●	
Namihei			△	△					△		
Chikaramochi-ya				△							
Hostel YUIGAHAMA + SOBA BAR			●	●	●	●			●		
Inamuragasaki & Shichirigahama Area											
yoridocoro KAMAKURA			●	●	●			△	△	●	●
SICILIANA	△			△	●			△	△		
Kamakura-yama Area											
24sekki	●	●	●	●				△	△		●
Raitei	●		●		●	●		△	●	●	●
Raitei Tea House			●					△	●	●	●
le milieu				△		●	●	●	△		
Kita-Kamakura Area											
Hanalei	△		●	●					△		
Hachinoki Kitakamakuraten	●	●	●	△	●	●	●	●	●		●
Hachinoki Shinkan			●	△	●	●	●	●	●	●	●
Kousen	●										
Enoshima Area											
The Market SEI	●	●		●							●
Iglu Hyouka	●	●									●

INDEX CHART

Restaurants, Cafes, Take-outs & Groceries

Area & Shop Name	P	C	T	BR	L	C	D	B				Eng	Eng							
Enoshima Area																				
iL-CHIANTI CAFÉ ENOSHIMA	184				●	●	●		O/7	●		●	△	●	●	●				
Eno-maru	185				●	●			W				△	●	●					
NAKAMURAYA YOKAN	186		●			●			O/7,IR	●	●	●	△	●	●	●			●	●

Shopping

Area & Shop Name	P		Eng				P			
Kama kura Sta. East Exit Area										
Ikustam	068	O/7			●					●
Funikura	068	M-Th,IR								
Patagonia Kamakura	070	O/7	△		●			△		●
nugoo Kamakura ninotorii Store	071	O/7	△		●					
nogoo Kamakura Wakamiya-Oji Store	071	O/7	△		●					
Kimono Kuroudo Miyamoto	072	O/7	△		●	●	●		●	●
Hakko-do	073	O/7	●	●	●	●	△	△	●	
Hachiman-do	074	Wed	△		●			△		
Kamakurabori Museum Store	078	M	△	●	●	●			●	
Kama kura Sta. West Exit Area										
Masamune Sword and Blade Workshop	094	Tue			●			△	●	
Yuko-do	095	M,IR			●					
Moyai Kogei	096	Tu	△		●	●				●
Yuigahama & Hase Area										
Second Hands Sosuke	142	M	△		●			△		●
Inamuragsaki & Shichirigahama Arra										
R OLD FURNITURE	156	M,Tue	△							
JONAS GLASS VISION	157	IR	●	●				△		●

Museums & Other Cultural Facilities

Eng English explanattion for the exhibitions is provided, or English speaking staff available.

Area & Shop Name	P	C		Eng			P			
Kamakur a Sta. East Exit Area										
Kimono Kuroudo Miyamoto	072		O/7	△		●	●		●	
Tsurugaoaka Museun , Kamakura	077		M, IR	●	●	●		●		
Kamakura Kokuhokan (National Treasure) Museum	077		M(*), IR	△				●	●	
Kamakurabori Museum	078		M	△	●					
Kaburaki Kiyotaka Memorial Art Museum	079		M(*), IR	△	●			●	●	
Kamakura City Kawakita Film Museum	080		M(*)	△	●				●	
Kamakura Sta. West Exit Area										
Kamakura Museum of History and Culture	099		Su, Holi	△					●	
Zaimoku-za Area										
Shimizu-yu (Public bath)	116		M(*),W(*),F(*)	△				●		
Okuda Style Surfing	117		O/7	△		●				●

■ Museums & Other Cultural Facilities

Area & Shop Name	P	C	Closed	Eng	WiFi	Card	Parking	Wheelchair	Info	Photo
Yuigahama & Hase Area										
Kamakura Noh Butai (Noh Theater & Museum)	148	🎨	Su, Holi				△	△	●	
Kamakura Museum of Literature	148	🎨	M(*), IR	△				●		
Hase-dera Temple Kannon Museum	152	🎨	O/7				△		●	
Inamuragsaki & Shichiriga hama Area										
JONAS GLASS VISION	157	👍	IR	●	●		△			●

Museums close when renewing displays or holding special events.

■ Places to Stay

Area & Shop Name	P	CA *1	CH *2	PRICE *3	Cup	Eng	WiFi	Card	Parking	Wheelchair	Info	Photo
Kamakura Sta. West Exit Area												
Hotel New Kamakura	098	A	P/R, P/P	★〜★★		●	△		△		●	
Zaimoku-za Area												
Good Morning Zaimokuza	118	B	P/P	★	●	△	△	●	△		●	●
Kamejikan	119	B	P/R, P/P	★〜★★	△	●	●		△		●	●
Yuigahama & Hase Area												
hotel aiaoi	143	B	P/P	★★	△	●	●				●	●
Hostel YUIGAHAMA＋SOBA BAR	145	B	P/R, P/P	★〜★★	●	●	●	●			●	●
WeBase Hostel Kamakura	146	B	P/R, P/P	★〜★★★	●	●	●	●		●	●	●
Kaihinsou Kamakura	147	A	P/P	★★〜★★★	△	△	●	●	●			

*1:Category (CA) A:Hotel, B: Hostel, Guest house, B & B, Boutique hotel

*2:Charge (CH): P/R: Rate is charged per room. P/P: Rate is charged per person

*3:Price (P/R): ★:¥3,000〜¥7,000, ★★:¥7,000〜¥15,000, ★★★:¥15,000〜

■ Shrines & Temples

Area & Shop Name	Features	P	Sha-kyo	Zazen	Cup	Parking	Wheelchair	Info
Kamakura Sta. East Exit Area								
Tsurugaoka Hachiman-gu Shrine	800-year old symbol of Kamakura	075			●	△	△	●
Myohon-ji Temple	Surrounded by a thick grove	077						●
Kamakura Sta. West Exit Area								
Jufuku-ji Temple	Distinctive stone paving	099						
Zen-arai Benzaiten Ugafuku Shrine	Unique money-rinsing ritual	100						
Sasuke Inari Shrine	Primitive spiritual place	101						
Kanazawa Kaido Area								
Hokai-ji Temple	Site of end of Kamakura shogunate	107					△	
Okura Shirahata Shrine	Yoritomo's grave above the shrine	107					△	
Sugimoto-dera Temple	Old temple that protected the road	107						
Kakuon-ji Temple	Only open for guided viewing	108				●		
Zuisen-ji Temple	Rock garden created by Muso Kokushi	109				●		●
Jomyo-ji Temple	Tea house overlooking a rock garden	110			●	△		
Hokoku-ji Temple	Beautiful bamboo grove	111			●	●		●

INDEX CHART

▌ *Shrines & Temples*

Area & Shop Name	Features	P	Sha-kyo	Zazen	☕	🅿	♿	🗒
Zaimoku-za Area								
Komyo-ji Temple	Large main gate and wooden building	120				●		
Yuigahama & Hase Area								
Kotoku-in Temple (the Great Buddha)	The Great Buddha of Kamakura	149					●	●
Hase-dera Temple	Gorgeous eleven-faced Kannon	151	△		●	△	●	●
Inamuragsaki & Shichiriga hama Area								
Gokuraku-ji Temple	History of social action	158						
Joju-in Temple	Bird's-eye view of the sea	158						●
Kita-Kamakura Area								
Engaku-ji Temple	Introduced Zen to the common people	171	●*1		●	△		
Tokei-ji Temple	Long history as a nunnery	173						●
Jochi-ji Temple	Wild, rocky ancient rear garden	174				●		
Meigetsu-in Temple	Iconic round window	175			●			
Kencho-ji Temple	The oldest Zen training monastery	177	●*2	●*3		△	△	

<"Shyo" (Sutra copyig) and "Zazen" (sitting meditation)>

○ : No Japanese language skill necessary to participat

△ : Participant has to have some level of Japanese language skill or be accompanied by someone who does.

***1: Hours: 10:00am-11:30am, 1:00pm-2:30pm on most days.**
Venue: Hojo or Zouroku-an   Fee: ¥1,000

The sutra used for copying is the "Enmei Jikku Kannon-gyo" (Ten Verse Kannon Sutra) which takes about 20 minutes to copy using a brush pen.

***2: Hours: 10:00am-3:00pm on most days.   Venue: Hojo   Fee: ¥1,000**

There are two kinds of sutras: one is the "Hannya Shingyo" (The Heart Sutra) which takes about 60 minutes, and the other is the "Enmei Jikku Kannon-gyo" which takes about 20 minutes using a brush pen.

*There is no instruction, so you are expected to learn how to do "sha-kyo" before participating.

***3: Days and time: 4:30pm-5:30pm every Friday and Saturday.**
Venue: Hojo   Fee: Admission fee only

- At irregular intervals, there is a 20-minute long discussion in Japanese, but translation is not available.
- Please arrive at Hojo by 4:15pm. Entering late or leaving in the middle of the session are discouraged.
- Written instruction is provided in English, but there is no verbal instruction. You are expected to learn about the basics of zazen meditation before participating.

  (Sessions may be cancelled or changed without notice. No reservations are required.)

- Kencho-ji Temple has zazen sessions for English speakers several times a year.
  Please check their website for details: https://www.kenchoji.com/news/#2542

ACKNOWLEDGEMENTS

The idea for this guidebook was ignited by the wish to share the places and shops that are dear to us with our visitors from overseas; it has taken us two years to fulfill that desire. Despite our small production team whose members were simultaneously engaged in their own respective work or projects, we were able to successfully complete this book thanks to those who lent a hand in creating our promotion videos, translating, editing, and much more; the steadfast commitment and support of friends, family, and members of the local community; and the warm crowdfunding contributions of our supporters.

To each of our production team members, we express our thanks from the depth of our hearts and send out wishes that *Local Focus* will serve as a tool for those who come to Kamakura and Enoshima to make their visit more meaningful and enjoyable. We also hope this guidebook will aid visitors from abroad in creating connections with the local communities.

Finally, we would like to acknowledge the samurai warriors, monks and priests, cultured figures, merchants, the hard-working townspeople, and all other predecessors of Kamakura and Enoshima who built and lived in these towns; and to those pioneers and all of those who will visit these towns with this book in hand, we say "*arigatou!*"

LOCAL FOCUS Production Team
Mariko Miki, Sae Yamane, Sosuke Hirai
Sarah Goff, Taisuke Yokoyama

Special Thanks to:

Evelyn Peralta Locatelli　Hiroichi Yanase　Koichiro Hoshi　Masahiro Yoshioka　Naoki Iwatani　Rika Oai　Takamitsu Sakamoto　Takehisa Shimoda　Yukako Nishikawa

Chief Translator/Copy Editor (English text): Norie Lynn Fukuda-Matsushima

Proofreader: Marie Isako Fukuda

Promotion Video Crew:
Go Nakamura　George Kodama　Hideyuki Iwasaki　Kazz Tsuji

Kamakura City Board of Education, Cultural Assets Division
Kamakura City Tourist Association　Fujisawa City Tourist Association
Enoshima Electric Railway Co. Ltd.

Staff

Mariko Miki   Producer/Writer

Over a span of twenty years, while working in public relations, Mariko hosted a nature program for swimming with wild dolphins in the ocean. She established The Blue Co., Ltd. to help spread awareness of lifestyles that are harmonic with nature.

Skin diving, Outrigger canoeing, Permaculture

In Kamakura, I have a community of friends with whom I share a love nature and the local area. I love the unique shops with owners who are committed to quality and who are filled with passion for their work. I also love the quiet Zen temples surrounded by greenery.

Sae Yamane   Editor/Writer

Brought up in Tokyo, Sae is an editor and writer on the topics of travel, food, and personalities, and is also a Bach Flower Essence practitioner. She runs a small cafe located close to a beautiful beach in Hayama.

Surfing,Tai-chiJapanese Tea Ceremony, and Kimono

I love the fresh green of Kamakura in the early summer and sunset views with Mt. Fuji in the distance as if floating above the sea. Kamakura is a place where people of refined sensibility gather, and where many people fully enjoy life in balance with nature.

Sosuke Hirai   Graphic designer

For most of his career, Sosuke was primarily involved in the production side of corporate advertising. As a Kamakura resident of ten years, he immersed himself in advertising work and personal fine art works. Since moving to Hayama 15 years ago, he has been involved in many local events and productions.

Furniture making, DIY, Gardening

Kamakura is a perfect environment to enhance creativity while admiring the sea and mountains. It also has a rare quality of locality that is conducive to expanding one's community.

Sarah Goff   Photographer

Sarah enjoys living in nearby Zushi and traveling the world while experiencing different cultures. Since her studies of photography at college in San Diego, CA, she has pursued her passion in photography for over 15 years.

Running, Relaxing on the beach, Woodworking

I enjoy hiking the many historical trails, finding unique Japanese treasures at the local antique stores, and the tranquility of Hokoku-ji Temple.

Taisuke Yokoyama   Photographer

Ever since the 1960s, the life of this Kamakuraite has revolved around surfing. As a photographer, he is known for his book, *surfers*, a collection of photographs of world famous wave riders.
In spring 2017, Taisuke established *Surf Magazine*, a Japanese surfer's magazine.

Surfing

Kamakura is a historic town that has both sea and mountains, and is also close to the city. I love the sea in the beginning of autumn, after summer crowds have disappeared. I also love early mornings at temples when no one else is around.

LOCAL FOCUS
A Japan Guide to Nature, Culture, and Community
Vol.1 Kamakura & Enoshima

Published by arigatoubooks
(The Blue Co., Ltd. arigatoubooks Division)
1-6-3 Unit-A Akiya, Yokosuka City, Kanagawa Prefecture, Japan
E-mail: localfocus55@gmail.com

Producer/Writer: Mariko Miki   Editor/Writer: Sae Yamane
Art Director/Chief Designer: Sosuke Hirai
Photographers: Sarah Goff, Taisuke Yokoyama

2st edition, 2019   ISBN 978-4-9910605-1-9

www.localfocus.info

A portion of the proceeds of LOCAL FOCUS will be donated to
Kanagawa National Trust Foundation

arigatoubooks